Playwork Voices

Playwork Voices

In celebration of
Bob Hughes and Gordon Sturrock

Edited by
Wendy Russell, Bridget Handscomb
and John Fitzpatrick

The London Centre for Playwork Education and Training

First published in the UK in 2007 by
The London Centre for Playwork Education and Training

Edited by Wendy Russell, Bridget Handscomb and John Fitzpatrick

ISBN 978–0–9554320–1–9

Published and Distributed by
The London Centre for Playwork Education and Training
Block D, Barnsbury Complex
Offord Road
London N1 1QG
ncpelondon@aol.com

Design, typesetting and production by
Action Publishing Technology Ltd, Gloucester
Printed in Great Britain

Contents

Foreword

It was a privilege to be asked to be involved in this project to celebrate the work of Bob Hughes and Gordon Sturrock. Over the years the London Centre for Playwork Education and Training has worked with both Bob and Gordon and, most recently, commissioned and published Bob's latest work, *PlayTypes – Speculations and Possibilities* which also involved Gordon as its editor.

There is no question that throughout our association all of us involved with the LCPET have at different times been challenged, enthused, confused and inspired by their writings and seminars. We have individually and collectively participated in this joint production and are delighted to announce the publication of *Playwork Voices*.

One of the exciting outcomes of this venture has been how willing people were to contribute and the wide variety of offerings. We feel that this sort of publication may well herald the start of a tradition that recognises the wealth of creativity and diversity that exists within the playwork world and acknowledges the importance of exchanging ideas and stories.

The London Centre for Playwork Education and Training
April 2007

Notes on Contributors

Sarah Atkinson BA (Hons), MA, PGCE

Sarah Atkinson is a Principal Lecturer at the University of the Arts London where she is Director of Programmes for the Foundation Studies in Art and Design at the London College of Fashion. Her interest in play and its impact on creativity in both children and adult learners developed through working with Gordon Sturrock on a number of educational projects. She is currently involved in further researching methodologies of teaching in art and design.

Arthur Battram

The playground of Arthur Battram's mind is a wonderfully complex place. He says that he learned everything he knows of complexity theory and management when he was a playworker himself. One cannot doubt it. His presentations are voyages through unexplored territories, new horizons unfolding to reveal fresh concepts, perspectives and ideas, guided by his urgent enthusiasm to preserve the endangered worlds of children's play. Read his *Navigating Complexity*, written while he was at the Local Government Management Board – you will see a playworker at work. He is now a freelancer who facilitates senior managers in exploring new ways to think about teams, to innovate and strategise. He writes and teaches, devises and runs powerful and effective training, and helps 'playpeople' and their organisations to improve their work in all manner of ways. Through it all, runs a playfulness and a multifaceted passion for creativity that is rivalled only by a playground full of playing children or the complex arc of a wave, so it is.

Mick Conway

Mick Conway has worked in play since 1978, firstly at Bermondsey Adventure Playground, where he learned (the hard way) that children are the experts in their play. The journey of enlightenment continued through working at and setting up projects at Hackney Play Association for the next eighteen years, then working at London Play and now Play England.

Over the years the work of Bob, Gordon and other amazing play thinkers was sometimes a puzzle but always an inspiration to him. They redrew the maps of play thinking and created new maps of uncharted territory in his understanding of children's play.

Keith Cranwell

Keith Cranwell is Senior Lecturer in Youth and Community Work at the University of Greenwich. He was Programme Leader for the UEL/Thurrock BA in Playwork and Youth Studies. He has published work on the history of play organisations covering nineteenth- and twentieth-century topics.

Annie Davy

Annie Davy is fascinated by human development and seeks to make connections between people, disciplines and a diversity of life ways, with a particular focus on human ecology and the natural world. She has worked in the fields of playwork, childcare, education and lifelong learning as a teacher, playworker, regulator, trainer, project manager and author for 25 years. She says that she has gained some of her most profound personal learning from informal situations, through involvement in community projects, festivals and in playing with family and friends. She takes any opportunity to spend time in the natural playgrounds of the forest or the beach.

Don Dare

Don Dare is the pseudonym of Dan Dore. Born in Blackpool between the Wars, he played for Burnley during their successful FA Cup victory in 1952 before turning to writing. His previous works have included the successful and critically acclaimed post-modern ironic *PlayTypes – Who'd have Thought It?*, *Psycholudics? My Arse* and of course his bestseller *The Ambiguity of Ray*. He also collected an Oscar in 2003 for his screenplay *Oi You, Leave my Monkey Alone!*

He has contributed the first chapter of his latest book featuring the eponymous heroes of his successful series *Fen Man and The Cowboy* in recognition of all that Bob and Gordon must have learnt from him. Don Dare is also known as John Fitzpatrick.

Perry Else

Perry has played in many settings over the years including (in chronological order) tin baths, backyards, garages, cemeteries, estate roads, fields, adventure playgrounds (Sheffield), art college, bands, galleries, adventure playgrounds (London), after-school clubs, community groups, sports centres, holiday playschemes, adventure playgrounds (Bristol), policy groups, development trusts, arts projects, conferences, council chambers, consultancy projects, seminar rooms ... and always on beaches and in woods. Perry has presented papers at many conferences, contributed to key playwork publications (*Best Play* and *Making Sense of Play*) and developed materials that are used in many training courses throughout the UK. Perry is the Course Leader for the BA (Hons) Playwork course at Sheffield Hallam University. In his spare time, he organises the conference 'Beauty of Play'.

Bridget Handscomb

Bridget has been involved in playwork since 1981 when undertaking an Introduction to Playwork course led to extremely enjoyable and challenging employment on Adventure Playgrounds. She has worked in the playwork field for over 25 years in both the voluntary and public sector. She currently works for a local authority in youth and play services and as a freelance playwork trainer in the London region. She is a self-confessed play-obsessive.

Jacky Kilvington

Following attendance at a workshop run by Gordon Sturrock many years ago, Jacky became a 'playwork warrior', always fighting the cause for children's play and playwork. She now works freelance as a playwork trainer, mentor and adviser. She has a wealth of experience working on both practical and theoretical aspects of playwork.

Pete King

Pete has in his brief lifetime been an office junior, administration assistant, gardener, a full-time student, a landscape gardener (albeit only for two days before he was sacked for being rubbish at it), a conservationist, a qualified science teacher, a playgroup assistant, after-school club assistant, after-school club supervisor, a holiday playscheme worker, a part-time explainer, a play development worker, a play development officer, a play development manager, a freelance playwork trainer, an NVQ assessor, a part-time student, a university lecturer and is currently a project development officer. This collection of job titles may constitute the vague remnants of a career, although it probably resembles more a visual cacophony of a man who has no idea of where he wants to go. Maybe that is why for the last ten years play has been at the core of what Pete has been involved with? Whatever Pete does, one thing that always remains true is, as according to Hakim Bey, freedom is a psycho-kinetic skill.

Stuart Lester

Stuart has been very fortunate to have got away with spending his life playing and constantly trying to ignore the voices off-stage that say 'playtime over, get back to work'. He has escaped these voices for many years by being a playworker, mainly on Adventure Playgrounds and local community based play projects. Stuart is currently Senior Lecturer in Playwork at the University of Gloucestershire and an Independent Playwork Trainer and Adviser.

Ian Macintyre

Ian has been a playworker since 1979 mainly on Adventure Playgrounds. He has also worked with young people and community groups on estates and festivals and managed Hackney Play Association's Design and Build Project. He has been involved in mainly play-related training courses and conferences as a participant and trainer.

He has taken many career breaks including living in a Buddhist community, working abroad, making furniture, sand-blasting, basic building and other freelance work and doing a Philosophy degree.

He moved to Brighton six years ago. Whilst working as a Residential Social Worker with autistic young people, managing the Census and driving old people around, he attempted to prove the need for an adventure playground (that would employ him!).

He did a Management course at Sussex University and finally obtained a playwork qualification (APEL). He returned to work in London two years ago and is currently Senior Playworker at Glamis Adventure Playground.

Sandra Melville

Sandra Melville's working life in play started as a volunteer on the Triangle Adventure Playground in London. From here she was co-opted to the Management Committee of the London Adventure Playground Association becoming vice-chair, responsible for Training. In 1981, she took up the post of General Secretary and remained with the organisation up to her retirement in 2004, having become Director when LAPA went national as PLAYLINK in 1993. Her role in leading the organisation through many changes allowed for a rewarding variety of activity (though rather too many committees), but throughout, her constant inspiration was the idea that all children should have wonderful places to play.

Maureen Palmer

Maureen Palmer is thoroughly rooted in playwork. Her feet are solidly planted. Her practice has grown from years of face-to-face work and has blossomed into training and supporting playworkers on their sites with their children. Her work is largely in Islington, where she is employed. Refusing to be cowed by the perception of the constraints put upon play work by health and safety requirements, she has undergone the required training of a health and safety inspector and works with children, playworkers, and line managers in embracing and subverting the agenda. She is well known for the video interviews that she did with adults who had grown up on the playgrounds that she worked on, inviting them to reflect on their memories of their playing and the effects that they feel those days had on their adult life. She is a dynamic and intelligent woman who breaks all the moulds, so she is.

Mel Potter

Play Person 1979 – 2000
Mel Potter – Play Person, was born as a playground volunteer into a poor play site family in Wolverhampton during the hard winter of 1979.

Because there was no one else available, he quickly advanced to full-time family member, then family mentor. He was eventually summoned to London (largely owing to the absence of more appropriate family members) where he tried to 'make a difference'.

He is survived by his 400 or more adoptive children (the exact number is unknown because a simple head was good enough in those days) and by several Play People whom he originally introduced to the work.

He was deeply affected by his encounters with the mysterious 'guru of play' whom he referred to as 'Yoda' (due to the uncanny likeness) right until the end.

Any similarity between Mel Potter – Play Person and any other Mel Potter living or dead is entirely coincidental.

Wendy Russell

Wendy Russell was offered her first adventure playground job in 1975 by Stephen Rennie, who advised her not to wear her platform shoes to work. She has worked in playwork ever since, in a number of guises, including playworker, play officer, play researcher, playwork trainer (but never in platform shoes). Currently she divides her time between being Senior Lecturer in Playwork at the University of Gloucestershire, working freelance, and her own research into play and playwork.

Stephen Smith

Stephen Smith has a degree in Playwork and Youth Studies. He began working with disabled children and young adults almost nine years ago at Barnardo's as a volunteer and is now a Senior Project Worker managing after-school clubs. He has nearly ten years' experience of providing sensory music sessions using the didgeridoo and has developed some highly innovative therapeutic work, which he has shared at conferences and events around the UK.

Jayne Shenstone (Stansfeld)

Jayne's playing started in earnest one afternoon in 1982 at Riverside Adventure Playground Cardiff after finishing at Art College.

'That summer we went around the world, each week to a different continent, we made stuff, fought, acted, tried weird food, shut our eyes, made things up, played chain tag in the dark, laughed till it hurt,' she recalls.

Since then she has worked with children and young people through playwork, youth work, community arts, teaching, play development, and latterly project management; in Wales, Nottingham, Wiltshire, Hertfordshire and Suffolk.

Michelle Virdi

Michelle came to playwork from a background in personnel and race equality. She has worked within a local authority play service since 1987 and has been actively and passionately involved in playwork education and training at a regional and national level for the last ten years.

Becky Willans

Becky Willans has a degree in Playwork and Youth Studies and is currently completing her PGCE. She is a lecturer on the BA (Hons) Playwork and Youth Studies, the Foundation Degree in Playwork and Therapeutic Playwork and the Foundation Degree in Playwork and Youth studies programmes at University of East London/Thurrock and Basildon College. Prior to teaching, Becky worked in a variety of play settings as a Senior Playworker and on a one-to-one therapeutic basis with children and young people with Special Educational Needs and disabilities.

Penny Wilson

Some years ago, playwork found Penny Wilson and grabbed her by the collar, shook her about a bit and has been leading her down unexpected paths ever since. She holds most dear her time at Chelsea Adventure Playground, the first of the inclusive adventure playgrounds established by Lady Allen of Hurtwood. The hand on the collar has dragged her to present at conferences and workshops and most recently and dramatically, she has been pulled across the Atlantic to work as a playworker advisor and trainer in New York, Chicago, Washington and Michigan.

She is employed as an inclusion worker by the Play Association Tower Hamlets, PATH, where she is trying to support play projects to open their services up to disabled children. She also trains and writes about play. It is her passion, so it is.

Ali Wood

Ali Wood has been working with children and young people in a variety of capacities for over thirty years – these include youth work, community development work, children in care and children in hospital as well as playwork, but it is children's right to play that has been her driving passion. Ali runs her own consultancy, which is based in the West Midlands, and is involved over the UK in playwork education and training, assessment and verification and research. She holds an M.Ed. (Comm.Ed.).

Introduction

Playwork Voices: In Celebration of Bob Hughes and Gordon Sturrock

It's all Brian's fault. Or you could say it's all Meynell's fault for bringing Brian over here. Anyway, it all happened in a typically accidental play-work way. We were walking down the street after listening to a presentation by Brian Sutton-Smith at the Birmingham NVQ conference in July 2004. He had mentioned the tradition of Festschrifts (a new concept to us and explained later) and we were commenting on what a good idea it would be to celebrate our own eminent thinkers in the play-work world. There was no hesitation in recognising that there were two people who richly deserved this sort of accolade: Bob Hughes and Gordon Sturrock. Then, in a classic playwork way, we went our separate ways and nothing happened!

It is in the 'nothing happening' phase that hidden roots begin to grow and the seed of an idea germinates and develops. So it was that this notion began to form in our minds. It took over a year to appear as a commitment to action and another month to emerge as an invitation to playwork colleagues to join us. The response was an overwhelming and resounding 'yes'. The incredible journey with a rare band of troubadours has had its ups and downs; its moments of intense activity and inertia; and that feeling of apprehension and achievement in keeping the ball in the air as it passes from one team member to another.

Throughout this experience themes arose and connections were made, and at the heart of this book are two central ideas: firstly, the special place that Bob and Gordon occupy in the playwork field. Both have been theorising and writing about play and playwork for thirty-odd years and there is no doubt that they have both had a significant influence on how we understand and talk about our work. Give or take a year or three, both are close to that magical moment of qualifying for a bus pass, although somehow we don't think that they will be living life in the bus lane just yet. We won't say any more about them here, as other contributors in this book do that far more eloquently.

Secondly, playworkers are a very special bunch. Play is central to childhood and, if post-industrial so-called 'developed' countries were not organised in the way that they are, adults would normally have only a small part to play in supporting children at play. In one sense playworkers are there so that children can be children; yet the current social policy focus of the Children's Workforce is on helping them on their journey to becoming adults. Each sector within the Children's Workforce will of course make claims to its own distinctiveness; in this, playwork is no different. Yet many in playwork, whilst operating within the context of *Every Child Matters,* have always known that the way we understand children and their play is quintessentially unique. The nascent but fast-growing body of knowledge that playwork theorists are developing also recognises this uniqueness, but for some reason, it seems so elusive, so very difficult to communicate to others. It is because of this that we have recognised the importance of developing our own language, our own ways of articulating what we do, our own voice. This publication is a contribution to that process, the process of finding a voice for playwork.

What on Earth is a Festschrift??

A Festschrift is an academic tradition. It is a celebratory publication, published to honour key academics. That publication is a collection of papers written by colleagues, past students or researchers and the papers are a gift to the person being honoured.

In true playwork tradition, however, we are doing things slightly differently. Not only are we honouring two people at the same time (very collective, very playwork), but also we wanted to ensure that the voices of a range of people from across playwork, and not just academics, were heard (very inclusive, very playwork). So what we asked those who have contributed to this publication for were stories of how Bob's and Gordon's work has influenced them. Some of the contributors to this publication are not writers nor academics, and some are. They are all, however, passionate about play and playwork, open to new ideas, and, most importantly, were willing to have a go at this kind of adventure.

This publication is a collection of their voices, and it represents, as Gordon would say, how Bob's and Gordon's thinking has played through them. Inevitably, and rather wonderfully, this has given rise to some very personal stories, firmly rooted in each contributor's personal, subjective experiences. Some of these experiences are specifically situated, some are more general musings. All contributors have made every effort to ensure that their stories, while being *their* stories, do not mistell or misrepresent other people's stories. If this is the case, it is unintended and we apologise in advance.

We are very pleased to present to Bob and Gordon and to you this delightful mixture of musings from a collection of people who have been touched by the work of Bob Hughes and Gordon Sturrock. These are all people who are immersed in the playwork sector and their contributions range from academic theorising (to extend, interpret or contest), through memory and personal reflection, to playful storytelling, all inspired by Bob's and Gordon's work.

The Contributions

We open our collection with a cartoon created by **Mick Conway** that encapsulates a feast of ideas and information in a way that words alone cannot convey – particularly the esoteric spirit of Bob as ancient philosopher surrounded by evolution's detritus and Gordon as shamanic silverback carrying the child within. We are sure that each time you look at this gem, you will spot another subtle reference and another layer of meaning will be revealed.

Next, **Sandra Melville** talks of her journey from an intuitive connection with playwork to a deeper understanding through the work of Bob and Gordon. She reflects on how their influence affected her own work in playwork, firstly on an adventure playground management committee and then with the London Adventure Playground Association (LAPA) and its successor, PLAYLINK.

We move on to a theoretical cocktail of tale telling. **Stuart Lester** illustrates combinatorial flexibility in action with a shaken-and-stirred *mélange* of ideas about playworkers as storytellers (actual and imagined, external and internal), through Hermans' work on the dialogical self to recent research in neuroscience. Mirror neurons and emotions blend with internal dialogue and rational decision-making in an analysis of a playwork scenario and the many voices that tell us how to respond. If you look hard, you might find a very hungry caterpillar ... (that turns up as a butterfly later on).

In a more autobiographical and confessional tone, **Ian Macintyre** provides an astute and perceptive tale, bringing Bob's theorising on consultation and participation to a critical appraisal of his work in this arena, concluding that his approach had little to do with the play or empowerment of children and everything to do with (albeit well-intentioned) adult agendas and egos.

Next, **Annie Davy** wonders whether our contemporary pursuit of a discrete definition of playwork might be the wrong quest, and that playwork is as difficult to pin down as the elusive butterfly that emerges from our earlier caterpillar. Rather than identifying what is special about playwork, perhaps we should be selling playwork approaches as relevant to other sectors within the Children's Workforce.

Adult agendas also feature in **Pete King**'s account of the work he carried out for his Masters degree in trying to reach a definition of free play that playworkers can use in their work. He shows how specific techniques (namely Bob's IMEE method of assessing the quality of play environments and Gordon's use of *tulpa*, a Tibetan custom of bringing forth a life form) can be adapted to look at the power relationships between children, playworkers and organisations in the facilitation or restriction of free play.

Time now to focus on our past. **Keith Cranwell** looks at the origins of adventure play in the community and particularly at the spirit of the play movement in which Bob and Gordon began their work. Highlighting the relationship between adventure playgrounds, delinquency and the counter-culture of the era, this chapter shows how adventure playgrounds and playworkers were in tune with the spirit of the age. Some of the debates around freedom of expression and empowerment still remain today and although the context for play provision has changed in some ways, the notion of play as a tool against delinquency (and its contemporary cousin antisocial behaviour) remains.

From playwork history to Bob's and Gordon's past, we are delighted to present an offering from the renowned mystery writer **Don Dare** who offers us a rare glimpse into Bob's and Gordon's early days of collaboration. A true, first, never-before-told-to-anyone, exclusive tale of the Fen Man and the Cowboy, complete with Dana, *jouissance*, toilet humour, a ghostly player, exploding chemicals, nursery rhymes and *tulpas*. Every play type included, guaranteed. Just spot them. Go on.

After such a boys'-own tale, **Ali Wood** and **Jacky Kilvington** ask whether there is a missing female perspective in playwork theorising. Using Perry Else's Wilber-inspired integral play framework, they consider play, playwork and playwork theorising from biological, psychological, anthropological and sociological perspectives. Careful to draw the distinction between male/female and man/woman, they consider whether a focus on the place of emotions and relationships in children's play might yield an alternative view of play types and play frames, ending with a consideration of the affective play environment.

Different ways of understanding and talking about play are also at the heart of **Jayne Shenstone**'s exploration of the relationship between colour and feelings, thoughts and actions. Drawing on ways of talking about colour and combining these with theories about visual, auditory and kinaesthetic modes of communication leads to some experimental and divergent models, culminating in a transformational model of play.

Returning to the theme of storytelling, **Maureen Palmer, Penny Wilson** and **Arthur Battram** present their own unique voices and those of the children and young people with whom they have played, interweaving these with fragments from the Playwork Principles, literature and philosophical musings on life, the universe and everything. A truly multivoiced piece delivered with wit, warmth and welly.

Bridget Handscomb offers a playful playwork version of Alex Glasgow's 'Socialist ABC' that celebrates the quirky, ludic and obscure language of play and playwork theory and practice – with a sting in the tail worthy of the original.

With a welcome and rare focus on a way of playing perhaps more often seen in girls than boys, **Sarah Atkinson** wonders why dressing-up play has received little attention from the theorists. Drawing from the literature on fashion and from her own experience of dressing-up play with children, Sarah discusses how the way we dress influences both how we feel about ourselves and how others perceive us, and how playing with dress allows both adults and children to play with identity and try on new ones for size.

Communicating about playwork's identity is a theme picked up in **Wendy Russell**'s chapter where she presents a journey through a maze of avenues and ideas to challenge the intrepid traveller. She navigates a complex series of twists, turns and dead ends, exploring and developing the concept of framing as an approach to understanding and articulating more about play and playwork.

Finding his own place in the frame was important for **Mel Potter.** He talks about his first job as a playworker and the rich rewards that playwork gave him – certainly not of the pecuniary variety. Despite parental incomprehension bordering on disapproval and lack of career opportunities, playwork, he says, has 'a way of getting under your skin'. The immediate and fundamental attraction of the work was augmented for Mel by attendance at PlayEducation conferences and a sharing of thinking and talking about play and playwork.

Stephen Smith and **Becky Willans** reflect on the way in which Bob's and Gordon's work has helped them identify how the play of disabled children and young people might be restricted. They illustrate this with the case of Layla, who was considered as naughty, spiteful and horrible. Drawing on aspects of Neuro-Linguistic Programming and the concept of play cues to help them understand and respond to Layla's different ways of communicating led to a better understanding of how she wanted to play and how the playworkers could support her in this.

Michelle Virdi and **Bridget Handscomb** chase our elusive butterfly in their reflections on the essence of playwork or the playwork 'way'. They consider their individual and shared journeys that have brought them to their current understandings of learning, development and reflective practice in playwork. They highlight how those who support playworkers through training and education can learn from and mirror the processes of play and playwork rather than being restricted by notions of 'packaging, templating and blueprinting the knowledge'.

To wrap it all up, in a playful homily, **Perry Else** uses Frank Capra's *It's a Wonderful Life* as a framework to consider what playwork might have been like without Bob's and Gordon's contributions, with some wacky Web wanderings and wonderings.

All in all, this adds up to a rich and diverse choir of playwork voices. Each one of us has been touched by Bob's and Gordon's solo and collective songs. We hope you enjoy these offerings.

Acknowledgements

We would like to acknowledge the help and support of those who have made this publication possible: firstly, Bob and Gordon themselves, for without them there would have been no Festschrift and no book.

Our heartfelt thanks go to the London Centre for Playwork Education and Training for publishing and underwriting this venture, and particularly to John Fitzpatrick, for offering ideas and support beyond the call of duty; all those who have written contributions as a gift to Bob and Gordon, and those who have undertaken the difficult task of critical reading of each other's work and particularly to Perry Else whose input has been invaluable; to Brian Sutton-Smith for planting the seed of the idea, and to Meynell for having the foresight and pluck to ask Brian to speak at the Birmingham NVQ conference, July 2004; to Annie and Sue who have made it possible to develop and maintain the surprise element and who must have immense patience and under-standing to put up with those two; to Colin and John, who made it possible for Wendy and Bridget to take on this gargantuan task, who kept things running smoothly in the background and who were, mostly, very understanding; finally, to all the children, young people and play-workers whose voices can be heard in this book.

Bridget Handscomb and Wendy Russell
March 2007

Chapter One

2007 – A Play Odyssey

Mick Conway

Primeval urges soon lead him to explore rock 'n' roll and swing, eventually to be played out when he becomes a disc jockey on an oil rig and then a youthworker far to the northwest, but first...

..at the edge of the forest, an enigma appears...

Meanwhile...

I must read...but what?? That ancient tablet is complete twaddle, and this new ambiguity that's just mysteriously appeared from nowhere is totally impenetrable! How do we become what we are? And where is everybody?? Am I just a lone organism on a hostile planet???

1. THOU SHALT NOT PONDER UPON THE BONES
2. THOU SHALT NOT EAT THE FRUIT OF KNOWLEDGE
3. THOU SHALT NOT DRINK THE WATER OF LIFE
4. NO BALL GAMES

Ontogenesis suddenly fast-forwards...

...do this??

Words too short...need big long words...like...like...essential and pertinent paradigmatic espousal of ludic tropes encompassing a cognitive rationale. Alternatively, why not just make it up as the playing 'I' goes along? And there's always the gnomic shamanic option!!!

Inevitably, a meeting of minds...

We appear to be surrounded by frames...containing...returns from Play Hughes? Must fully develop this cyclic ludogogic paradigm Elsewhere!!

Hallo mate - love the Colorado hat! Magic to meet a thinker who retains the child within!! Been reading your thoughts...mind-blowing stuff! Fancy joining me on a journey to the wilder shores of play type possibilities and speculations? I'm thinking the triune brain, recapitulation theory and an enriched day out on the beach!

Bob, the essence as I see it is to posit therapeutic meta-frames both built from _and_ encompassing unplayed-out material. But how to arrive at a full synthesis of our own impact on the playing other??

Deep stuff Gordon - but basically I'd just use intuition, memory, experience, evidence ... and whatever else comes to hand to cope with the consequences of gravity. Can I pose another eternal question: Are we nearly there yet? And hazard an answer: Yesss!!! I can see the sea!

Chapter Two

From Intuition to Understanding

Sandra Melville

This is Bob Hughes talking about his start in playwork in 1970: 'I had no idea what I had to do ... I walked onto an adventure playground one day and there were two hundred children there and I just kind of got on with it.' A few years later I walked onto an adventure playground as a local mum and found myself a member of a management committee with responsibility for employing staff. I had no idea either.

The founders of these neighbourhood playgrounds were inspired by a generalised vision of what a play space should be like, responding in part to what children chose for themselves and in part to their own instincts about what was good fun. There was a political edge to the provision created to foster children's autonomy and this attracted workers with a strong commitment to ideas of freedom and independence and to the adventurous, moderately anarchic atmosphere of the playgrounds.

Looking back, it seems as if we just about managed, relying on our intuition and often flying by the seat of our pants. As a group of local parents, we saw it as our job to recruit resourceful individuals with the energy, creativity and personal authority to manage the complications of day-to-day life on the playground. They had to be people who enjoyed and respected children and who wanted to spend their working days in play. As the local committee, we saw it as our role to negotiate the some-times contentious relationship with local residents, explaining and protecting spaces that were dedicated to children's use.

Photographs from the 1960s and 1970s show adventure playground sites with haphazard-looking high structures, rough terrain and features such as the burnt-out carcass of a car. These physical features, added to the fact that we catered for a very wide age range and attracted some of the more alienated local youth, are a reminder that, as both workers and volunteers, we were in a risky business.

Nevertheless, the playgrounds then were a comparatively novel phenomenon. There was a measure of support from neighbours, local authorities and funders who accepted for reasons of their own the value of what we were doing. Often these reasons had more to do with diverting local youngsters from antisocial behaviour than with any appreciation of the value of free play to every child or any recognition that children have entitlements in their own right.

Charged with responsibility to sustain funding and good neighbourly relations, committee members ran with any argument that would find favour on behalf of playgrounds, providing we were not diverted from what we wanted to do for children. If this meant accepting grants designed for Intermediate Treatment schemes for young people actually or potentially in trouble with the police, then so be it. For good or ill, accountability criteria were less onerous then and it was possible to attract funding on the basis that the project was seen to be generally 'a good thing' and reasonably well run, even if it was not particularly well understood. We were not called upon to explain play or justify our approach to playwork. The subject did not come up at our meetings, even after Gordon Sturrock joined our playground committee.

In London we were fortunate to have the backing of the London Adventure Playground Association (LAPA) which had been set up in 1962 for mutual aid by the five original London playgrounds. By the mid-1970s, there were more than twenty-five London playgrounds and LAPA had negotiated funding from the boroughs, notably from the Inner London Education Authority (ILEA), the largest education authority in the country and one of the most progressive. The funding secured playground salaries together with capacity in the Association to provide support services. There were similar playground groupings elsewhere in the country but nothing on this scale and this gave LAPA a certain standing nationally, despite its regional focus.

As the number of playgrounds grew, we could no longer rely on a supply of inspired individuals prepared to spend their working lives on the rewarding but often uncomfortable and always demanding task of running adventure playgrounds. The ILEA agreed to fund salaries for an in-service training scheme. The aim was to bring people with no playground experience to the point where they could apply for assistants' jobs after a year. With the need to develop training came the need to start thinking about and articulating what this work was all about.

Even so, the course elements of the training scheme concentrated heavily on personal confidence-building and the development of physical skills ranging from structure-building to kite-making. Placements on playgrounds, which constituted the main element of the training, were immensely useful in exposing trainees to the experience of senior workers. However, as former LAPA trainees have reminded us, we did not really address Bob Hughes' original question, 'What do I have to do?', let alone the more searching 'Why?' With hindsight, it could be said that what, in effect, LAPA was doing was replenishing the supply of resourceful individuals.

Meanwhile, the world around us was moving on. By the time I took over as General Secretary of LAPA in 1981, many playgrounds had been an established feature of their neighbourhoods for almost twenty years. They were clearly valued by their users, some now the second generation, but their ethos was increasingly out of joint with the times. They were no longer new and exciting to charitable funders who, in any case, were becoming anxious not to get locked into long-term revenue funding. There was increasing pressure on local authority resources. Social work, youth work and the under fives sector were developing their professional practice and all had views on play.

It was becoming urgent to be able to communicate, authoritatively, the distinctive nature of what we were doing to a variety of different audiences. The difficulty was, as one sympathetic ILEA grants officer pointed out to me, there was no discrete 'body of knowledge' to draw on. Though there had been competing theories and debate about children's play from the end of the nineteenth century, we had no specific analysis nor language to substantiate our claims for the importance of children's play throughout childhood or to explicate the nature of spaces and playwork that would foster play. What we did have was a fierce commitment to a set of values that underpinned our way of working with children and gave the work its particular character. This was proving to be no longer convincing on its own.

It is in large part due to the sustained work of Bob and Gordon that it now seems hard to make the imaginative leap back into those times. It is no accident that they both have a background in adventure playgrounds. Both are infused with that spirit of independence and the characteristically dogged determination to continue against all odds. Adventure playgrounds were the one form of supervised provision that had been conceived specifically for children to play in their own way. They were the right place from which to start developing the theory.

Throughout my time at LAPA (and PLAYLINK as it became), I was lucky enough to have access to the thinking of both of them and to be able to debate their developing ideas. Though we regularly disagreed, they were both enormously influential on my work and the work of the organisation. They provided coherent analysis and a rationale to replace individual intuition and interpretation. It was hard going at first – for them to articulate in simple terms the core of the ideas they were grasping for, and for me, and I suspect others, always to understand what they were getting at.

I was impatient for the thinking to be translated into robust concepts – clear, usable theory to explain and protect the provision and the practice on behalf of children; for, with the tremendous political drive behind education and childcare that grew throughout the 1990s, the pressure was really on to identify what was distinctive and valuable about provision solely for what we came to call 'free play'. (Interestingly, this was not a concept that we had to engage in the early days of adventure playgrounds, which were recognised simply as places where children could play. I hope the need for the term will fade away as play itself comes to be commonly understood.)

One of the problems PLAYLINK faced was that, in a sense, the idea that play is important for children had been successfully sold to politicians and others. Everyone seemed to be agreeing with us. It was common to hear the assertion, almost a mantra, in public policy arenas concerned with children in the 1990s. The trouble was that there was no agreement about what play was or why it was important.

Play was therefore conceptualised by different professional groups in terms of their own interests and expertise: play as a tool for learning in the classroom; play as a therapeutic tool for children injured by their life experience; play as a natural way for children to fill their time in their early years; play in local parks and playgrounds as a way for children to run around and 'let off steam'.

Most of these interpretations put the professional in a highly interventionist role in relation to the child's play. Even in the case of parks and playgrounds, it was the adult imagination at work in the design, creating fenced off spaces and garishly coloured play structures, some built literally to resemble a castle or galleon, as if to instruct children where and what to play.

In effect, there was no common understanding of the role of professionals creating, or working in, a setting where children came to play. The notion that children's autonomy in play might be both functional for their learning and development and essential for their enjoyment, an idea fundamental to the work of both Bob and Gordon, was not generally appreciated.

The Children Act 1989 required local social services departments to register and regulate staffed provision for children under eight and so brought adventure playgrounds and similar play settings within the regulatory framework for the first time. This increased the pressure to find a way to distinguish the nature and purpose of play provision, particularly provision where children come and go at will. Put crudely, we had to oppose the idea that an inspector should expect to observe a good deal of busyness by children and playworkers interacting together all the time, but we had to do it by suggesting what quality playwork should look like, and why. The results of these debates varied wildly across the country in terms of disseminating the ideas and impact on the provision.

When Ofsted became the regulatory authority under the Care Standards Act 2000, the opportunity was created to make our points at a national level rather than case by case in each local authority. This created both a context and a necessity for consistent theory throughout the country. As Bob and Gordon were refining their ideas, we were able to draw on them to make the case for an approach to the registration and regulation of adventure playgrounds and other open access play provision that would protect their essential nature. It was a case which Ofsted accepted, at least at the strategic level, without too much difficulty (though failure to grasp the principles at local level remains a problem in some areas).

For me, the second crucial idea underpinning the work of both Gordon and Bob is that of complexity, though they give expression to it in different ways. Bob's mode is an analysis of the many different ways in which children play and why – his play types. Gordon's mode, developed in conjunction with Perry Else, is the play cycle. Taken together, respect for children's autonomy and recognition of the complexity of their play indicate the need for playwork that is knowledgeable, subtle, observant and responsive, and for play spaces that are full of possibilities.

In a sense this brings us right back to the first days of adventure playgrounds with the crucial difference that the practice we followed instinctively then, we now increasingly understand and can articulate. The implication is that this understanding of play is transferable to other settings and other disciplines – the other important difference between then and now. It is no longer necessary to privilege one type of provision over another. In a properly ordered society (still some way off, I admit) this understanding of play will become part of the common knowledge and children will be able to find the play experience they want and need in all sorts of settings, and all over the place.

In the meantime, I salute Bob and Gordon for their individual contributions to the well-being of generations of children. I feel privileged to have been able to draw on their developing knowledge and ideas to substantiate my own work in making the case for play in public policy, and, disagreements notwithstanding, I am so glad to have known them both.

Chapter Three

Telling Tales

Stuart Lester

The aim of this chapter is to explore the dialogic nature of playwork and the development of a 'constructed voice' (Belenky *et al.* 1986) as an informed and passionate playwork perspective. Such a voice arises from the ability to align our subjective narratives, based largely on feelings, insights and memories, with relevant theory and to analyse critically the significance of this for our practice encounters.

The title of this piece provides a clue to two interconnected themes:

- Telling tales may refer to the ability of playworkers to narrate their stories of practice, to appropriate threads of other voices and to construct voices that resonate with passion and 'sparkle' (Bakhtin 1981). As we shall see, such dialogues have both an internal and external dimension.
- 'Telling' in another sense refers to the significance of the 'stories' narrated by Bob and Gordon in providing meaningful perspectives and enabling the development of a specific set of tools and resources that position a playworker in relation to the words, narratives and discourse of others.

A Personal Narrative

People are natural storytellers; throughout history, across ages and cultures humans have used stories or narratives (myth, folklore, fairy tale, legend, epic, opera, movies, biography, novel, plays, personal anecdote, etc.) to give meaning to their lives (Sarbin 1986).

As human beings we are constantly engaged in telling tales:

People make sense of their lives via story lines or narratives that are available at particular cultural moments. No life fits neatly into any one plot line and narratives are multiple, contradictory, changing and differently available ... some help us tell our lives well; some break down in the face of the complications of our lives and times.

(Lather and Smithies 1997, p. 125)

Narratives are intimately connected with understanding ourselves and fashioning our identity; stories represent who we are. A narrative or story is not simply an objective reconstruction of personal experience but an expression of how it is perceived. As such, it is based on the story-teller's life experiences and recounts selected parts of his/her life. We may see that narrating, or telling our personal stories, is pivotal for the person's sense of self and it takes us further than simply describing the world. Storytelling positions us in the world.

Thus, as a playworker, I tell many stories to a wide range of real and imagined audiences. Telling these stories features not simply my voice, but intimately connects to the voices of others. I cannot tell my story of being a playworker without telling children's stories of play. Equally, my telling of stories draws upon other voices that have been highly influential in shaping my ability to tell these tales.

Of course, this is a complex tale, and does not follow any 'once upon a time ... and they all live happily ever after' pattern. It is accidental, opportunistic, non-linear, and at times apparently random and an emotional roller-coaster. Yet our stories need to make sense to ourselves; we need to construct a 'sensible' and coherent life story. As such, rather than a linear narrative, these multiple storylines represent an emergent unfolding tale that is dynamic and fluid, in which countless treasured and valued stories are continuously modified, transformed, reconstructed, relived and retold.

Telling my tale involves many intertwining narrative threads. Stories of magic, wonder and beauty mingle with darker tales that represent intense dissatisfaction and frustration, often arising from a struggle with the underlying paradigmatic assumptions; sometimes my beliefs appear at odds with other increasingly dominant narratives of children's play and of adult roles in working with this process. Inevitably, all good stories contain tension, subplots, twists in the tale and dramatic peaks and troughs as they meander to some resolution; but they are held together by a sense of continuity and coherence. Initially half-formed ideas grow through practice and experience into some deeper perspectives that also become connected with the voices of others, providing 'tools' that strengthen principles and associated actions, giving rise to new voices and languages.

This telling of my tale, then, explores the very nature of telling tales and the development of our ability as playworkers to develop tales worth telling.

Playwork as Dialogue and Storytelling

We live in a 'story-shaped' world, in which social and cultural values, histories, myths and so on provide 'libraries of plots' that help us interpret our own and other people's experiences (Sarbin 1986). Narratives, thus, are stories of our 'self' as a person situated in the social, cultural, historical and institutional contexts in which we live. We select and tell our stories according to our position in relation to the listeners and audience.

The notion of a positioned or situated storyteller takes us away from looking at dialogue as a pure mental process, something that happens inside us, to recognition that dialogue is a form of 'mediated action' (Wertsch 1998) that involves two central elements: the person who is doing the acting and telling; and 'cultural tools', or the physical and semiotic instruments, resources and artefacts that are appropriated from the culture and used by the agent to accomplish a given action (Tappan 2005).

To tell a story requires a voice directed at another, whether real or imagined, using signs that are expressive of culture, history and ideologies. Our dialogues are mediated actions in both form and function. How, then, do playworkers construct their stories and identities? What cultural tools do they use and how is one selected over another?

Playwork Voices

Playworkers are increasingly presented with 'standards' that describe specific tasks and functions, a prescript of practice designed to achieve appropriate outcomes. Having defined what a playworker does, the next step is to ensure compliance through training, inspection and regulation systems. This approach represents a powerful technical tool designed to mediate the actions of the playworker.

Yet, at the same time another perspective has emerged, like a caterpillar crawling along and nibbling away at these 'prescripted stories' with a deeper and richer narrative, perhaps best summarised by Gordon's rendition of the playing child that:

contains ideas of evolution and adaptation, of environment and ecology, of deep laws, of nature and nurture, of genes and inheritance, of emotional repertoires, of identity and self.

(Conway *et al.* 2004, p. 2)

Such a perspective offers the opportunity for a different way of relating to the world; but it is not simply about children's play: playworkers themselves are immersed in these ideas of evolution and adaptation, deep laws and processes. The playworker is a subject whose inner life will influence and be influenced by his/her encounters with the playing child; both the child and the playworker emerge from this process changed in some way. The playworker, as with the child at play, is both being and becoming. As Bob eloquently expresses:

When we see a child playing with a flower, or in the dirt, or skipping or playing tag, we should remind ourselves that what we are looking at is the child-like result of a deep and irresistible urge to interact with and have knowledge of the world and everything in it.

(Hughes 2001, p. 13)

A broader and deeper perspective of children's play must inevitably involve a similar appreciation of the complexity of being a playworker. As playworkers, our positioning alongside children's play sees us as being intimately connected with a deep and irresistible urge to understand the world and our place in it. The idea that play is at the very centre of our being takes an appreciation of the playworker role into totally different territory.

The Playwork Brain at Play

At this point the story starts to get a little complicated. Perhaps this is inevitable given the fertile, verdant vegetation that our caterpillars have led us through. The next stage takes us into the luxuriant field of neuroscience with a brief introduction to two themes:

1. Dominant views of the adult/child polarity emphasise the incompleteness and immaturity of the child against the complete, rational 'grown-up'. Yet during the past two decades, the idea that the mature brain can alter its function and structure in response to experience has gained acceptance (Rakic 1998; Gritti *et al.* 2002). Research suggests

that new neuronal connections in different brain regions occur in adult mammals, and that these regions actually contain adult stem cells (the progenitors of neurons) that display a 'multipotency' much broader than expected (Gritti *et al.* 2002). What this research indicates is that our brains continue to show plasticity throughout our lifetime and it may be speculated here that the suggested role of play in maintaining neural plasticity in children (Sutton-Smith 1997) may also apply to adults.

2. Gallese *et al.* (2004) propose that our brains contain neural mechanisms (called mirror neurons) that enable us to understand directly the meanings of actions of others by internally simulating these without a cognitive reasoning process. That is, we intuitively understand the actions of other subjects by matching their actions through our own neuronal responses (Rizzolatti *et al.* 2001). A similar mechanism is involved in our capacity to experience and empathise with the emotions of others. Obviously, this mapping process is not the sole way that we come to understand actions or emotions; the simulation initiates a whole series of internal events that adds further value to this initial impression, as we will explore later.

Of course, this is all highly complex, but it may speculatively suggest that as playworkers, we are intimately connected to a child's play through this neural mirroring. A child's play triggers an internal psychosomatic replay, initiating a series of ripples that conjure up memories, emotions and body responses. Specific neural clusters enable us, initially, to establish a personal reading of children's play, and then to continue to carry out acts of simulation in response to this connection. Our very contact with the playing child instils in us a sense of being at play. As Sutton-Smith (1997, p. 60) proposes, the brain is engaged in 'a ceaseless inner talking that is like fantasy', and extends this through the theory of 'neural fabulation', which suggests that 'the brain is creating some kind of inner fiction, or is at play with itself'. Deleuze (1997, cited in Prout 2005) comments on the way that children maintain a continuous stream of chatter as they engage in their activities; such activities may be seen as 'dynamic trajectories of practice' and their auto-conversations, as mental 'maps' of these trajectories, are constantly changing and shifting. So, too, the playworker constructs his or her fabulations and readings of the play, the brain in a state of constant dialogue and story-making with itself, creating a continuous succession of profile changes (Damasio 1994).

Embodied and Embedded Voices

This fabulating brain cannot be reduced to an isolated organ sitting in a skull, but is connected to the entire organism and situated within the world. Our connections with the play of the child initiates a continuous dynamic and reciprocal interaction between three permanent and inter-twined modes of bodily activity (Thompson and Varela 2001):

1. Organismic regulation (homeostasis) of the entire body, essential to being alive and sentient. It is evident through our emotions and feel-ings, body regulation and responding to basic drives and instincts.
2. Sensorimotor coupling between organism and environment, expressed through our perception, emotion, and associated actions that arise from this.
3. Intersubjective interaction, involving the recognition of the inten-tional meaning of actions and linguistic communication of others.

Thompson and Varela (2001) note that the human brain is central to these three modes of activity, and it is also reciprocally shaped and structured by them throughout the lifespan. The nervous system, the body and the envi-ronment are 'highly structured dynamical systems, coupled to each other on multiple levels' (ibid., p. 423) and are so thoroughly enmeshed – biolog-ically, ecologically and socially – that they should be viewed as mutually embedded systems rather than defined through a binary of internal/exter-nal. Our narratives as playworkers are constructed through these three modes and perhaps can be illustrated by the following:

A story of playwork
A playworker stands in the middle of an adventure playground, casually observing children's play on the rope swing, watching as children 'deck' (jumping on each other) with all the usual chal-lenges, teases and threats that accompany this form of playing. As more children manage to cling onto the rope, the cries of the chil-dren become louder, laughter and screams are interspersed with 'squeals' of pain and comments about each others weight, accompa-nied by jostling behaviours to try and get others to fall off the swing and so on until the swing gradually comes to a halt and children disentangle themselves, many of the group falling to the sand beneath the swing.

As this action unfolds, we may envisage the playworker having an internal commentary, a dialogue with him/herself, about this situation. Of course, this is only one situation that the playworker encounters during the play session. Throughout this period there will be a multitude of dialogues, some imagined and internal, others real and external. The content of these dialogues represents the playworker identity; they are the voices the playworker uses to give meaning to experience, to position him/herself in time and space and to take appropriate actions in response.

The Inner Voices of the Playworker – Telling Tales to Ourselves

Two forms of dialogue structure our daily experiences: imaginal and actual. These forms are certainly not separated but rather, exist side by side and are intimately interwoven; they are both part of our narrative construction of the world (Hermans 2002). Even when we may be 'silent' (that is, not speaking to an external other), we maintain an inner dialogue that carries out endless chatter with our conscience and all the people and things that inhabit this state.

Fogel *et al.* (2002) comment that the dialogical self is composed of multiple I-positions, each interacting with the other and each having a unique perspective on the individual's experience. As Hermans *et al.* (1992) explain, the 'I' has the possibility to move in response to changes in situation and time; the 'I' in one position can disagree, understand, ridicule the 'I' in another position. There is an active voice in the multiple self (Hermans 1996). These voices '... take turns in an internal dialogue, like interacting characters in a story. They agree or disagree and tell stories from their own perspective'. (Lewis 2002, p. 177).

Imaginal interactions certainly have a pervasive influence on real interactions; they offer a playing forward of how you might approach someone, a rehearsal of what you might say or a replay of what has already been said and done and how you might have handled this differently, and opportunities to check feelings about the situation. Let us look then, at two possible dialogues that might take place in relation to the playwork story:

Dialogue 1

The start of the play sees the playworker in a state of some vague and indeterminate pleasure in this scene: 'The children appear to be getting on with things and enjoying themselves.' However, as the action unfolds and the noise levels increase, the playworker becomes increasingly anxious and there appears to be a sense of foreboding: 'It looks like it might be getting out of hand', 'remember last week when somebody ended up crying', 'I wish you older ones would stop teasing each other', 'what if my manager walks in at this point?' 'why don't the other play-workers do something, why am I always having to deal with these situations?' and so on.

Dialogue 2

The start of the play sees the playworker in a state of some vague, inde-terminate pleasure: 'The children appear to be getting on with things and enjoying themselves', and as the action unfolds and the noise levels increase, the playworker becomes more tuned in to this, 'I wonder what might happen now', 'did you see the laughter on the child's face as they screamed in pain?' 'wasn't that a creative tease issued by one child to another', 'what an amazing response from the child', and so on.

Of course, these are highly stylised dialogues, and there is every possi-bility that the playworker employs all of these voices within the scene, giving rise to a complexity of call and response patterns. The inner dialogue is an attempt to resolve the author's conflict and tension; there needs to be some resolution to this conversation. Multiple voices play together, but one dominant voice will emerge and lead to some form of assessment of the situation and plan of action.

What Informs these Voices?

Lewis (2002) proposes a neural account of the brain's ability to talk to itself, highlighting that this is not a multiple and simultaneous voice but is turn-taking. He suggests that the prefrontal system of the brain is central to initiating and maintaining these internal dialogues. The prefrontal cortex is in a 'privileged position' among other systems as a recipient of many signals about the external world, the internal body state and previous and current body states; 'the entire prefrontal region seems dedicated to categorising contingencies in the perspective of personal relevance' (Damasio 1994, p. 181). Lewis (2002) identifies two independent attentional areas in this system that may be implicated in internal dialogues: the orbitofrontal cortex (OFC) and the anterior cingu-late cortex (ACC); each of these has a different connection to the motor circuits. The ACC is associated with monitoring and evaluating potential actions, resolving conflicts and selecting attention. The OFC appears to hold attention to threatening or rewarding aspects of the environment. Both of these regions serve as 'interfaces' between the prefrontal cortex and the limbic system, a region of the brain that is intimately involved with the mediation of emotions. The vertical connections between the prefrontal cortex and limbic structures of the brain (often referred to as 'paralimbic') are crucially important for 'integrating the cognitive and emotional aspects of psychological functioning' (Lewis 2005, p. 259).

The two attentional positions (ACC and OFC) are not active at the same time but the capacity to switch subjective voices rapidly and completely between the two areas does permit autonomous voices to become engaged in something like a dialogical exchange:

> The internal monologue implies the presence of another person, because it is directed toward an imaginal (but unspecific) sense of that person and it adjusts and updates itself through a changing anticipation of how that other person will respond ... The switch of subjectivities between attentional systems permits the interjection of enormous emotional intensity and novelty into internal dialogues, and this may provide the creativity to carve out unique dialogical frames.
>
> (Lewis 2002, p. 188)

Lewis (2005) indicates that there is a 'trade-off' between these systems that may see, in crude terms, supremacy of emotions over cognitive processes or vice versa. Where emotions dominate, there is likely to be an emotional colouring that becomes strengthened with time. This elaboration of the emotional response becomes more readily called upon to assess future uncertain situations.

An Emotional Response – the Embodied Voice

The internal dialogue, as Lewis (2002) suggests, is emotionally driven. We adopt our subjective positions according to how we feel; the imagined dialogue establishes continuous feedback loops to monitor current body states. Emotions establish a set of preferences for future situations, what Damasio (1994) refers to as 'somatic markers'. In categorising the situations we encounter, we draw upon 'dispositional representations', a neural 'memory' of what it felt like in the past. These are not simply bodily responses but also occur through '*as if* body loops' (Damasio 1994), an implicit non-reflexive simulation mechanism that Gallese

(2003) suggests may be triggered by the observation of the behaviour of others.

These markers do not make decisions but signal to the prefrontal cortices and may act as a bias towards a reasoned response. Without emotions, rationality cannot work: 'no logic determines salience: what to notice, what to attend to, what to inquire about' (De Sousa 1987, p. 192). Equally, Lewis (2005) comments on the way that the brain connects through *vertical integration*; our primitive agendas for survival flow up the neuroaxis while at the same time the regions for planning and knowledge flow down from the cortical regions. As Lewis (2005, p. 260) notes:

> If not for the bottom up flow, the brain would have no energy and no direction for its activities. If not for the top down flow, recently evolved mechanisms for perception, action, and thought would have no control over body states and behaviour.

Vertical integration explains the way that the brain coordinates itself in response to a significant change in internal or external events that trigger an emotion and thus require the initiation of a cognitive and/or motor response.

Returning to the playwork scenario, we can see that there are powerful emotions being triggered that will affect the possible actions taken. In the first situation the reading of the play draws on an understanding of adult responsibility, a 'face value' impression that the children's play is not 'nice' and so on. Anxiety, fear, concern about children getting hurt and our potential culpability in this situation, based on these emotional triggers, are likely to give rise to justifications and actions for curbing this kind of play. The internal dialogue is voiced around adult responsibilities, issues of safety and seeking to control behaviour. As Lewis (2005) observes, a tendency to process information with a negative emotional bias (i.e. anxiety) leads to increasing activity in the limbic and lower-brain circuits, and this activity feeds back to the cortical systems that increasingly attend to the anxiety-relevant aspects of the situation.

Given that the internal preference system is inherently biased to seek better than neutral situations, to avoid pain and seek potential pleasure (Damasio 1994), the playworker strives to seek a better state of being. This can be achieved by responding to the cause of their anxiety through curtailing or controlling the play. Thus, children become the object of concern, positioned as 'the other'. Of course, this is problematic in playwork terms: 'How can the other be seen as the cause of one's discomfort but still be attended to, responded to, empathized with, and emotionally connected with?' (Miehls and Moffatt 2000, p. 341).

The second dialogue offers an alternative reading that provokes a different emotional response. Interplay of memories and experiences, of ideas and intuitions initiates voices that seek to enter into (unspoken) dialogues with children. We might find that there is both an internal and external dialogue based on subjective emotional feelings and the simulation of feelings in other subjects giving rise to 'spontaneous emotional communication' (Schore 2001, p. 314). As Schore notes, this level of communication enables resonance between participants, a synchronisation of affect. Here the playworker is attuned to the moment-by-moment rhythmic structures of the play and at the same time conversant and conversing with their own, subjective, fluid, emotional states.

While this communication will not remove the uncertainty, it will help to lessen any anxiety that might arise from this. In this mode, the playworker has more time and energy to muse with the playing children, to play with their own tentative ideas about what is happening and to participate in feelings of uncertainty and 'unknowing'. A state of curiosity and elation as the play unfolds initiates a rapid generation of multiple images, which in turn brings about a greater range of cues available to judge the situation and make inferences about what is going on. Accompanying this will be a greater enhancement of motor efficiency and increase in exploratory behaviours; we become more attentive to the play, our sense of wonder and curiosity remains alive (but, as Damasio also points out, the extreme of this may be found in manic states).

In contrast, when we are anxious and fearful about the play, we will have narrow and less efficient inferences, we become over-focused on the cause of our anxiety, our motor capabilities are inhibited and ease of action reduced (again, Damasio highlights the extreme form of this as depression).

Thus, the positions that these 'I' voices adopt are based on a reading of the situation, informed by past experiences and events, giving rise to an emotional response. Such a perspective depicts the self as a dynamic multiplicity of different or opposed (voiced) 'I' positions that send their emotionally laden messages to each other internally, but also are constructed in relation to an external audience (real or imagined). The audience becomes another layer of our voice; we adopt 'I' positions in relation to our perception of the people listening and involved in the dialogue.

Voices in the World: the Embedded Voices of Playwork

Our voices are not simply an internal dialogue, a specific aspect of mental functioning cut off from everything else, but are very much part of the wider environment. The dialogical self is spatially structured and embodied, populated by the voices of other people, and historically and culturally contextualised (Hermans 2003).

The multiple voice is a representation of a collective of voices. Dialogue is informed by many social languages, including professional jargon, languages of different age groups, passing cultures and fashions, and the language that serves the dominant sociopolitical purposes (Hermans and Kempen 1995). Whether or not we are aware of it, these social languages influence our unique voices. Thus, the playworker, when giving an opinion about playwork, is aligning with the voices of others from diverse collectives.

Yet these heterogeneous groups and the voices that are employed to tell their stories are not equal in power or authority. The voice of one group may be hegemonic and suppress the voices of others. Alongside this are counter voices that provide alternative dialogues and seek to challenge existing orthodoxies. We may see that our distinct voices – the collective and the personal – may at times be at odds:

> Social positions are governed and organised by societal definitions, expectations and prescriptions, whereas personal positions receive their form from the particular ways in which individuals organise their own lives sometimes in opposition to or protest against the expectations implied by societal expectations. (Hermans 2001, p. 263)

Dialogue may be seen as both internally and externally power-laden. As part of a process of turn-taking, voices are able to take initiatives and display their views in asymmetrical patterns. There are many ways in which one of the parties can be said to dominate communication and some people have more opportunity to exert power through dialogue than do others.

A Dominant Voice

Bakhtin (1981) makes the point that only when we invest words with our own intentions and unique accent can we claim to own the words of others. Prior to this point the word exists in other people's contexts, serving other people's intentions: it is from there that one must take the word and make it one's own ... Language is not a natural medium that passes freely and easily into the private property of the speaker's intentions; it is populated – overpopulated – with the intentions of others. Expropriating it, forcing it to submit to one's own intentions and accents, is a difficult and complicated process.   (Bakhtin 1981, p. 283)

Bakhtin distinguishes between two discourses, 'authoritative' and 'internally persuasive', and the distinction between the two can be found in the degree of ownership that one accepts for what one says (Tappan 2005). Dominant stories are likely to arise through authoritative discourse, where another's words are recited by heart and through that recitation make demands that it has an authority fused to it. Bakhtin (1981, p. 341) explains: 'It is not a free appropriation or assimilation of the word itself that authoritative discourse seeks to elicit from us, rather it demands our unconditional allegiance.'

Tappan (2005) notes that such discourse is distanced, it cannot be changed, doubted or altered. As such there can be no true dialogue, and no play with the context that frames it. It becomes a 'sacred story' (Clandinin and Connelly, 1995) to be transmitted and never questioned. Thus, playworkers may face demands to make utterances that are representative of a prevailing authoritative discourse, invested with a power and social forms shaped by the use of power, that inevitably condition and impact practice through both subtle and less subtle means. Here we find legislation, codes, policy agendas and regulations scripted into playwork, often with no 'substantive place for conversation about what is being funnelled down' (Huber and Whelan 1999, p. 387).

Hermans (2006), drawing on the work of Lysaker and Lysaker (2002), comments on a disorganised self-narrative of the 'monologue', where the dialogical capacity is seriously reduced, rigid and immune to any evolution, transformation and ability for shared understanding with others.

Once these authoritative stories are in place they direct attention from the unique dynamics and relationships in any given situation towards more generalised and stereotypical patterns. Fogel *et al.* (2002) argue that all dialogues, whether real or imagined, form into regularly recurring routines, or 'frames'. These frames, while recurring in a relationship over a period of time, may show regularities but do not remain the same; there will always be some variability, as Fogel *et al.* (2002, p. 192) comment, 'more like an improvisation rather than following a script'. Yet some frames become rigid, relatively unchanging over time and stuck with familiar patterns. A rigid frame limits opportunities for growth through the process of the 'I' positions adopting resistant or coercive stances.

Perhaps the first playwork dialogue uses a language that is externally authorised, unquestioned and directed internally as a form of regulation. What is missing is any connection with the playing children as a subject; children feature only as an object of concern in their internal dialogues.

In contrast, when one appropriates and owns the words that are spoken, they become internally persuasive. Bakhtin (1981, p. 345) highlights the nature of ownership:

> In the everyday rounds of our consciousness, the internally persuasive word is half-ours and half-someone else's. Its creativity and productiveness consist precisely in the fact that such a word awakens new and independent words, that it organises masses of our words from within, and does not remain in an isolated and static condition ... it enters into an intense interaction, a struggle with other internally persuasive discourses. Our ideological development is just such an intense struggle within us for hegemony among various available verbal and ideological points of view, approaches, directions and values.

Thus ownership can be seen as a creative process marked by an emerging separation between an internally persuasive and an authoritarian driven discourse. This can be an extremely difficult and uncomfortable process at times (although we should also acknowledge that at other times it can be highly pleasurable), but the struggle with other discourse is of crucial importance to the construction and emancipation of the individual voice. In this creative frame, new narratives are constantly being written to replace the old (Fogel *et al.* 2002).

Listening to the Voices – Tools for the Job

A dialogical approach regards communication as a process in which participants work collaboratively to produce shared meanings, both internally and externally. Our internal dialogues draw on a range of cultural tools to seek to resolve some of the inner tensions and conflicts associated with being a playworker. Playworkers are not individuals, alone in their actions, but are continuously a part of a society in which others are indirectly co-construing their individual actions. In performing their actions there is always 'another' present (internal or external, real or imagined). This presence initiates a dialogue, a process of question and answer, of agreement or disagreement (Hermans and Kempen 1995). Let's look at another situation:

A playworker visits the local play 'scrap' resource centre and explores the resources, selecting various materials and identifying what children will be able to do with them, carrying out an internal dialogue along the following lines:

'What can I plan for children to do tonight?'
'Ah, here are some bobbins, we could use these to make puppets'
'What else do I need to do this?'
'Sponge balls would make really good heads'
'This material could be used to make costumes,' and so on.

At the same time, another playworker is checking the shelves and appears to be selecting very similar items but with a different internal commentary

'I wonder what children might do if they discovered some of these lying around in the play setting'.

The articles collected are the same, but the agency and mediation of these are formed in two different spaces. Markova (2006) discusses the idea of a 'third party', as a voice from outside that participates symbolically in our internal voices. When we extend this, we may see that the first playworker's agency is mediated by thoughts, writings and tools that reflect a dominant discourse about children's play based on control, productivity and purpose, what Sutton-Smith (1997) refers to as 'progress rhetoric'. The communication frame is rigid in the sense that it leads to a highly ordered and causal dialogue. The second playworker's dialogue is talking and listening to different voices and the multiple 'I' positions implicitly hold a narrative with children's play. Their agency uses a different set of tools and symbolic voices that clearly accept that uncertainty is a desirable state. In appropriating tools we may find there is a difference between 'mastery' as a process of following instructions, codes and prescriptions with a high degree of skill and accuracy and 'owner-ship' as a representation of our ability to make the tools our own (Tappan 2005).

Telling Tales

And so as this tale draws to a close, it is time for some resolution to the themes presented here. What is suggested is that our playwork identity is embodied and embedded; neural, somatic and environmental elements mutually interact to form our ways of being a playworker. This being is shaped in a shared intersubjective space in which, as Gallese (2003, p. 525) suggests, when we observe other acting individuals and

> face their full range of expressive power (the way they act, the emotions and feelings they display), a meaningful embodied interpersonal link is automatically established by means of simulation.

The mirroring of children's play through neural simulation triggers dispositional representations: we draw on our memories and experiences, and in learning to read this simulation we invest it with meaning – it is how it plays through us (Sturrock 2003).

This intersubjective space is populated by many voices, real and imagined, silent and spoken, historical and contemporary, competing for our attention. Some of these voices are more powerful than others, authoritative tools that seemingly demand to be obeyed.

The telling contributions from Bob and Gordon have added significant 'third-party' voices that speak symbolically with our internal dialogues. They provide a referential *'inner alter'* (Markova 2006), someone to talk with as we seek resolution to our practice encounters.

Their explorations of evolution and adaptation, of environment and ecology, of deep laws, of nature and nurture, of genes and inheritance, of emotional repertoires, of identity and self provide a powerful counter-hegemonic voice, a mediational means to transform, and be transformed by, our actions. These tools have amplified our sense of self in dialogic relationship with children's play, providing an ever-deepening awareness of our emotional and ideational responses as we continually seek to give meaning to our experiences.

From this dialogic perspective playworkers begin to speak with a constructed voice (Belenky *et al.* 1986), to narrate their stories with passion and a growing confidence to articulate their meanings, to engage in dialogue, to dare to play and be human, to embrace the uncertainty and tension and welcome this as a vibrant part of being a playworker.

The drive to make sense of children's play in terms of those 'deep laws' has provided many more voices, signposts of possibilities and increasing opportunities for dialogue. They have added to an internally persuasive voice that accepts continuity and discontinuity as an essential part of the play process; creativity, fascination and curiosity must be complemented by apprehension, doubt, uncertainty and tension.

Adapting from Daloz (1999) we may see that the contributions of Bob and Gordon act as a guide to accompany the journey of our play lives. We trust these voices, not with any degree of certainty but because of their own playfulness with possibilities, their continuing quest. They embody our hopes and passions, interpret arcane signs, warn us of possible dangers and hazards that lie along the route and show us a multitude of delights along the way.

And so finally back to the caterpillars and their guided journey through the lush vegetation, floating ideas that soar and resonate, leading to wonderful transformations. We may seek to avoid these, like the caterpillar who sees a butterfly and says to a fellow caterpillar, 'You wouldn't get me up in one of those'. But of course to do so would deny the very existence of those deep laws that are at the heart of children's play and human existence.

Chapter Four

Notes from a Playworker Who Wanted Children to Play His Game

Ian Macintyre

It's like remembering a bad dream: images of children with clipboards, pens and questionnaires. Children with cameras, children in hard hats, children with spirit levels and even one holding the Chancellor's big red budget box aloft with a menacing grin. These images of children being hailed as *'expert architects'* that are now a familiar sight in many children's publications, often disturb my morning journey to work. Oh why won't you let me forget – leave me in peace! Like the offspring of the Stepford Wives these impossibly together children are not only *designing their own play spaces*, they are *experts in behaviour*, should be *consulted about playworkers' salaries* and could even show the Chancellor of the Exchequer a thing or two about *fiscal policy*.

This article offers the personal reflections of one playworker on how easy it is, despite the best of intentions, to get caught up in the heady world of adult agendas such as consultation, participation, targets and outputs. Drawing on my own experiences, I will argue that unless we are clear about what we are trying to achieve, and prioritise time to reflect, discuss and record what actually goes on on our playsites, we are likely to prioritise activities that can lead to an adulteration of children's play experiences.

I first came across the idea of adulteration of play through the work of Bob Hughes, who attributes it to the work of Gordon Sturrock and Perry Else (1998). Bob (Hughes 2001, p. 163) interprets adulteration as meaning '... the hijacking of the child's play agenda by adults with the intention of substituting it with their own'. Bob Hughes' work has provided playworkers with ways on which to reflect and understand different essential ingredients of play. In 1999, Bob carried out an evaluation of Hackney Play Association's (HPA's) 'Design and Build (D&B) Project', and it was this report that helped me get my feet back on the ground, reminding me what the role of a playworker should be. I should make it clear at this point that I am only referring to the Design and Build Project that I managed in Hackney between 1996 and 1999 and not about the project at any other time past or present.

With this report in mind, and with the help of Carse's (1986) concept of finite and infinite games, I am going to explore how playworkers can resist the adulteration of children's play and make sure our work facilitates quality play environments and supports the play process.

Many moons ago I had a great opportunity to lead the D&B project. HPA had secured Lottery funding for the D&B project to promote the ideas later expressed in *Best Play* (NPFA *et al.* 2000) practice by taking practical and theoretical ideas out to playsites. HPA was in the process of developing what was to become *Quality in Play* (Conway and Farley 1999), in an attempt to protect and promote play. Central to this agenda was recognition of the rights of children as autonomous individuals with views and expertise about play who should be consulted and involved in any developments of 'their' play space.

So What was Design and Build about?

I had a healthy budget and some of the best playworkers in the business with whom to work. I saw D&B's role as involving children and playworkers in analysing and changing their play environments. I thought I was more than ready to put into practice some of what I had learnt and, as with many male playworkers, I quite liked building big structures.

D&B took resources and materials to playsites, where we introduced ourselves, played games and talked with the children and playworkers about what was good and not so good about their particular site. We took children on trips to experience other playsites. Back on their playgrounds we used a Play Environment Audit that I had adopted from Bob (Hughes 1996). Children were given pens and paper on which to mark their favourite areas, the worst bits, exciting areas, quiet areas, smelly areas and so on. We did practical planning exercises, making maps, models, videos and questionnaires and discussed possible improvements using themes such as: what kind of fun, for whom and what is going to go wrong?

Many different and colourful things were to some degree or other designed and built by children. The permanent projects included murals, building various play structures such as swings, slides, sand pits, walkways and camps. The temporary sessions involved turning up and making a fantastic mess on estates and at festivals with a vast amount of cardboard, cloth and, in the latter days, a huge amount of water and several pumps straining the suspension of our van. These sessions were the easiest to organise, the most fun and arguably the most successful. However, this essay is about the conflicts and anomalies that can arise from involving children in playground design and not what Bob called this 'travelling thespians' aspect – that is another story ...

I was hugely proud that under complicated restrictions we enabled children to lift mechanically a telegraph pole over six metres high for a big swing. We even made voting fun! It took about a year for D&B to settle down with a relatively stable staff team experienced at producing fairly simple end products from the fantastically free imaginations of children. The more slick we became, the more I became aware of the contradictions and paradoxes of our top-down approach to consultation. Were we involved in clever workshop planning and engineering and not play? Or, in Bob's words, had we become examples of playworkers 'who wanted the children to succeed in spite of themselves'? (Hughes 1999, p. 8)

Originally, I became involved in adventure playgrounds because it was fun. I was not interested in play theory, I was interested in being involved in playing: making hills and tunnels, a raku kiln, building go-carts and a lot of other stuff that was as much about my own playing as that of the children (what Sturrock and Else, 1998, refer to as 'unplayed-out material'). I knew that play was more than mucking about and keeping fit. It enabled children to express themselves and er ... err ... social interaction was good for them, but that was about it. In 1996, I got hold of *Play Environments: A Question of Quality* and *A Playworker's Taxonomy of Play Types* (Hughes 1996a; Hughes, 1996b). I had never heard of this Bob Hughes but he made me think! He helped me make sense of what I felt my job was and I started to believe that there was a way to talk about the whys and wherefores of play that was spiritually and scientifically sound. I thought that it made sense because it was not just all heady thinking. His heart was in the right place because his feet were on the ground of an understanding of the *feelings* of play. I saw Bob's articulation of play types and analysis of what contributes to and/or detracts from a quality play environment as radical and useful tools.

At D&B I wanted to involve children and playworkers in this epiphany so I designed Play Environment Audits and Play Types Spidergrams that I thought children and playworkers could understand. But I had not fully thought it through. I rushed out with my new toy and tried to educate children and playworkers about Play Types and Play Environment

Audits without spending enough time reflecting on where the children and playsite were at.

I therefore have photos of children with tools proudly smiling for the local paper in front of 'the boat designed and built by children'. *Yes,* the children had decided that they wanted a boat. *Yes,* they had designed and built it. *Yes,* they had enjoyed much of the process, but how much leading or adulterating of children's play did I do?

- YES – D&B was a lot of fun for children and adults, taking exciting new opportunities all over Hackney, and we successfully involved children in designing and changing their play environments.
- OH NO IT WASN'T – It confused two conflicting aims: designing and building play structures that fitted adult defined criteria and empowering children under the auspices of consumer choice. Of course, the adults won out and the children ultimately had little real say in the final designs and limited input into the actual building work.
- BUT the children liked using the clipboards. They loved being involved in planning and designing their playspace and we piloted the use of Play Environment Audits and used Play Types with playworkers and children.

Going up to accept the 'Children's Involvement' award at London Play, I knew that we had won the award not only because we had built some great stuff with children, but because we had presented the project well. Whose needs were being met by this project, adults' or children's?

Towards the end of the project we had Bob in to do an evaluation. Although we had 'by and large achieved our aims' (Hughes 1999), the main flaw that Bob identified was 'the deviation into participation' (Hughes 1999, p. 11) – something that I was keen to encourage! He commented that the project 'unintentionally "adulterate[d]" children's ideas by getting children to draw things and then subjecting them to an adult selection process of what was and wasn't feasible' (Hughes 1999, p. 10). Although I really wanted Bob to do the evaluation, being interviewed by him felt like being in the head teacher's office. Yes Bob, some of the permanent structures we built were 'formulaic', but there were time constraints and we were working with people unused to analysing, let alone changing their playgrounds. Did he not see the wonderful bottle top rattle shapes strung out across rope walkways, or the buttons on the

Bat Pole? Yes, we had imposed our own interpretations on the children's ideas and selected and adapted them, but we needed to get them built within a short timescale with finite resources and to conform to Health and Safety standards and be of some play value in the longer term. On reflection, although I was a little hurt, I understood what Bob was saying and how right he was. Obsessed with my new toy, I had forgotten some fundamental play principles.

Whose Games?

There was a fundamental contradiction between the open-ended exploratory *process* that is central to play and my desire to involve children in the work of designing and building permanent *products*.

It is not only how and why we consult children that is important, but how we interpret and respond to their various behaviours (that provide the answers) as they play in different environments. The following story illustrates how we can get things pretty wrong at times.

When a school contacted D&B for help in remodelling their playground, I was far too involved with my new game to notice that their colourful pie charts indicated that although the teachers said children were constantly complaining that the playground was boring, over 70 per cent of the children indicated that they did not want any changes.[1] It transpired that the first question the children had been asked was, 'What is missing from the playground?' The children had taken the question literally. Seeing that the covered area, the drinking fountain, the benches and even the painted hopscotch lines were still on the tarmac, they concluded that everything was still there, nothing had been stolen, and so they ticked the 'nothing is missing' box by which the teachers understood that nothing needed changing.

The planning of a park in East London involved thousands of local children writing and drawing on reams of paper. Much later, only a few of the things from the wish-list were installed, one of which was a BMX track that is rarely used, most children preferring, or required, to play with their bikes and friends near home.

It could be argued that this is a necessary learning cycle; but what is being learnt and who is doing the learning? Children at play should have the *opportunity* to reinvent the wheel constantly but adults, especially playworkers, seeking to create spaces for play should understand some fundamentals. I have found James Carse's (1986) concepts on finite and infinite games useful here.

Finite games

These are games that have obvious beginnings and ends, rules, goals, winners, and winnings. Chess and Association Football are finite games. The purpose of finite games is to win.

Infinite games

These have beginnings but no obvious ends, flexible rules and no permanent winners. Players can make the rules up as they go along and move the goal posts. The purpose of infinite games is to keep the game going. Infinite games involve the *active* revelling in the *now*. Play on playgrounds should involve infinite games and be 'freely chosen, personally directed and intrinsically motivated' (Play Wales 2005).

So:

- Play is essentially about the *now*. Play is an infinite game. To be able to understand this you need to remember what play feels like (like being able to stand in the feet of a child, preferably with the mud oozing between your toes).
- Planning is a finite game with many rules and constraints that negate the *now*.
- The role of the playworkers is to use their experience, understanding, knowledge and adult abilities to create opportunities for children to play.

How do we Know what Children Want?

As most consultations start from simplistic premises they can produce straightforward 'wish lists'. Yes, kids want a skateboard park, a dance machine and to go on the Internet, and better still, a youth club, a swimming pool and an Asian young women's centre; but often, children find activity programmes restrictive and choose not to go, preferring to hang out on the streets making their own entertainment, doing grinds and ollies on improvised skating poles and ramps, discussing who is in, out or whatever.

The teachers with their pie charts, the community artists, the design consultants and D&B asked the children what they wanted because it was 'the children's playground' and 'their playpark'. This kind of muddled thinking is not a very good starting point. If it really is their playground why are adults involved at all?

One wet evening after a discussion about how much I was paid, some of the children came to the conclusion that they could spend the money much better. We worked out that sacking the playworkers, cancelling the insurance and liquidating all the assets would net them about £6,000 each. They had a number of exciting investment opportunities and were more than willing to accept a one-off payment – cash, cheque, whatever! Beyond the universal human needs for food, clothes, shelter, freedom from harm and right to express opinions (as expressed in the United Nations *Convention on the Rights of the Child*, 1989), young people, as people with less power and lots of potential, need environments in which they can thrive. Their needs should be understood and respected, but do we give them our wages and the keys?

Consulting children is so much flavour-of-the-month that to oppose it seems antidemocratic or authoritarian. Many wordy documents describe a commitment to user involvement. Whilst they might meet the needs of the funding bodies, do they really procure for young people what they asked for, want or need? Most adults I know are very sceptical. They do not believe the consultations or promises of politicians or community workers who ask them what they want. They know who is going to win these finite games.

Playwork should focus on creating *opportunities* for play where children can '… determine and control the content and intent of their play, by following their own instincts, ideas and interests, in their own way for their own reasons' (Play Wales 2005).

Try to ensure that children's voices are heard and their rights are respected, yes, but do we have to do this by designing clever activity programmes that are more about getting them to play our games? Involving children in a process over which they have no real control is not what play should be about. Providing forms, tick sheets and planning exercises all have their place as do diversionary activity programmes for bored teenagers, anger management courses, art and craft, but these are finite games and not the infinite games of play. Playworkers should ensure 'the play process takes precedence' and should 'act as advocates for play when engaging with adult led agendas' (Play Wales 2005).

We need to be able to understand a range of play behaviours and be able to discuss what is happening on the playground before we begin to think about consultation. That way, we can create opportunities and spaces for genuine answers. Consultations often meet the needs of adults who, like me, were getting paid!

So How do Playworkers Find Out What Children Want?

The way that some adults view and investigate youth culture is reminiscent of explorers or missionaries. From deepest East Africa, East London and East Brighton come reports of cultures with strange behaviours, exotic dress and tribes of fantastic monsters with weird rituals recorded by surveillance cameras. Listening to some 'experts', one could conclude that we are under attack from an alien hooded species fuelled by strange drugs, music and video games who communicate through a range of electronic devices; but is the schism between young people and adults so wide that we are living in different worlds, or is it possible for us to stretch our memories and our feelings back to understand what it might be like? Are we able as adult playworkers to try and understand what infinite play can mean for children in the twenty-first century?

Well, here is something that Bob Hughes prepared earlier to help us do this and it works! Intuition, Memory, Evidence and Experience, IMEE (Hughes, 1996a).

At the heart of most good playwork training is IMEE, a tool designed to help playworkers reflect on and analyse their practice.

IMEE starts with Intuition. Intuition is about how we feel about children's play, our instant gut responses to situations. Playworkers can wonder what would happen if, for example, we handed over the keys or turned all the furniture upside down. We can use our Memory of what we liked and disliked when we were children. Playworkers can think about the best, most exciting and influential moments from our childhoods, asking questions like: 'what did you do when you were young, with whom, who was in control, where do young people do this nowadays?' For most people, certainly those of my generation, the more positive play experiences occurred in a place of their own choosing, often in the absence of adults and the worst or most boring experiences often involved a dominating adult presence.

Using Intuition and Memory in this way can help playworkers to understand young people in a different way from the external, pedagogical, anthropological adult with their approach that looks at young people as an alien species.

We can then go on to reflect on and use our Experience as playworkers. What happened when all the materials were ready and what were the best experiences during the summer playscheme, what sorts of game work, with whom and why, who was being disruptive, of what and why?

Finally, playworkers can use the Evidence from both the academic literature and their playwork practice. Collecting and recording evidence to make a coherent case for play involves an understanding of play and an ability to describe it. This evidence could include what the children say they want, but much more importantly, playwork should involve ongoing research into how children actually play. We need to be clear about whose needs are being met and to be aware of the historical, social, cultural and religious frameworks we are using as well as the framework the funders are using and the framework the children are using. For example, I knew a group of play providers who *knew* that young people needed to know about their culture through the Torah. Their practice reflected this. I also know of playworkers who are concerned to teach children to be better citizens and other playworkers who are interested in sport. Another example I can think of is the desire to reduce racism by exposing children to 'African Culture', misunderstanding the fact that Africa is a continent where genetic, social, political, geographical and cultural diversity is huge and most Africans live in cities. Teachers and playworkers take children to an African Village (in East Sussex!) to dress up in 'traditional African' (Nigeria/Ghana) dress and experience traditional (precolonial, central/east) African architecture. Whilst playing with stereotypes can be fun, it is bad history, bad sociology and bad psychology.

Whilst these activities can be justified, playworkers should resist these agendas and be able to justify their work using the Playwork Principles (Play Wales 2005). IMEE helps us to do this.

Using IMEE to get to the Heart of the Problem at D&B

Intuition

I almost squashed my intuition because I had a task to complete. I knew that we could only hold the children's attention for so long and that the faster and more fun we were, the easier it would be. I should have been braver and listened to that uneasy feeling that we were just motoring through. I think the more the environment changes and has surprises and secret stuff, the better – as long as we are not precious about how children choose to play with it. It is the *how* and *when* that is important and interesting. Let's give children real choices by providing lots of stuff for them to choose from.

Memory

We used and abused many different consultation methods and came up with very creative ways of getting from A to B to achieve the end products I thought D&B needed in order be successful. We spent a lot of time creating activities to enable children to play our finite games and not enough time watching and thinking about what the children were doing and what they might want to do. We made it clear to the children involved that their views and designs could only have so much influence and final designs needed to be based on practical issues such as time, cost, health and safety; but we hoarded and polished 'trophy quotes' to show how much the kids had done: 'Oh yes, this is a good one, this is what one of the boys wrote ...', 'Look at this photo, it's great ...'

We also forgot to remember what play is like. Children were interested, for a while, and they liked the attention, but they were only fully engaged when they were 'doing their bit'. They just wanted the opportunity to rush out with the hammers and start. We therefore became very good at quickly selecting, simplifying and rationalising the wonderfully irrational ideas they came up with. Tasks were parcelled out in manageable chunks and then dig, saw, nail, bish bash bosh, job done. All that planning and preparation and what did they want to do? Muck about with the video and throw paper around!

If we want to avoid frustrated children pushing at the boundaries of what they are allowed to do and playworkers frustrated by children's 'bad' behaviour, we need to remember and understand that mucking about, making up and changing the rules is vital and natural. Play is about being able to do it *when* and *how* you want.

Experience

My need to come up with a coherent design and a safe end product, coupled with time pressures and my pride, meant we tried to get children to play our games and work to our agendas. Many of the things that I had learnt about play became confused by my desire to involve children in activities that would produce end products that could be built by the inexperienced, be safe, not cost too much *and* be of some play value in the longer term. We all knew the Theory of Loose Parts'[2] (Nicholson 1971), but did not have time for such a messy process, so we reduced the number of variables. We became very adept at getting from discussing and modelling to hammering and sawing as quickly as possible. Rather than designing out most of the play and chaos, we should have designed it in! Rather than attempting to understand children's play, we wanted them to understand us and play our games, so, for example, we simplified sixteen Play Types down to three: games with rules, imaginary games and mucking about.

Evidence

Asking children at play what they want is like stopping a band in full flow and distributing questionnaires to the audience as to whether the music should include:

- more lead vocals
- less guitar
- other – please specify …

… and, like D&B, arriving with diagrams and felt-tipped pens asking children what they wanted.

I'm not saying that we should not ask children what they want, but that playworkers should have a grounding in what play is and the tools to define and discuss what makes a good play environment. We should also draw on our experience to develop effective play environments. Like music fans who love the whole sound and understand how it is put together, playworkers should be able to empathise with and analyse the different rhythms of play.

Play is:
- 'a process that is freely chosen, personally directed and intrinsically motivated [whereby children] determine and control the content and intent of their play, by following their own instincts, ideas and interests, in their own way for their own reasons' (Play Wales 2005);
- a *process* through which children learn to define their environment (Children's Play Council 1998);
- a natural *drive* that will normally be expressed without direction or interference (Hughes 2001);
- what children and young people do when they are not being directed by adults (Children's Play Council 2002);
- 'scientific research' (Eibl-Eibesfeldt 1970, cited in Hughes 2001).

Bob has given us a way of thinking about our roles as playworkers that enables us to keep our feet on the ground and our heads in the sky. We can talk about what we think children are up to, BUT it is crucial that we watch more than we ask, show or tell. I am not saying that we forget about asking young people their views because we think we know that what they want is the latest PS2, or what they're talking about on My Space. Instead, we can observe them closely so that we can empathise with them and can understand the flavour of the dreams we had and they are having.

What is Getting it Wrong?

Playworkers should not be concerned about children getting it right. As Maslow (1970) points out, whilst food, clothes and shelter are important, once these needs are met it is the higher needs for what he called 'self-actualisation' that are crucial. The more control that we have over events, the more interested and motivated we are. Given the opportunity, we all know how long a child will be engrossed in 'meaningless' play – aeons. Using IMEE to analyse our work can help to ensure that playworkers have their feet firmly planted in an understanding of and empathy with children's experience and can use their heads to explain why play is important.

Where I work now, much more time is spent on creating a physical and emotional environment that offers a range of play opportunities. We make sure that we provide a relatively clean, safe and caring environment with a lot of loose parts (Nicholson 1971) and then we trust the children to get on with it. This does not mean that at times we don't focus on play types that we think are under-facilitated. The children still run around and kick and hit balls, but maybe by putting time into creating quieter areas, we facilitate adventures such as dinosaur nests and eggs being discovered. We do not design particular activities for particular children, as we believe that where and how they choose to take part in a play opportunity is the most important thing. As Bruner (cited in Conway and Farley 1999, p. 8) points out: 'The main characteristic of play – child or adult – is not its content, but its mode. Play is an approach to action, not a form of activity.'

Organisations that aim to produce things (factories, schools or D&B workshops) can find the inclusion of people with different skills, aptitudes or needs difficult. Timetabled workshops with predetermined rules, or an activity that has a predetermined outcome or *product*, can restrict creativity and inclusion because the child is not in control of the *process*, whereas, a quality play environment gains from including more diversity, as play is about the *process* rather than the *product*.

If play types are genetically programmed biological drives as Hughes (1996a) suggests, it means that they are crucial and universal. We all seem to be born with wonderfully similar needs that lead us in beautifully different directions. Playworkers should be the champions of diversity and resist the desire to simplify. Play is an activity that crosses boundaries; that is why it is so important to our development. I believe that it is the role of the playworker to see that appropriate adults are able to hear, see, feel and respond to the concerns of young people[3] rather than 'enabling' young people to play adult games.

Bob and others have helped us to define our profession and develop a language that enables playworkers to think and talk about the wonderful complexities of play. I have used IMEE many times with many different people and it never fails to remind me that we have often forgotten more than we know about play and childhood. From the questions, the thoughts and the laughter that IMEE instigates, we realise that playwork is much more complex, interesting and important than providing activities for children. Playworkers seeking to understand what children want should be wary of responding to the loudest voices and the latest fads. Playwork involves an ability to 'listen' on all channels (Marchant *et al.* 1999), to listen to more than just speech because communication involves a whole array of different signs, symbols, gestures and behaviours.

I have tried to outline how I was one of those playworkers who 'wanted children to succeed in spite of themselves' (Hughes 1999) because I forgot children's needs and how, by stopping, listening and reflecting on the works of Bob Hughes, I think I remembered some of what I had forgotten. This has enabled me to see how important it is that I honestly discuss and question whose needs are being met by my playwork rather than accepting, or hiding, inconsistencies.

Let's copy the majority of children and ignore the emails, poster and proposals offering the chance to 'have your say', 'come and have a chat', or 'cotch with the councillors'. Most are not about playwork. I believe the job of a playworker is to create and preserve environments for children's play and to oppose non-play agendas and even at times to shout out 'The emperor's got no clothes!' Children's jobs are to use, change, interpret, mess it up – in other words play with the environment. Rather than trying to knock a round peg into a square hole, we could give children hammers and the freedom to create their own holes.

Notes

1   I am grateful to Mick Conway for pointing this out.
2   'In any environment, both the degree of inventiveness and creativity, and the possibility of discovery, are directly proportional to the number and kind of variables in it.'
3   Traffic-calming and Homes Zones are arguably better environmental modifications worthy of playworkers' attention rather than making hats or the colour or position of a bit of equipment.

Chapter Five

Playwork: Art, Science, Political Movement or Religion?

Annie Davy

Defining Playwork – to Catch a Butterfly

> You are sitting … it is a silent evening. The sun has gone, and the stars have started appearing … don't even say 'this is beautiful' because the moment you say that it is beautiful, it is no longer the same. By saying beautiful, you are bringing in the past, and all the experiences that you said were beautiful have coloured the word. (Osho 2002).

'Playwork' is seen as a relatively new vocational and increasingly professional sector. In its embryonic state, tiny but flourishing in the recent rapid development of children's services in the UK, it has struggled to define itself, not only in terms of what playworkers do, but also in terms of what playworkers need to understand and what they hold as core values and principles to underpin their work. My question here is: should the sector be trying so hard? Is it flapping into, rather than flying away from the butterfly nets?

What we know about play?

One thing all playworkers are agreed upon: playwork makes children's play its core business. The phenomenon of play itself may be as old as the planet, and has certainly been happening for as long as mammals have inhabited the earth. Academic fields from across the sciences, humanities and the arts have attempted to describe and circumscribe 'play' in its various forms and through multifarious definitions.

Everyone wants a piece of play, but play is intersubjective by its very nature, and eludes ownership. It is particularly difficult to capture the spontaneous and various quality of play in a definition – although it is right that as playworkers we keep trying, and adding to the definitions in existence. It can only ever be truly experienced in the present, and can lose its essence in being described and coloured by past experience or future plans. Play is interdisciplinary creativity – essentially experiential – defying any definition that attempts to confine it to a specialised field of study or work. It is the breath between inertia and productivity– the empty speech bubble, the journey across the zone of proximal development (Vygotsky 1978) or of human potential.

Play might be seen as a spiritual (but not religious) pathway to greater understanding of human beings' place in the world and in the cosmos – our connection to earth and that which is unexplainable and greater than what we know. 'Spirit is that which animates the inanimate, defies the determinate, flickers between order and chaos. In short as playful as it gets' (Kane 2004, p. 323).

A professional tool?

Many professionals who work with children work with play as a process for achieving the outcomes they seek: most notably early years teaching, psychotherapy and other therapeutic professions. Biologists study play as a window to understand human and animal behaviour and development. Most if not all areas of artistic endeavour would acknowledge the playful element of the creative process.

An art like cooking?

In 1621 Robert Burton said, 'Cookery is become an art, a noble science . . .' Playwork might also be seen as akin to cooking. It draws on the sciences – an understanding of the elements, the key ingredients, the flavours of the world that make it endlessly variable and delicious. However, playworkers, like cooks, need to draw on innovation and intuition if they are to respond to the play tastes of the children they serve. They may learn from their mothers, grandfathers, visiting playwork chefs, books or celebrity programmes on TV, but essentially no theoretical base, knowledge or understanding will do of itself. Playworkers must draw on their experience and their own creative resources, create their own dishes, make their own mistakes, bask in the joy of their contribution to the experience of others. If they are good chefs, they will think about what went wrong or what went right, get feedback, consult others and be always willing to reflect, learn and develop. The proof of the pudding is in the eating, the saying goes, and so it is with playwork. It is in the practice that you realise the benefits and the outcomes – and these will be different from day to day, from minute to minute and from place to place. It is from the practice that we find the innovation, the insights and the understanding.

> The qualities of an exceptional cook are akin to those of a successful tightrope walker: An abiding passion for the task, courage to go out on a limb and an impeccable sense of balance. (Millar, 2002)

A distinct skills sector and professional development route?

Playwork is a term currently recognised in the UK by Sector Skills Councils. National Occupational Standards have been produced for people who work in adventure playgrounds, after-school clubs and leisure centres, or as play rangers in parks and in other settings. The playwork sector has its own nationally recognised training and professional development pathways from Playwork National Vocational Qualifications (NVQs) and nationally accredited courses to foundation degrees to postgraduate research. However, the sector is very small – both in terms of employment opportunities for which a playwork qualification is specifically required, and in terms of its own specific theoretical base and published research.

The playwork sector has struggled to describe how playwork differs in theory from what other people do, who work with children in different contexts but also recognise play as an important process in their work. Nursery school teachers, therapists and artists of various kinds may all describe themselves as playworkers at times.

National Occupational Standards and NVQs have prescribed the functional competencies required of a 'Playworker' and in doing so tried to describe what playworkers do. Although the context in which the majority of playworkers work is largely out-of-school childcare settings, playworkers also have a duty of care, in the legal and ethical sense, whether they work in a formalised out-of-school club environment or in a more open-access setting such as an adventure playground. National Occupational Standards and NVQs in Playwork have therefore tried to cover the legal, administrative and managerial aspects of most of these jobs, which often involve a contract of care with parents whilst the child is in the play setting. As such, many of the playwork standards have become barely distinguishable from childcare standards. Combine this with the elusive qualities of play itself, and the uniqueness of the playwork pedagogy can be easily lost or ignored.

The playwork sector might state that its type of playwork is different in that the focus is to facilitate children's play as its *primary purpose*, without other specific developmental objectives or agendas. This is tricky as we are currently living in a social and political climate where we are constantly required to justify all children's services or work with children in terms of specific outcomes with supporting measurable evidence of achievement. As play itself is so difficult to define in any universally accepted form, the playwork sector has been grasping around a range of disciplines for its theoretical underpinning and measurable descriptors of any sort.

Playwork, in trying to distinguish itself as a separate vocational and professional development pathway and thus competing as a skills-based sector alongside the giants of education, childcare, social care, and to a lesser degree youth work, is in danger of become insular and didactic. It loses out in separating itself from others who might be seduced into valuing play in their work. In an attempt to underpin a uniquely playwork-orientated pedagogy, the playwork sector has turned to discussion of values and principles as a framework for professional development and training. As an intrinsically grass-roots, democratic and peer-led *movement* (rather than the skills based sector it has aspired to become), these discussions have often taken a political turn. Attempts at sector-led consensus in terms of discussion around values and principles have compounded didactical extremism with in-sector wrangling. The results thus far appear to have, to use another cooking analogy, 'diluted' some of the more radical and interesting ideas so that what has ended up in the National Occupational Standards and related publications, are rather bland general statements that do not reflect or do justice to the rich and diverse practice developing in the field.

More of a movement than a sector?

As an eclectic conglomeration of individuals and organisations, mostly in the voluntary sector, with a shared passion for children's right to 'unadulterated' play, perhaps playwork is better described as a *movement* rather than a discrete professional sector. Like the peace movement, the playwork *movement* has its spokespeople but no one organisation or individual holds the mandate to prescribe its values or codes of conduct or claim a monopoly on the understanding of relationship between play and being human.

Discussions on playwork values and principles are often inextricably linked to wider sociopolitical and cultural issues around concepts of childhood, human rights, institutions, public space or educational and psychological methodology: what is, and what is not, 'good for children'.

On a national level the playwork *movement* contributes significantly to the political debates around childhood, most recently in fairly high-profile discussions about the impact of growing up in a risk-averse society. It also touches on nearly all the cornerstones of children's policy, whether about health and concern about increasingly sedentary lifestyles, or community safety and children's access to public space.

Rather than trying to define itself too narrowly as a separate sector, those advocating a pedagogical approach that puts play, and particularly children's right to play, at centre stage might do as well to form stronger alliances with those who share their values about play, about creativity, about what it is to be a child and about what it is to be human.

Advocacy for the importance of play in children's lives should surely extend into all areas of children's services; for example, in:

- reinstating recognition of and greater attention to all kinds of play within schools and beyond – creative thinking, problem-solving, the arts and sports, for a start
- developing school grounds into play-rich environments for lunchtimes, break times, after school, holidays
- defining quality in childcare in play terms and embedding a play-based pedagogy in all training for work with children
- reclaiming outdoor play space to enable increased access activity for all children
- transforming urban spaces with the introduction of more informal play, place spaces, better guidance for developers and renewal schemes – working with nature and responding to what children find interesting
- the playwork sector needs to recognise its power as a movement – and seek alliances to influence all work with children to move toward a more play-based pedagogical approach. In doing so it will need to acknowledge its differences rather than seek consensus or containment in narrow definitions, codes and practices.

Most important of all, the sector also needs to stay close to playwork practice for its survival. It is the practice that provides the tap root, the energy and the conviction. Playwork, like play, should rightly be process-driven, difficult to define and experiential and should not be overly prescribed or contained. Try to pin it down, and, like a captured butterfly, it dies.

To Bob and Gordon – with my personal gratitude for the paths you have helped form in my personal playwork mind maps: for your creative 'minting' of playwork words and concepts, your scientific exploration of human behaviour and responses to the environment, your maverick political activity and your presence as bearded gurus of a playwork movement.

With love, Annie

Chapter Six

The Free Play Matrix and the CAOS System –

How the IMEE process and Tulpa creation were used in qualitative research on children's free play

Peter F. King

The aim of this paper is to explain how aspects of both Bob Hughes' and Gordon Sturrock's contribution to playwork were incorporated into my three-year study of free play. This paper will begin with a brief account of the creation of the six factors of free play. This is followed by a detailed account of how both the 'IMEE' and 'Tulpa creation' tools were used in case study research. The information gained from the case study research will be discussed with a definition of free play and the development of the Free Play Matrix (King 2005), the hypothetical interaction between the child, the playworker and the organisation. More recently, the research is being used to develop a multiagency framework for play in the creation of the Child-Adult-Organisation-Society (CAOS) Free Play System.

Introduction

Free play has been an expression that has been used and described for over a century in relation to play theory (Bowen and Mitchell 1927; Mitchell and Mason 1934; Huizinga 1949); playwork (Bonel and Lindon, 1996; UKPlayworkers 2003); early years (Cass 1971; Cowe 1982); education (Smith, 1994); creativity (Nachmanovitch 1990); anarchism (Kropotkin 1886 as cited in Walter and Heiner 1988) and playwork practice. From this diverse list, I found over twenty various definitions of free play to be in existence. How adults interpret free play will thus depend on which definition of free play is being used.

I investigated this variation in the definitions of free play in relation to playwork environments as part of my Masters in Research with Leeds Metropolitan University (King 2005). The work of both Bob Hughes and Gordon Sturrock contributed to the research methodology. This involved modifying Hughes' (1996) concept of Intuition, Memory, Experience and Evidence (IMEE) and developing a self-administered questionnaire which then drew on Sturrock's (2003a) use of a Tulpa creation as part of a Therapeutic Playwork course delivered at the University of Gloucestershire.

Before going into more detail on how their work was incorporated into my research, I would like to take this opportunity to explain briefly how I have come to know both Bob Hughes and Gordon Sturrock, whose contribution to play and playwork cannot be underestimated, and which is reflected in the Playwork Principles (Play Wales 2005) that underpin playwork practice.

I first met Bob Hughes at the 'Yellow Pages Celebration of Play' in 1999. Listening to Bob, his passion for play was so evident that I telephoned him the next day and had a 20-minute conversation with him about children's play and the project I was working on at the time. More recently, Bob very kindly read a draft paper I had prepared on free play that eventually formed the basis for my three-year research. I first met Gordon Sturrock in 2002 at the PlayEducation event in Newtown, Cardiff; however, it was the following year at the NVQ conference in Birmingham, after hearing Gordon's paper on the 'Ludic Third' (2003b) that I first grew interested in his writing. My interest developed further whilst studying on the Therapeutic Playwork course run by Gordon. Gordon has always encouraged people to put forward their ideas on play, something I personally found helpful when carrying out my own research.

The Six Factors of Free Play

When analysing the many definitions of free play, it became apparent that each definition had a distinct focus or factor. In total, I identified six factors in relation to the 'how, where, why and who' of the child's free play:

1. Goals – play can be either goal-oriented or non-goal-oriented
2. Spontaneity – play occurs as and when it happens
3. Organisation – play is organised by the player

4. Freedom – the player has total freedom in their play
5. Choice – the player has total choice in their play
6. Time – play is set by the time limits of the player involved

(developed from King 2005)

The use of these six factors helped develop a coding system to determine playworkers' perception of free play. This perception was not only how individual playworkers themselves viewed free play, but also how they thought children and the organisations they work for perceived free play. These initial observations were also compared with how playwork ers perceived children as seeing any restriction of free play and with researcher observations of the playworkers' own restriction of the child's free play.

This multiperception of free play was carried out through qualitative research using playworkers as case studies. The methodology involved:

(a) each playworker undertaking a self-evaluation using a modified version of IMEE as described in Hughes (1996);
(b) the creation of a Tulpa using information gained from the self-administered questionnaire;
(c) interviews with each playworker;
(d) observing the practice of each playworker to identify the level of restriction of the child's free play;
(e) obtaining copies of the organisation's policies and procedures to assess their impact on free play.

An outline of how Hughes' IMEE was used will be described first, followed by the development of a questionnaire and the subsequent use of Tulpa drawn from Sturrock (2003a).

IMEE

Play Environments: A Question of Quality was written by Hughes (1996) as a process for creating and assessing the quality of children's play environments and was the forerunner to *First Claim* (Play Wales 2002). In this publication Hughes introduces the concept of IMEE (Intuition, Memory, Experience and Evidence). IMEE is a reflective tool that

relies on [playworkers'] use of their **intuition** (I), their personal childhood **memories** (M), their **experiences** of working/being with children in play situations (E) and on what they have gained from whatever research and other data or **evidence** they have read (E). (Hughes 1996, p. 30).

For the purpose of this research, respondents used the IMEE process to gauge how they perceived free play and how they thought children perceived free play. In addition, I was interested in how playworkers thought children's free play was restricted in play settings. The whole process involved:

Step 1: Playworkers listing up to twenty reasons why they felt free play existed.

Step 2: Playworkers using the reasons identified in Step 1 and placing them under themes/headings as identified by the playworker.

Step 3: Playworkers listing up to twenty questions they felt children would ask to attract them to free play.

Step 4: Playworkers listing up to twenty questions they felt children would ask that would restrict their free play.

Step 5: Playworkers using the data identified in Step 3 and placing it under the headings/themes as identified by the playworker in Step 2.

Step 6: Playworkers using the data identified in Step 4 and placing it under the headings/themes as identified by the playworker in Step 2.

(King 2005, based on Hughes 1996)

The playworkers were given a workbook to complete, along with a booklet providing guidance.

The themes identified by the playworkers varied; one case study identified four themes in Step 2, compared to fifteen themes by a second case study. As the themes identified varied between the case studies, a different approach was used in order to compare the results.

The information obtained from each of the six-steps of the IMEE process in this research was coded using the six factors of free play. This was achieved by placing each of the reasons given for free play (Steps 1, 3 and 4) into one of the six factors and comparing this with how the playworker categorised their own headings/themes. The more reasons placed in each of six factors of free play, the more prominence that factor was given. The end result produced a hierarchal order of the six factors of free play, which showed that there was a difference between how the playworkers themselves perceived free play and how they thought children would perceive free play.

The next stage was for the Tulpa to be created from information obtained from the playworkers' self-administered questionnaire.

Tulpa Creation

In 2003, Gordon Sturrock delivered a higher education module on Therapeutic Playwork at the University of Gloucestershire. Two of the aspects explored on this module were 'lifeworlds' and 'Tulpa creations'. These two approaches identified whether the playworker's own life experiences influence their responses to children's play. This in turn would enable the playworker to identify their 'repertoire of responses' in relation to the child's 'play cycle' (Sturrock and Else 1998). The concept of the Tulpa was used and modified for this research.

The word Tulpa is from the Tibetan language and is a term that applies to the creation of a 'thought form' (Sturrock 2003b). This was a concept used by Sturrock for the Therapeutic Playwork module where a fictitious adult personality was created and matched to a fictitious child personality. Once matched, the next step was to try and identify how the two would react in a play environment, where and how they would get on, where clashes might occur and to identify the *'buttons and triggers'* (Sturrock 2003a) that may cause any clash. The model assumes that playworkers will project their own thoughts and feelings onto the creations and so make those thoughts and feelings manifest[1].

I modified this concept of the Tulpa[2] for the case study research. Firstly I constructed a questionnaire that consisted of an open-ended set of questions for playworkers to reflect on the various stages of their life and write down a small descriptive account for each question. The format consisted of the case study providing information about themselves under the themes of:

- your character
- your family
- your home environment
- your play environments
- your school environments
- your work environment
- your likes and dislikes

• your interests

From the information provided I then created a Tulpa of each play-worker case study in order to identify if any themes materialised in relation to free play. The reason for using the Tulpa was to identify factors that may influence the playworker's perception and observed practice in relation to free play based on their own personal experiences, likes or dislikes. This was based on the concept of 'unplayed out material' (Sturrock and Else 1998, p. 49) where 'the attraction to many of the work [playwork] may be that they have, themselves, unworked out material that they feel impelled to express'.

Once the playworker had completed the IMEE process and the Tulpa questionnaire, the playworker was sent a case study interview workbook to complete. When this was completed, a telephone interview was arranged to discuss their answers. The interview included the play-worker being asked to place in hierarchal order their own preference of the six factors of free play, how they think children would place them and finally how they thought the organisation would do it. This was done in order to compare the original IMEE order of the six factors of the importance of free play as viewed by the playworker, compared to how they ordered the factors when interviewed, both for themselves and their perceptions of children (as explained above).

The final task was to observe the playworker in their practice. The observations that took place of the playworker case studies were focused on restriction of any of the six factors of free play with regards to the children playing. Whenever factors of free play were being restricted by the playworker, then that factor, or factors, was recorded. For example, a child who may want to draw outside may have been asked to go inside, indicating that the organisation factor from the six factors of free play may have been taken over by the playworker. The observation used a mark sheet based on the six factors of free play to identify which factor was being restricted and how the restriction took place. This was carried out to compare observed restriction of free play with the playworker's self-assessed IMEE restriction of free play.

Once all the data had been collected, all the results from the IMEE process, Tulpa creation, interviews and observations were compared. The IMEE process provided comparisons between what playworkers thought and what was observed in practice. The Tulpa creation was used to try and identify if anything in the playworker's play or work history could influence how they viewed free play. Although the number of case studies used was low, it was shown that factors from the Tulpa creation could influence their interpretation of free play, which in turn influenced their practice. This influence on their practice had both a positive and negative effect in relation to the playworker working to organisational policies and procedures. By using the six factors of free play through the IMEE process, Tulpa creation, interview and observed practice, it became clear that the playworker's perceptions of free play – that is, their own personal perspective, how they said the child views free play and also how they said the organisation views free play – were different. This has led to the development of the Free Play Matrix.

The Free Play Matrix

The construction of the six factors of free play in conjunction with the use of Hughes' IMEE process and Sturrock's Tulpa creation identified the complex nature of trying to define free play when it is being influenced by three different perspectives:

- the child's perception and implementation of free play
- the playworker's perception and implementation of free play
- the organisation's perception and implementation of free play (often through the organisation's policies and procedures) in play environments

This complexity is one that Petrie (1994, p. 38) has identified with regard to play and care provision:

> In part, complexity resides in the matter of perspective. In addition to the parental points of view, we could also consider the perspective of children, of different government departments and of the staff who work the provision.

Potentially any of these three viewpoints (child, playworker or organisation) could be controlling any of the six factors of free play. In addition, the child, the playworker and the organisation could potentially influence each other. For example, as well as having their own perception of free play, the child will also have a perception of how they think playworkers or the organisation view free play and may organise their play to other agendas away from their own. This interaction can be set out in the Venn diagram below.

   If the six factors of free play can be controlled from one of three sources (the child, the playworker or the organisation), then potentially one may have more control over any of the six factors of free play compared to the others. When we compare the perception of free play between the child, the playworker and the organisation, it can be demonstrated that the child often has the least control over their free play whilst the organisation has the most.

The child

The child has control of all the six factors of free play in area 1 of the Venn diagram. This situation is what Hughes (2001, p. 68) determines as adult-free play, where 'children gain a perspective on life that is their own'. However, in play environments such as out-of-school clubs, open-access schemes and adventure playgrounds, adults are present and their presence may interfere with the child's own perspective of life. Thus, the importance of the adult minimising their restriction to any of the factors of free play is fundamental in enabling children to have complete, or as much as possible, control over the six factors of free play. Potentially, the

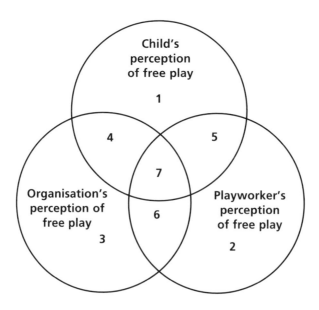

Fig. 6.1   Hypothetical interaction of the six factors of free play between the child, the playworker and the organisation in a play environment. (Modified from King 2005)

child could have control of the six factors of free play in areas 4, 5 and 7; however, they would need to be able to dominate over both the play-worker and the organisation. This is unlikely to occur owing to power dynamics, as will be discussed later in relation to the CAOS system.

The playworker

The playworker controls the six factors of free play in area 2 and poten-tially in areas 5, 6 and 7 of the Venn diagram where the playworker can dominate free play from his/her own agenda (area 2); the playworker can dominate free play thinking she/he knows what is best for the child, or the child's free play based on the playworker's interpretation (area 5) or the playworker can dominate free play by working together with the organisation (area 6) or with the organisation and the child and with the playworker being dominant (area 7). Hughes (2001, p. 63) states that adult intervention is 'an infringement of the child's biological and psychic integrity'. The adult's presence in the play space may mean that the 'play function of the child is overtaken ... by the wishes, hopes and aspirations of the adult' (Sturrock 2003b, p. 5). The play history of the adult may influence how the six factors of free play are controlled, and in turn, this may work with or against the playworker in relation to the organisational policies and procedures.

The organisation

The organisation has control over the six factors of free play in area 3 and potentially in areas 4, 6 and 7, where

- the organisation can dominate the six factors of free play from its own agenda (area 3);
- the organisation can dominate the six factors thinking it knows what is best for the child, or the child's six factors of free play based on the organisation's interpretation (area 4);
- the organisation can dominate the six factors thinking it knows what is best for the playworker's practice, or the playworker's practice is based on the organisation's interpretation of the six factors of free play (area 6), or
- the organisation can dominate by working together with the playworker and the child, with the organisation being dominant (area 7).

Where the playworker has much autonomy regarding organisational policy, their practice can reflect their perception of the six factors of free play and this could be influenced by their own play history and life-world. In contrast, where playworkers have little control over organisational policy, their practice may actually go against their perception of free play, so they become frustrated.

These different perceptions of free play in relation to the six factors of free play have been used to construct a definition of free play.

A Definition of Free Play

If the six factors of free play are used to determine a definition of free play, it is up to the player as to how each of the six factors is implemented. For the child with complete control, and as long as the adult and organisation fit within the child's play, then this can be defined as pure free play. If, however, an adult or the organisation determines the controlling factor, no matter how well-intentioned it is, this is not pure free play but *pseudo-free play*.

Dewey stated that free play is the 'interplay, of all the child's powers, thoughts and physical movements, in embodying, in a satisfying form, his own images and interests' (Mellor 1957, p. 23). Expanding on Dewey's concept of the interplay of all the child's powers, I proposed a definition of free play as:

> Pure free play is where the individual person (child, young person or adult) through the interplay of all their powers (body and mind) has complete internal and external control of the organisation, goals, time, freedom, spontaneity and choice of their play. (King 2005)

It is very unlikely that a child would have complete control over the six factors of free play; therefore, this definition may never be achieved in a setting. However, in a play environment where adults or an organisation are influencing any of the factors of free play, it may be possible for the adult or the organisation to identify what factors they are controlling and realise the need for children to have back the control of that factor or factors of free play.

In relation to the child, adult, organisation or even society, if any of these factors are dominated or restricted by other people or an organisation, then a hybrid or *pseudo-free play* will exist. This has led to the development of the Child-Adult-Organisation-Society (CAOS) Free Play System. This system is a framework for multiagency partnership working for individuals and organisations involved in play, for example, playwork, early years, education, youth work and community work, to provide not only a consistent interpretation of free play but to enable them to determine which factors of free play are being controlled by whom.

CAOS Free Play System

When the child has complete control over the six factors of free play, then the child has complete control over their free play. However, this scenario may be rarely achieved, particularly in organisations or learning environments where adults are present. (It is recognised that there may be some situations where a child's free play may be controlled by another child[3] or they may decide that they want an adult or the organisation to control their six factors of free play[4].) The concept of the 'Manchester Circles' (Lester and Russell 2004) can be adapted to demonstrate the influence of power using the six factors of free play in relation to the position of the child, the adult, the organisation and society.

Based on Bronfenbrenner's (1979) ecological model, the Manchester Circles consist of four concentric circles representing:

- the playing child
- the organisation (further broken down into the physical environment, the role of the playworker and the human environment)
- the organisational framework and
- the wider context. (Lester and Russell 2004)

The place of the playing child within the Manchester Circles has the child with the greatest influence. My use of the Manchester Circles concept has the four concentric rings made up of:

- the child (C)
- the adult (A)
- the organisation (O) and
- society (S)

This makes up the CAOS system which is seen in the diagram below.

Ideally, as with the Manchester Circles, the child should have control over the six factors of free play thus allowing them the greatest influence in their play. However the control of the six factors of free play can be through:

- The child him/herself (C)
- The adult (for example, a playworker) (A)
- The organisation (for example, the organisation who employs the adult or owns the building where children play) (O)
- society (for example, the influence of government legislation) (S)
- any combination of the child, adult organisation and society.

If we return to the example of the child drawing outside, who is then moved inside by the adult, the child's decision to draw outside would have been made by the child controlling all six factors. However, the adult playworker interrupting the child's play by moving him/her is

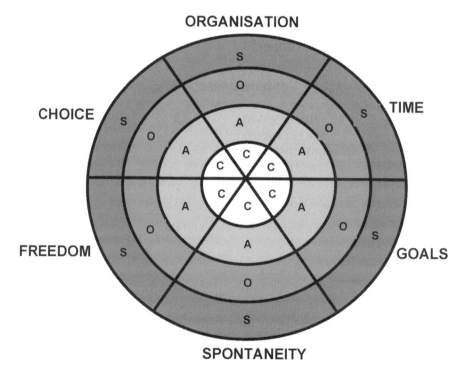

The CAOS Free Play System

Fig. 6.2   Key: C = child; A = adult; O = organisation; S = society

evidence of the adult controlling the organisation of the child's play. In turn the organisation (setting) may have rules controlling where the child can play, and thus curtail his/her freedom.

This CAOS system demonstrates that unless the child is controlling free play through all six factors, as soon as one or more factor is taken out of the child's control, then a hybridised version of free play exists, *pseudo-free play*. Ideally, the child should have control over the six factors of free play; however, in reality, a hierarchy of power exists where the Child may have the least power, followed by the Adult playworker and the Organisation and Society having the most power. The argument for this would be when a government initiative results in play environments being controlled by organisations and adults to meet society's agenda, not the child's intent. The model also shows how misguided or manipulative (whether consciously or unconsciously) adults, either in collusion with organisation policies or on their own, may dominate free play by taking control of the environment and rules.

This view is based on the control and use of children's play to meet adult engineered social policy (Holme and Massie 1973; Cranwell 2003) in conjunction with the prevailing social construction of childhood. Moss and Petrie (2002, p. 59) describe the dominant adult perception of childhood as the 'child being poor, weak and needy' as opposed to being seen as 'strong, competent and powerful' (ibid., p. 101). Well-meaning adults therefore 'protect' children from the harm they feel children may experience without their expertise.

With regard to the challenge of providing play spaces for children, Hughes (2001, pp. 67–8) states:

> The march of the built environment has so reduced the child's opportunity for adult-free experience, that we feel driven to make special provision so that it can happen. But play provision and the playwork that takes place there will only be special if it ensures that children are able to play, and that means that it has to facilitate an adult-free, often socially unacceptable, fundamentally biological process.

This point is important when considering the interpretation of the six factors of free play in relation to multiagency partnership working in developing play policies and strategies around children's play. An all-encompassing play strategy will need to recognise that in some environments where children play, some of the six factors of free play will be controlled by the adult, organisation or society, for example playgroups, schools and youth clubs. There needs to be recognition that not all settings can be as flexible as those where playworkers are present. However, if we are not to support the 'poor, weak and needy children' (Moss and Petrie 2002, p. 59), it is important that children should be able to control the six factors of free play in any environment where children's play will take place.

Conclusion

'Everything in nature arises from the power of free play sloshing against the power of limits' (Nachmanovitch 1990, p. 33). Pure free play is where the individual person (child, young person or adult) through the inter-play of all their powers (body and mind) has complete internal and external control of the organisation, goals, time, freedom, spontaneity and choice of their play (King 2005).

In relation to the playworker, the organisation and wider society, the child has limited power and influence when playing within settings controlled by those three agents. If an adult or organisation determines the controlling factor, no matter how well-intentioned it is, this is not free play but pseudo-free play.

Use of the modified IMEE and Tulpa creation processes shows that many factors affect the playworker's real and perceived influence on playing children. This influence may be in collusion with other factors or it may be the adult's own choice.

The CAOS Free Play System suggests that children should be able to control the six factors of free play in any provision for children's play. The System provides a challenge to adults, providers and multiagency groups where for free play to exist, the child needs to control all six factors. If this is too much to ask, then at least the adult, organisation and society can share power with children.

The research presented also shows how well-intentioned, though misguided or manipulative adults, either in collusion with organisa-tional policies or on their own, may dominate the play by taking control of the environment and rules. What the research does not show is how conscious and deliberate that influence and control is, nor the extent to which it pervades the play settings described, and which may result in the dissatisfaction with such provision reported by both children and some playworkers; that is a task for another time.

Acknowledgements

This work could not have been achieved without the influence of Bob Hughes and Gordon Sturrock. The use of their work in the design of the qualitative methodology of my research into free play was invaluable and my thanks go out to both Bob and Gordon.

I wish to acknowledge many people who have helped and influenced this paper:

- Sue Palmer for supervising my three-year research and all those involved in the research process;
- Perry Else and Wendy Russell for providing a critical playwork response and for editing this chapter;
- Liz King for painstaking proof-reading of the early drafts.

Their contributions have all been invaluable.

Notes

1   Thanks to Perry Else for making this important point.
2   The use of the Tulpa to produce a fictitious thought form could be questioned with regard to non-fictitious information being gained from the case studies. However, as a third party was used to create a thought from the non-fictitious information, the word Tulpa is still being used. My thanks to Wendy Russell for raising this point.
3   If a child is happy for another child to control their six factors of free play, then that is the choice of that child. My thanks to Wendy Russell for bringing this to my attention.
4   If a child is happy for an adult to control their six factors of free play, then that is also the choice of that child. My thanks to Perry Else for bringing this to my attention.

Chapter Seven

Adventure Playgrounds and the Community in London (1948–70) –

An appreciation of the ideas and actions that shaped the spirit of the 1960s play movement

Keith Cranwell

The philosophical drive that inspired the play movement of the 1960s, that made it a movement, and made play an issue is no longer there. The philosophy remains, buried in the fading constitution of play organisations everywhere, but the hope has gone. (Hughes and Williams 1984, p. 8).

The community that engaged in the drive for a play movement is today perhaps more divided than in the 1980s when Hank Williams and Bob Hughes began to develop a theory of playwork in *Playtimes*. The bureau-cratisation of playwork and its use as an agent of childcare within the scheme for children's services have made the work appear more prescrip-tive and bound to external governmental constraints that have repressed the creativity and potential of playwork. The idea that organising play was a dissenting presence that had the capability to invalidate dominant norms, needs and values as the spirit of play that was forged in that period remains strong, and is what we celebrate in this publication and recognise in the work of both Bob Hughes and Gordon Sturrock.

In this essay I intend to take a historical look at the origins of adven-ture play in the community and explore some ideas about how organised play arose in the 1960s. The term 'spirit of play' is useful for a number of reasons. Firstly, I believe that it is central to appreciating the work of Bob and Gordon as their lives are imbued with it.

Secondly, the term crops up in discussions of classical play theories and exists as part of the cultural politics of play. In particular, it was a term that had a currency in the 1960s and 1970s to express an attitude towards power and imagination. Thirdly, it gives an opportunity to show that community activists were partners in play but their work was overlooked. Fourthly, in much the same way as conversations I have with Bob and Gordon play with ideas, this work is offered in that spirit.

   This paper sets out to explore the extent to which community, child-centred education, youth counter-cultural politics and delinquency provided significant arguments that promoted the Adventure Playground (APG) cause and looks at how the National Playing Fields Association (NPFA) assisted in their development between 1948 and 1970. The paper is divided into four parts. The first section discusses the state of organised play immediately after the Second World War. The second section looks at the early examples of the adventure playgrounds that were initiated by Lady Allen of Hurtwood[1] and the NPFA. The third part discusses the relationship between APGs, delinquency and the New Left and the final section looks at the how APGs became accepted as community initiatives.

Pre-Adventure Play – Post-war Provision of Children's Play

In the 1944 Education Act clauses 41 and 53 placed a duty on every local authority to provide leisure-time occupation that included 'play centres and other places ... for recreation and social and physical training'. In 1947, a Ministry of Education circular required Local Education Authorities (LEAs) to produce local development plans for these services. What this tended to mean was that government was able to create a 'principle non-interference' at a local level (Davies 1999, pp. 23–4). The effect of this left the level of play-centre provision to be decided at the discretion of the individual local authority, as it had been since 1907.

   In the immediate post-war period, there were three types of organised children's play provision. Firstly, there were fixed-play-equipment playgrounds in parks and other open spaces. These could be both unsupervised or supervised facilities and were often situated some distance away from children's homes. The local authority parks departments managed this type of facility. In some areas the park authority also ran Playleadership schemes, which were open-air supervised programmes of outdoor games and sports activities run by recreation officers with qualifications in sports and organised games. These facilities were free and open for all children under twelve using the park. In innercity areas, supervised after-school play centres provided a free indoor recreational facility held in schools, Settlement buildings or 'play rooms' on housing estates. The function of this type of agency was to provide working-class communities with informal childcare. Since 1940 in London, the LEA has managed this provision in schools. Playrooms and play flats served a similar function on housing estates and might be part-funded by the LEA but run by voluntary bodies such as the Save the Children Fund. The play-centre provision was offered close to where children lived.

There were also children's activity groups and youth clubs. These groups included youth provision such as the scouts and other uniformed groups and junior youth clubs. These were generally once-a-week evening meetings run by volunteers that took place in school, church or community rooms. In addition, various sports bodies organised youth teams using sports facilities and playing fields. The uniformed groups and sports clubs provision provided structured activities that were graded according to age and in some cases according to gender.

The post-war state of children's supervised recreation provision was a combination of organised after-school recreational welfare, structured games, and social education. The more formal the requirements of a children's leisure organisation the more likely that it was that it would be organised according to age groups and/or as gendered activities. The play centres service provided a predominantly recreational welfare service for the after-school care for the under elevens. In contrast, youth clubs were recreational social clubs for the over elevens. In 1945, the models of children's recreation services showed a preference for organised play activities and play provision as a form of compensatory education for working-class children.

The adventure playground entered into this rigid world of fixed-equipment playgrounds, organised games and structured activities for working-class children as a supplement, 'a means of supplying the vitamins to the child's inadequate recreational diet' (Mays 1957, p. 6). The adventure playground essentially promoted a fresh view of the potential of play as part of child development.

The Experimental Phase (1948–60)

In 1948 the adventure playground was introduced into England through the efforts of Lady Allen of Hurtwood, whose visit to John Bertelson's 'junk playground' in Emdrup, Denmark inspired her to champion this new type of play provision. Between 1948–49, seventeen playgrounds were established (Benjamin 1961, p. 8). Lady Allen argued that APGs had three functions. They provided a way for communities to recreate in the city the kinds of play environment that parents had when they were children. The APG answered critics who felt that working-class children's use of their free time was 'empty and purposeless'. In addition, the APG met the needs of children who did not enjoy organised games, playground asphalt and mechanical swings. What had impressed her at Emdrup was the wealth of play opportunities that were provided through the use of waste materials, and its lack of manufactured play equipment. The range of activities that could be provided included construction of dens, experimentation with natural materials such as earth, sand, water and fire, all supervised by a benign play leader. The adventure playground was seen as a 'pro-child' physical environment matched by 'pro-play' creativity and imagination led by the child (Cranwell 2003).

The APG was the first leisure facility that cut across the artificial segregation between age groups to offer a space in working-class neighbourhoods that could accommodate children and young people from 3 to 18 years. Groups such as the Under-14s Council embraced the APG as an experimental urban play space and supported several individual voluntary initiatives in London. In the late 1940s and 1950s many of the first playgrounds were short-term ventures that were built on land prior to redevelopment and had a life of three to five years. Up until the 1960s problems of funding, unsuitability of the sites and poor leadership all perpetuated a view that this provision was a short-term experimental measure (Benjamin 1961, p. 9).

The initial ideas that supported the development of the adventure playground came from several sources. Through the work of Anna Freud (1942) and Melanie Klein (1937) child psychology provided evidence of the importance of play in understanding children's problems. In the post-war period child-centred approaches to education gained ground, particularly in primary education (Selleck 1972; Cunningham 2002). Social reformers were also attracted to the APG as it appeared to reach delinquent children who were not attracted to any of the existing after-school provision. In addition, APG developments made a link between delinquency and working-class children's play provision in the community, which highlighted the need for proper planning of play space within housing and open-space developments.

Delinquency, Counter-culture and the APG 1950–70

In 1949 a London County Council conference on delinquency recorded that crimes by the under 14s had risen from 10,874 in 1938 to 16,574 in 1948, a rise of 58 per cent (LCC 1949), and linked the problem of juvenile delinquency to the lack of parental supervision in the home. This was felt to have occurred because both parents had to work, thus depriving working-class children of a normal home life. However, part of the cause of the disruption to children's home lives was due to the post-war redevelopment of cities. The 1943 County of London Plan recognised that there were four defects that needed to be remedied to provide an adequate environment for Londoners: traffic congestion, the depressed state of housing, inadequacy and maldistribution of open space and the jumble of housing and industry in the inner city. All of these issues directly or indirectly affected children's lives. The post-war reconstruction of London created a separation of housing from industry, which meant that parents had further to travel for work, increasing the amount of time they were absent from home. There was the need to build 750,000 new homes, with overcrowding in a further 500,000 dwellings leading to children spending more time on the street. There was an insufficient number of out-of school clubs and although the LCC released land for conversion into games pitches, these facilities were distant from the neighbourhoods where they were needed. The concern to maintain traffic flows and traffic congestion undermined any thoughts that may have existed to extend play streets as options to increase play space. The priority to repair damage to schools made it difficult to use school sites as supervised playgrounds.

The post-war clearance of bomb sites left areas of London derelict and this wasteland was ideal for children's play as they were often out of sight of adult supervision and were perfect for building dens, lighting fires and playing war games, all behaviours that were considered anti-social (Humphries 1997, pp. 80–81). Children's trespass into empty bomb-damaged houses was interpreted as housebreaking, whether it was to use the stolen laths as swords, loose bricks for a playhouse or wood for fires. These social crimes were seen as creating an environment of petty theft (Stimson 1948, p. 71). Research into delinquency had established a relationship with family disorganisation and suggested that new approaches to addressing the problem were needed (Spencer 1964, p. 4). The issue was to refocus the problem of juvenile delinquency away from work with the individual child and to see the problem as arising from the social isolation of families that were part of the strains and stresses of a community in a redevelopment area (Spencer 1964, p. 24). This approach proposed community-based solutions, which the APG could be adapted to meet. The APG, as had been observed from the Danish example, provided a permissive and 'protected' space on the child's home patch where s/he might access a range of activities that included den building, campfires and 'risky play' often viewed as anti-social behaviour.

In 1952 Lady Allen wrote to *The Times* in response to an article on juvenile delinquency identifying the APG as the only type of facility that 'begins to solve the problem for a child between the age of nine and fifteen' (Benjamin 1961, p. 23). According to Lady Allen, the APG addressed the issue of providing constructive hobbies that could not be carried out in the overcrowded homes and a place to meet in groups to play with friends.

The association of APGs with juvenile crime continued a long tradition of linking philanthropic playground development as an antidote to street crime without regard to substantiating the claims (Cranwell 2001). Play organisations such as the NPFA acted in the role of social reformer and asserted that the playgrounds could prevent children from hurting themselves or doing damage to property.[2] In the period 1950–80 there are a number of examples of attempts to connect decreases in children's street crime to the appeal of the APG (Buck 1965). It formed part of a funding strategy and arguments to justify the role of playgrounds (Andrews 1983).

This social-reformer approach to justify the provision of adventure play may be contrasted with 1950s APG pioneers, such as Joe Benjamin and Pat Turner, who saw themselves as progressive educators (Turner 1961). The progressive educators used their work with children on APGs to show that there was an alternative way to work with delinquents. They placed the work of the APG in the wider social context of why children needed a play space that could handle the 'normal' behaviour of children living in a constrained or abnormal environment where their needs were displaced by traffic or the effects of living in high-rise dwellings.

In 1956 Pat Turner was appointed the first playleader on the Lollard

Street Adventure Playground, which was run by a management commit-tee chaired by Lady Allen. He identified that the appeal of the APG was that there was 'no formal authority – only the authority the children give me of their own free will' (Turner 1961, p. 15). Joe Benjamin, who ran the Grimsby Adventure Playground in the 1950s and later became manager of the London Borough of Camden play service, saw himself as a benev-olent policeman whose main role was not to intervene save for safety reasons or to deal with bullying behaviour (Benjamin 1992). These men highlighted the importance of being free of rules and regulations other than those they negotiated with the children.[3] Pat Turner took a radical stance on the role he had with other agencies such as the police, teachers or social workers. He stated that he was prepared to discuss children informally with them but he was concerned that to do more would compromise his relationship with the playground children (Turner 1961, p. 106).

In the late 1960s liberationist educators such as Lambert (Lambert and Pearson 1974) viewed their role as that of facilitator working in the chil-dren's domain rather than as teacher (ibid., p. 159). The spirit they invoked created an attitude towards play as a way of life that was cele-brated in Richard Neville's, book *Playpower* (1970). This book captured the idea that there was the possibility for young people to create an alter-native do-it-yourself culture (Neville 1970, pp. 13–14). In this new world imagination could seize power (ibid., p. 37). It was a form of 'comic anar-chism'. The adventure playground, Colin Ward argued, was an example of a living anarchy and children's play was a form of protest where shoplifting, was 'scrumping from Woolworths' (Ward 1978, pp. 96–105).

Neville cited the emergence of the Arts Lab Movement in 1967 and its growth to 150 in 1969 (Neville 1971, p. 41), the squatter movement and the actions of student protest and black power as evidence of the merging of politics and a way of life. 'Our programme is cultural revolu-tion through total assault on culture, which makes every tool, every energy and every media that we can get our collective hands on … our culture, our art … and the message is FREEDOM' (Neville 1971, p. 52).

Neville's vision of the power of play was a reaction to the centralised and technologised world that he observed in which work might be liber-ated as play. For him the 'play element fizzled out of culture in the nineteenth century when work was sanctified' (ibid, p. 211).[4] By engag-ing in play as work, temporary summer jobs on adventure playgrounds provided opportunities for students, in particular, to dabble in the ideas of play as a rejection of material values and to see the spirit of play as an attitude towards play as a way of life.

In the late 1960s, doing this work allowed playworkers to believe that they were acting out a form of liberationist politics that had gained popularity through the rise of the New Left as represented by Marxist cultural theorists such as Herbert Marcuse (see Volkwein 1991). In trying to resolve conflicts within capitalism that created a world that was dehumanising and repressive, it was necessary to release mankind from the rational and technological forces that curtailed personal freedoms. To do this, Marcuse felt that play/art was a liberating force. In this he was largely taking his ideas of the play impulses in society from Schiller[5] (Volkwein 1991, p. 360) who used the term to mean 'everything that is neither subjectively nor objectively contingent, and that still neither subjectively nor externally constrains' (Beiser 2005, p. 141). For Schiller and Marcuse play overcomes the constraints of an individual's physical needs, as we do not play from need and the constraints of reason, which limits our moral actions. Play is, then, a synthesis of these drives as it 'frees us from the constraints of the other' (Beiser 2005, p. 141).

In the 1960s, ideas about play were in tune with the 'spirit of the age' and covered not only developmental arguments for play but political and social motives of the playworkers. Play was symbolic of a way of life and an expression of freedom. However, at an organisational level it was the older social arguments of 'play as prevention' that were more successfully used to secure the development of adventure play.

The APG was central to 'play as prevention' arguments in the literature on vandalism where crime was cited as children's 'high risk play' or that play bodies could talk about the idea of policing through play (Andrews 1983). Evidence was offered to suggest that the adventure playground was able to channel or deflect aggression and vandalism as it was a setting where it was situationally acceptable (Ward 1973, p. 238). The APG, by offering the child unlimited opportunities for 'working off' antisocial behaviour in creative ways even though these actions might be externally interpreted as destructive, released the stresses the child experienced through urban living. The adventure playground was seen as a safe outlet for children's risky behaviours. This view suggests that the libertarian approach to organising children's play had a resonance with the nineteenth century ideas of the surplus energy theory of play proposed by Schiller and Herbert Spencer.

Throughout its history, the APG has attracted workers who supported a libertarian view of their work. This was interpreted as being outside of the accepted social welfare agencies of the State. This meant that delinquent young people could feel safe on the playgrounds but it also meant that there was a tension between meeting the needs of the delinquent and those of the wider non-delinquent child population. In the 1970s Bernard McGovern felt that the adventure playground was creating a new form of radical social work rather than providing a generic playleadership programme (Cranwell 2003). There was a strong sense of independence in the type of leadership that the pioneer playleaders offered, and the principles of choice they gave to children underpinned their approach to the work they thought was the best way to address this problem.

APGS and the Community 1960–70

By the 1960s, despite the support of the NPFA, of the original playgrounds only five were fully operational (three were Local Authority funded), eight had closed permanently and a further five opened part-time. Between 1964 and the late 1970s there was a gradual growth in the numbers of APGs. There were a number of reasons why this occurred and several of them were not aimed directly at promoting children's play. In 1960 the Albemarle Report was published which set up structures for the professionalisation of youth work and the Youth Service Development Council that had representation from major voluntary organisations. In 1967 the Plowden Report recommended a programme of developments of child-centred active learning in primary schools, greater participation of parents in children's education and the setting up of Educational Priority Areas that promoted community based play projects (Rogers 1980, pp. 84–91; see also Mitton and Morrison 1972). In 1968 the government set up twelve Community Development Projects that initiated a number of adventure playgrounds around the country (Thomas 1983). The Urban Aid Programme between 1969 and 1987 financed small-scale children's play programmes. The role of the NPFA regional officer team was to support, advise and guide local adventure play initiatives at grassroots level.

In the late 1960s and 1970s there was an extensive community work literature that recorded the 'struggles for play provision' and linked the cause of children's play to community development strategies (Baldock 1974; Thomas 1976; O'Malley 1977). The reason for this was that children's play activities and play space acted as a catalyst for community action. The provision of play facilities in the community was seen to have a multiplier effect on people's ability to act together. The focus on children's needs was a generally agreed goal that generated cooperation between families. In most working-class communities, there was a history of successful organisation of children's events, e.g. street parties. There was also educative purpose through involvement on committees. In addition, the problem-solving involved in setting up play provision brought together different inner-city communities. Furthermore, the Urban Programme provided a resource that provided local groups with regular funding for playschemes at Easter and summer. The playschemes on derelict land gave the impetus for an all-year adventure playground (Danby 1972). Some 75 per cent of the Youth Volunteer Force Foundation projects ran play programmes and six of the twelve CDP programmes were heavily involved in providing play projects. For many community workers play was their way into the community. Play was frequently the springboard for taking up local community issues (Thomas 1976).

Through Drummond Abernethy the NPFA developed a community work role. Drummond's reformist approach to the development of APGs sought to establish them as the 'hub of the community'. He had observed that the adventure playgrounds of the 1950s were often the only community resource in an area and that the Play Hut on the APG site could be used for a variety of purposes. At the Lollard St and Grimsby APGs initiatives to help old people had spontaneously developed and during the day under-fives playgroups were organised. There was also scope for schools to undertake projects on the playground. In 1965 the raising of the school-leaving age from fifteen to sixteen increased the provision of social studies courses that children might undertake in the community. Drummond also believed that since the reach of the APG was wider than youth services, it had contact with the so-called 'unclubable' young person who had no contact with other forms of provision. In addition, the fact that the voluntary management of the APG quite frequently included parents increased opportunities to support local families and for them to help the playground (Abernethy 1974). Abernethy saw the adventure playground at the centre of a holistic recreational leadership scheme for the whole community and not just a children's play facility.

However, there were limitations on the extent to which larger capital schemes for adventure play could be funded. Many of the adventure playgrounds were too small, lacked the necessary skills to apply for grants, or charities were unwilling to fund single playgrounds and this was hampering the sustainability of playground developments. In 1962 in London, the London Adventure Playground Association (LAPA) was set up as a charity to raise funds for playgrounds across the metropolis. In the 1960s LAPA initially supported eight playgrounds. As a pan-

London organisation representing APG the organisation was able to procure support as a youth organisation from the LCC that enabled it to run a playleader training programme, expand the number of playgrounds in London and establish a central resource centre to support the playgrounds. LAPA ceased to exist in 2004.

Conclusion

In the late 1940s the APG was a new child-centred play programme that represented a return to the ideas of rural play from an earlier era whilst at the same time promising to be the solution to the problems of post-war regeneration and the child's needs for a safe place to play in their neighbourhood. To justify support for this new type of playground, the leaders of the playground movement extensively relied on arguments that connected their role with the growing problems of post-war delinquency. The two approaches that emerged appealed either to a social reformist agenda of preventative work with delinquent young people or as a progressive education programme in the community. In the 1960s a third, liberationist position was fashioned from the New Left critique of the capitalist society and appealed to ideas of a counter-culture that emerged in the 1960s. Its role was to encourage new workers into the field and they took the movement forward into the 1980s.

These contrary forces within play mean that the APG battled with contradictions between the needs of creating a free play environment for all children and reaching out specifically to delinquent young people. By the late 1960s the APG was harnessed to meet the needs of community work programmes and support for antipoverty programmes. The adaptability of the APG to meet such diverse needs in the community is a strength and makes this type of provision relevant to meet the play needs of children today.

Notes

1   Marjorie Allen (1898–1976) was a landscape architect, gardener and children's advocate for causes as diverse as nursery schools, early childhood education and adventure playgrounds for handicapped children. Her marriage to Clifford Allen, a radical socialist and prominent figure in the 1920s–1930s Labour movement gave her access to important political arenas to gain support for her ideas. See Holman, B. (2001) *Champions for Children* (Bristol: Policy Press) for an overview of Lady Allen of Hurtwood's career.

2   The term and usage of social reformer is adapted from Selleck's categories

used in his study of the New Education movement of the late nineteenth and early twentieth centuries to describe the various interests that were engaged in promoting new ideas in the education of children. See Selleck (1968), *New Education*.

3 In the 1960s and 1970s Turner went on to develop one-o-clock clubs and adventure playgrounds attached to London Parks for the GLC.

4 Neville's ideas regarding the relation of work and play in the nineteenth century have parallels with the arguments used by Wood (1913) and the American play movement for the need for play organisations in the early twentieth century. See Wood, W. (1913) *Children's Play*. For an update on Neville's view of playpower today and its role in business, see Kane, P. (2004) *The Play Ethic* pp. 261–8.

5 Frederick Schiller (1759–1805) was a poet (*Ode to Joy*), playwright (*Don Carlos*) and philosopher whose definition of play is usually described as a surplus energy. Recent work on Schiller by Beiser develops a much more complex theory that links play to an engagement with moral education, aesthetics and politics.

Chapter Eight

Fen Man and the Cowboy Go To School

Don Dare

I'm not normally a praying man, but if you're up there, please save me Superman
                                                            Homer Simpson

It is hard to believe that this all happened over thirty years ago. That was when I first came across Bob and Gordon. At the time I could never have guessed the impact that they would have on my life. Of course, I didn't call them by their first names then. At the time it was Mr Hughes and Mr Sturrock. They weren't really that much older than I was, and there was little to portend the bearded wonders that they later became, except for their beards of course. If you close your eyes and try to imagine Bob and Gordon just out of short trousers, aged around twenty and a bit, (although Bob was slightly older than Gordon) (and still is), young and idealistic. Bob wore bell-bottom jeans and an unfashionable, even then, kipper tie adorning a flowery shirt. Less of a fashion victim, more like a total fashion motorway collision. What was most striking about Bob was his gingery red beard and his hair which seemed to grow at right-angles to his head. A bit like if Wurzel Gummidge played for the Incredible String Band. They turned up in an old VW Camper van (1966, split screen, VW blue). It backfired as it went up the gravel roadway leading to my school; coughing and spluttering till it stopped under the sign 'The Bellevue Academy for Young Men'.

Before the engine was turned off I could hear what sounded like *All kinds of everything remind me of you*, a rock'n'roll classic by Dana bought by mums and grans and my younger sister. I had even heard some of the teachers humming it around school. Surely I must have been mistaken!

When Bob stepped out of his van he wasn't wearing any shoes. It was the first time I had seen someone in real life, and not just an American hippie on the telly at a rock festival, walking around without shoes. It was also the last time, until many years later when I met another well-known fashionably challenged individual. Gordon, meanwhile, was wearing drainpipe jeans and a white T-shirt covered by a brown cowboy jacket with tassels hanging from it, like that character in 'Midnight Cowboy', and he was just as much out of place as that cowboy was in New York. To finish off the ensemble he was sporting a pair of brown riding boots. I looked around for a horse, but unless he had tethered it outside the school gates, there wasn't one. He also wore a badge on his jacket that informed me he was a 'sheriff'. The prat!

It was 1972 and I was in the fifth form of the Bellevue Academy. There was no reason on earth as far as I could find out why my parents had sent me to this institution. My father hadn't gone there, nor my grandfather or any other kith or kin, possibly because the Academy had only been established ten years previously and had not and as far as I could tell never would guide an enquiring young mind to Oxbridge and on to high office to lead the country against the miners or to the brink of bankruptcy with the International Monetary Fund.

The school was in the heart of the Cotswolds near Nether Hampton and nowhere else. It was mainly for boarders with a few day boys who must have lived in the woods or in some secret military establishment based underground, as there were no other houses until you hit Oxford almost 30 miles away. I don't know how much my parents paid for the privilege of abandoning me to the direct descendants of the Spanish Inquisition (or teachers as they preferred to be called), but whatever it was, it was too much. I had just been humiliated by Mister Jack Cunningham, the sports master, who once nearly played rugby for England. 'Nearly' meant that he watched them once at Twickenham. Lots of masters had clever or affectionate nicknames such as 'Potty Potter', formally known as Mister Potter the English master, 'BeUp', or Mister Standing for Latin, and of course Mister Ayres was called 'pubes'. However, Jack Cunningham was just 'that prat.' Anyway, I had turned up for rugby with two different coloured socks. I didn't know why I had different coloured socks in my bag, it was just one of those things. 'That prat' told me I was improperly attired for chasing a funny shaped ball around a muddy rugby pitch and putting my face uncomfortably close to other boys' bums. He made me pull my shorts down to my ankles and walk backwards to the school on my own whilst the rest of the boys roared with laughter as I tripped on the start of my journey.

*

'Now look Bob. We agreed. I choose the music here and it's your choice for the way back.'

'Yes I know, but Dana!'

'Dana speaks for all oppressed people around the world.'

'No, you pillock. Dana speaks for lovers of puppy dogs and kittens, weepy movies, mum and dad, snowmen with carrots for noses, Eric and Ernie, and other such sentimental rubbish.'

Gordon whined, 'But I love snowmen with their little carrot noses and coal for eyes!'

'Quick, cowboy, zip it! Someone's coming.'

'Will you stop calling me that? I'll have you know this jacket and these boots are de rigueur in Chelsea, Fen man.'

They both turned to look as the boy came closer. For some reason he was wearing odd socks, had his trousers around his ankles and was walking backwards.

'There you go,' said Bob, 'we have no language to explain that kind of behaviour.'

'Yes we do. It's called unhinged.'

'Be serious a moment. There must be a way we can define the way that children play.'

'Lighten up Bob, children play because they play. We don't know what goes on in their heads and we can't second guess that.

'You wait cowboy, one day the Government will recognise the importance of playing. They'll legislate so that everyone can play freely. When we get all this leisure time that machines are going to give us, childhood will be given the status it deserves. Treaties will be signed around the world.'

Gordon wasn't impressed. 'Ha Ha. Get off that cloud. What will we have? Nations rushing to sign up to *Every Child Plays*? Even then I bet our government doesn't sign up to it.'

Bob said nothing.

'What's that noise, Fen Man?' Gordon continued.

'What noise?'

'Oh, don't worry. It's just the sound of people sniggering behind your back.'

The boy approached them and spoke to Gordon. 'Howdy there, partner. Can I help you?'

'Yes, you can. young man. Can you tell us why you are walking around with your trousers around your ankles?'

'Oh my, have they fallen down again? They're always doing that. I thought I had lost the ability to walk properly. Don't you just hate it when that happens? Well that's me sorted,' he said as he pulled up his shorts. 'Now, how can I help you?'

'Well, you insolent little guttersnipe, you can have the privilege of directing us to the Head's Office.'

'Follow me hopalong and I'll take you there myself.'

And with that, the boy raced off with Roy Rodgers and Bob in hot pursuit.

*

Bob thought back to what had led them here today. It was after a series of meetings where he and Gordon had been speaking about play and its importance, arguing against people who said that play could not be defined and therefore could not be studied scientifically. A phone call had come from a head teacher who had heard from someone who had heard from someone else at a conference about a pair of young troubleshooters who had had remarkable successes with children, 'letting them run around and get hot and bothered and letting them do what they wanted to do and the school's atmosphere, behaviour and exam results had improved'. Although Bob tried to explain that that wasn't exactly what they did, the head teacher was in a flap and not listening, imploring Bob to come down to the school to meet him to discuss their 'particularly difficult and disturbing happenings'. Before Bob knew where he was, a date and a generous fee had been agreed, and the Head had arranged a week's stay at a local hostelry. Gordon, right from the start, had not been happy. 'But what are we going to do for a week? We don't even know why they want us to come to the school. If they want to discuss a play plan, why the indecent haste?' Bob had no answers.

When they did arrive at the Inn, Gordon's mood sunk further. To say the building was ramshackle would be to insult rams (and their hackles). They found a plaque, which showed, once they had removed the mud, that the Inn was a seventeenth-century coaching station on the Bath to Oxford route.

'It's alright for you, Fen man, this is a pretty decent joint where you come from, but I'm used to a more upmarket establishment. How you managed to escape when they flooded all the lands around Ely I'll never know!'

They carried their bags inside to be met with silence. This wasn't silence like in the films where strangers walk into a bar for all the locals to fall mute. With pentangles painted on the wall above the dartboard and the newcomers warned to 'beware the full moon and stay on the path', said in a quivering voice, no, this was silence as if no one was there. Not a soul – friendly or unfriendly, no one was there. It was only half past eight and the evening should have been in full swing with the locals supping their ales, swapping stories about sheep and abusing townies whilst the local farm lads raced their tractors outside the inn until PC Plod turned up and had a quiet word. They walked into the empty space and approached the bar and Gordon coughed loudly to try and attract attention.

'That's a bad cough you got there,' someone said from behind them, making them both jump. They turned around and came face-to-face with Moses. Well, they only called him that because he was a giant, dressed in a smock, hirsute and bearded, covered in dust and carrying two paving stones the size of which would have left room for a few extra commandments. 'I'll just put these out back and I'll be with you. Just building a conservatory, you see,' he said as he disappeared behind the bar, through a beaded curtain and into the beyond.

'I expect he's just gone to part the Red Sea,' Bob said to Gordon.

The beaded curtains swished again as man mountain returned. 'Now, are you the two young men that Mr Sampson from the school has booked in?'

'Yes, that's us' Gordon replied. 'Tom and Jerry. Bill and Ben. Sonny and Cher.' Bob willed Gordon to shut up but to no avail. 'Esther and Abi. Tweedle-dum and Tweedle-dee. Donny and Marie. But you can call us Gordon and Bob.'

Moses tutted. 'Just follow me, Batman and Robin, and I'll show you to your room. You'll have to share because of the building works but Mr Sampson said that would be OK, especially as you are "cosmopolitan" gentlemen.'

*

Bob was not happy. 'It's bad enough that I have to share a bed with you, but now this!'

The night had not been a good one for either Bob or Gordon. First, one snored and woke up the other and then vice versa. This was coupled with a tug-of-war as both of them tried to claim all the blankets. It didn't start well when Gordon revealed that he always slept in the nude and teased Bob about how this might awaken Bob's homoerotic fantasies so that he'd better keep on his side of the bed. 'If I was going to be homo-erotic, it wouldn't be with you, cowboy. Anyway, if you are going to do any gun-slinging, keep it on your side of the bed!'

The next morning didn't start well either.

'What are you on about now, Fen Man?'

'The toilet! You've blocked the toilet!'

'Don't fuss. It will disappear after a few flushes.'

'Now I know why you call it the Ludic Turd!'

'Ho, Ho very funny! How long has it taken you to think up that, then?'

'Ludic Turd! Do you see what I've done there, Gordon?'

'Yes, and do you know what Freud said about jokes, eh?'

'Yes, he said how many analysts does it take to change a light bulb? What, you're not going to guess? Well then, the answer is one. However, the light bulb has got to really want to change!!'

'Once again, Bob, do you know what Freud said about jokes, eh?'

'No. But now you're gonna tell me aren't you?'

'Freud says that a joke provides a unique window into the unconscious. So we look through your dirty window and see a classic case of fear of pooh!'

'It's not poophobia, Gordon. I just don't feel that any toilet should have to accept a gift of that size! And look, you can't go looking like the Lone Ranger. It's not a fancy dress party.'

'Once and for all, Fen Man, it is what well-dressed fashionable gentlemen are wearing in London.'

'That's as maybe, but I wouldn't dress my well in it.'

*

After a hearty breakfast they went to the bar to leave their key and from beyond the beaded curtain they heard a woman crying. Moses swished through the curtains angrily. 'That's my wife upset because of our doctor.'

'I hope everything is alright,' said Gordon.

'Well it will be when I catch up with the doctor. Cheek of it. Calling my wife a beast!'

'How strange,' replied Gordon, 'calling your wife names. What was said?'

'Well,' said Moses, 'He said my wife needed to lose weight as clinically she's a beast.'

They left the key on the counter and just made it to the van before collapsing in fits of laughter.

*

Gordon was pacing up and down the corridor. 'I feel like I'm standing outside a head teacher's office.'

'That's because you are standing outside a head teacher's office.'

'I know, but its reawakening memories for me.'

'Happen a lot, did it Gordon? Standing outside the head's office?'

Gordon hesitated 'Once or twice ... well, until I got expelled.'

'You were expelled! What for?'

'It wasn't my fault. It was the middle of winter and me and some friends were hiding out in the sports pavilion and I built a little fire to keep us warm. Unfortunately it got a little bit out of control and it set the curtains on fire.'

'You were expelled for setting fire to the curtains?'

'No, the sports pavilion burnt down ... and it was right next door to the caretakers' house and that burnt down too.'

'Bastards! They expelled you for that? That could happen to anyone who is seriously loopy.'

Further tales of Tom Brown's schooldays were forestalled, as the head teacher came along and ushered them into his office.

'Mister Hughes and Mister Sturrock. Welcome and sit down. I'm Mister Sampson, the head teacher here at Bellevue. I'm glad you could spare the time and come so quickly. Especially as I hear you are quite the TV star now, Mr Hughes, after your bit on 'Romperoom' with Miss Rosalind. We do not get Anglia Television in this area but I have heard good reports about her children's programme. Anyway, I hope that the 'Boar's Head' is suitable.'

Mister Sampson, in his flowing black don's gown, looked miserable. He looked like Delilah had just cut his hair.

'Yes thank you. It's, eh ... very comfortable. Now how can Gordon and me help?'

Gordon leaned forward. 'I'm sorry, Mr Sampson. Bob is a product of the Comprehensive School system and comes from a closed community, one may even call it inbred, and as such he does not understand common English usage such as 'Gordon and I'.'

Mister Sampson smiled. 'How very refreshing to find someone who is concerned with the way that language is spoken. In these times I ...'

'So how can I and Nancy Mitford help you, Mr Sampson?' interrupted Bob.

Mr Sampson took a deep breath and started. 'Well this is a bit delicate and I hope that you can guarantee confidentiality, as I wouldn't want this to get out.'

They both nodded, intrigued.

'It all started about six weeks ago. First it was small things such as all the chalk from the classrooms disappearing, followed by all the spoons from the refectory. I just thought that it was pranks and that we would find out who the culprit was and things would go back to normal. Then when I went to prepare for the school assembly all the chairs in the school hall were piled on top of each other and Mr Cunningham came to tell me that all the school rugby posts had been sawn in half. Then only last week, Mrs Jones, our school nurse, was locked into the medicine cupboard when she went in to check our supplies.'

'Well,' Bob said, 'I don't know how we can help you. We're playworkers ...'

'Yes, I know, but only two nights ago I assigned one teacher to sleep in each dormitory and had the rest of the school staff patrolling the grounds. The next morning all the staff reported that no pupil had left their rooms at any time. Yet when the school refectory was opened (and this involved unlocking padlocks which only myself, the deputy head teacher and the school caretaker had keys for), painted in red in four foot high letters on the wall was '**LET ME PLAY!**'

*

Bob was now in the refectory looking out of a window overlooking the school field watching some of the boarders playing, whilst Gordon was sitting at one of the tables scribbling away in a tatty notebook. They were intrigued by what Mr Sampson had said and looking at the scrubbed wall they could still see the outline of the words 'LET ME PLAY'. They didn't really have a plan at this stage, but had decided to lock themselves in the hall and wait until dark and the boarders had gone to bed before having a quick look around and going back to the 'Inn of Happiness' to discuss their next steps.

Bob looked over to Gordon. 'What you doing?'

'I'm inventing an affordable portable music enabler which will make me my first million. I'm thinking of calling it an iPoo.'

'Bollocks. What you doing?'

'Ooh get you, Mr Potty Mouth! What I am doing is preparing a lecture for the Institute of Very Clever People and I am up to ... ,' he said glancing down to his notes, 'The perception of the unreality of reality is the beginning of psychological realism. We are omnipotent beings able to transcend the existential despair of urgency.'

Bob sighed. 'Sometimes you talk a load of bollocks, Gordon. That last lecture I attended of yours when you were talking about rapture and jouissance left right and centre. Most of the audience had no idea what you were on about. I didn't until I got home and looked it up and found out that jouissance means 'orgasm' and the 'spilling of seed'. Why is it always sex with you psychoanalysts? You are such a wanker. You have so much to say, but you always dress it up in long words.'

'That's because, my dear Fen Man, I am a believer in the art of sesquipedality.'

At that point Bob gave up talking and resumed his observation.

'Anyway, what are you looking at?'

'I'm looking at the different ways that the kids are playing and trying to find words that describe it.'

'Budge over and let me have a look.'

They both looked out over the school playing field.

'Look over there, Gordon, at that group of kids who are standing around talking, laughing, shrieking and shouting at each other. And over there, at the group who are playing 'tag'. And there, those two boys who are burying themselves under those leaves. They are all playing in different ways but we haven't got the language to describe what they are doing.'

'Yes we have, Fen Man; it's called 'chatty play', 'running around play' and 'crazy play'. Oh and look over there. 'Robin Hood play'.

Bob wondered how someone so astute and clever could at times be so facile. They both went back to what they were doing.

*

Later Bob turned to Gordon, 'So how did you get involved with children and play? What was your motivation?'

Gordon thought for a minute. 'Well, when I was travelling around India, I went to an orphanage where I was introduced to a young girl aged about eight called Amina. She hadn't communicated with anyone since she arrived there three years previously. Not only had she not spoken but she hadn't smiled either. She used to sit and stare blankly as though her life happened inside her head and not in the outside world. I went up to her and looked in her eyes and started smiling.'

Bob noticed Gordon had tears in his eyes as he continued with his story.

'After about five minutes of this smile I saw creases around her eyes and mouth as she too started to smile and then she started to laugh and then I laughed and everyone around laughed at this miracle. That's when I realised I wanted to work with children and that's when I realised I had something to offer.'

They were both silent for a few minutes.

'You just made that up didn't you, Gordon?'

'Yep.'

They both went back to what they were doing.

*

Bob awoke with a start. It was dark and he had fallen asleep at one end of the table and could hear Gordon snoring from the other end in the darkness of the refectory. He went to the window to see if he could tell the time on his watch from the light of the moon and the stars. It was nearly half past eleven and still thirty minutes before the witching hour. He had hoped to be back at the Inn by now. He shook Gordon awake.

'What is it now, Skippy? Has Jimmy fallen down the mineshaft?'

'No, Cowboy, it's about time we were out of here. Let's do the rounds and get back to our room.'

'I love it when you take control, Fen Man!'

They gathered their things and just as they were about to open them, the refectory doors started to shake backwards and forwards as though someone was trying to open them without a key.

'Who's there?' Bob shouted.

The doors shook some more.

'Right, whoever it is, we're going to open the door and come out now.'

There was a boy's voice from outside, 'Let me in. I want to play!'

'OK,' Gordon responded 'We'll let you in to play then.'

The boy continued to shout and bang the doors asking to be let in and play.

'Come on, Bob. Get the doors open, quickly.'

Bob tried several keys in the lock before one finally turned. As it did, the boy outside the door went silent. Bob flung open the door just in time to see a shape disappear down the corridor into one of the classrooms.

They both raced out of the hall, down the corridor and in through a door marked 'Chemistry'. At the end of the laboratory on top of a desk was a boy wearing pyjamas, twirling around and around, with his hands above his head, singing out loud over and over again:

'Oranges and lemons say the bells of Saint Clements. You owe me five farthings say the bells of Saint Martins!'

Gordon sang out loud 'When will you pay me say the bells of saint …' He hesitated. 'Saint who? Bob can you remember?'

'Quick Gordon. He's slowing down!'

Gordon tried again. 'When will you pay me say the bells of Saint Nick'

'Saint Nick? Saint Nick? It doesn't even rhyme you twit!' shouted Bob.

The boy stopped still and glared at Gordon before starting to twirl around again, faster and faster.

'What did you do that for?' Bob demanded.

'Well, I must tell you about it some time. It's a new concept I'm working on about children giving out signals – invitations to play. I'm calling them play cues.'

As the boy twirled around, books, pencils, pens and glass tubes flew up into the air as though caught in a tornado. The cupboards opened up and chemicals were caught up in the maelstrom. Bob pulled Gordon down under a desk as small explosions ripped through the lab.

'Well Gordon, I thought that went well, eh? Your little play cue has invited an interesting response.'

Bob poked his head over the desk. The boy was still twisting around and two pots of chemicals collided into each other above Bob releasing a noxious, foul-smelling gas.

'Blimey Bob, pull yourself together,' Gordon spluttered. They both tried to hold their breath until the gas had dissipated.

'Listen,' said Bob.

'What?' replied Gordon.

'It's gone silent.'

They both peered over the desktop. The boy had gone, leaving the lab in a ruin of paper and broken glass with plumes of smoke.

'Quick, Gordon! He's gone out the back of the lab!'

They both raced through the door at the end of the lab into an empty corridor.

'Where's he gone, then?'

'Got any other songs you can start singing? Maybe you'll "cue" him and he'll come back to join in with you?'

'Leave it out, Bob, it's just an idea at the moment, and anyway, what we saw there isn't normal.'

'Yes I know, but I'm not clear what we saw there. We don't have time for a critical incident analysis, we need to find that boy before someone is hurt. How do we find one boy amongst so many?'

'Didn't you notice, Bob?'

'Notice what?'

'The boy was wearing odd rugby socks.'

*

They eventually found the boy in his dormitory fast asleep. The dormitory was being watched over by Mr Cunningham who was insistent that out of the twelve boys fast asleep, no one had left the room since Jenkins

Minor had needed the toilet at about quarter past eleven and that they had no right to accuse him of being negligent.

Bob and Gordon stood at the end of the boy's bed.

Bob whispered 'This is definitely the boy I saw in the chemistry lab ... 'What do you think, Gordon?'

'I agree but how did he get past that prat?'

The boy was tossing and turning in his bed and seemed to be talking, but only a few words were discernible.

Bob pointed to a line drawing chalked above the boy's bed.

'I've got an idea about what's going on here Bob, but it's a bit Jackanory.'

'OK, Cowboy. I'll make myself comfortable and then you can begin.'

'Well. Have you heard of 'Tulpas?'

'Isn't that somewhere Gene Pitney was 24 hours from?'

'That was Tulsa, you numbskull! A tulpa is a Tibetan mysticism. Tibetan yogis claim that through thought and through their imagination they can create a physical being. An other-worldly twin of themselves. The only problem is that sometimes the twin can be mischievous or even deadly.'

'OK Gordon, but what about that drawing and why does the boy keep asking to play?'

'Well' I'm trying to make sense of it myself.' Gordon thought for a minute.

'The symbol is called a sigil and can invoke the power of a spirit. I think we have a case here of someone who has seriously unplayed-out material. Something that has caused so much damage, it has become stronger than ordinary neuroses. Repressed-play experiences that have started to create a slippage from his unconscious when he is asleep and which has gone dangerously awry. These incidents have only happened at night and I believe that when the boy dreams he opens the portal to his inner world and releases his twin demon. His demon is the result of an interrupted and corrupt drive to play and therefore can only play malevolently.'

'So,' Bob said standing up 'The boy's neurochemical equilibrium may be seriously compromised.'

Gordon stared at Bob for a minute before continuing. 'Thank you "Brains'. We need to know something about this boy's history. Who is he? Where was he brought up? What is his family like? What has happened in his life to create this fracture?'

'Right,' said Bob, going up to Mr Cunningham. 'What's this boy's name?'

Mr Cunningham looked shocked. 'Surely you know who this is? If you don't, you must be the only people in the country who don't! Why that's …'

Nothing more could be heard as there was a mighty bang from an explosion in the school drive where Bob had left his camper van.

Who is the little weirdo?
Will Bob and Gordon work out the riddle of the Tulpa?
Can they break the secret code?
Do you know the way to San Jose?
Is grey the new black?

All of these questions, except the last one, are answered in Don Dare's latest book … Fen Man and The Cowboy go to School

Chapter Nine

The Gentle Art of Agonism –

Speculations and Possibilities of Missing Female Perspectives?

Ali Wood and Jacky Kilvington

In this chapter we will consider why we think there may be missing female perspectives in current playwork theory and what we think some of these perspectives entail.

This is not an attempt to dismiss what has gone before, but an endeavour to build on, colour and enrich understanding. We see ourselves as the mouthpiece of a collective of female agonists. 'Agonism implies a deep respect and concern for the other … this agonistic discourse will therefore be one marked not merely by conflict, but just as importantly, by [what we hope will be] mutual admiration' (Chambers 2001, p. 8). We would not be in a position to argue potentially absent perspectives, if we were not able to access current theory. Bob and Gordon are major contributors to this and we thank them for their work and their influence – both personally and professionally.

We should also state clearly that the terms 'male' and 'female' used herein are not interchangeable with 'men' and 'women'; although we do purport that generally, men are more likely to have 'male' traits and women to have 'female'.

Finally, we should specify that we are basing our contentions on the intuition, memory, experience and evidence IMEE (Hughes 1996) of many playwork women.

Why Might there be Missing Female Perspectives in Current Playwork Theory?

We will locate our arguments in the quadrants of the Integral Play Framework – adapted from the Wilber model by Else (2003, p. 48), in order to explain particular viewpoints, but keep a holistic overview.

	Feelings/Subjective	*Facts/Objective*
Me/self	A Feelings and thoughts *(Psychology)*	B Physical ability and skills *(Biology)*
Us/others	C Belief and culture *(Anthropology)*	D Relationships, power and control *(Sociology)*

Fig. 9.1   Integral Play Framework (Else 2003)

Quadrant A

For some time now, women in playwork have been having conversations and sharing feelings about aspects of play and playwork theory that have never been recorded or publicly debated and shared with male colleagues. We decided to air this at a recent playwork conference where we facilitated a women-only session. Forty-six women attended (and others who could not, contacted us separately) and the following questions were debated.

1. Why are there so few women writing, publishing, researching and presenting playwork theory?
2. What is the female perspective – if it exists – with regard to play and playwork (and what is male)?
3. What might be the female aspects of current theory and what bits might be missing?

Many women reported a sense of heightened expectancy, of collective conviction and of freedom and relief – 'about time too' was repeatedly stated, as though suddenly there was the chance to speak freely rather than covertly (although no-one felt or had been previously prevented from doing so). Discussions about 'female play' and 'female memories' and 'female intuition' ensued and spilled over outside the session. There was debate about possibly missing play types; social empathy and emotion displayed in play; the nature of 'choice' versus 'negotiation' or 'dominance' during play; the role of caring in playwork; gender differences in play; alternative play environments ... and some of these will be explored further in this chapter.

The articulated feelings and thoughts of all these women (and many more since) do suggest missing perspectives. Many women say they feel under-represented in descriptions of play. They feel intuitively that definitions of play have a male bias that manifests itself in individualism, control, freedom and adventure that does not wholly encapsulate female play experiences. One woman put it well – she had noticed that when describing play memories, men often talked about 'feeling like gods', 'being able to do what *I* wanted', whereas women often talked about the exuberant feeling of playing with others superseding what they actually did.

Quadrant B

Moving into the more scientific and objective quadrant; there has been much neurological research in recent years and some scientists claim evidence of 'concrete scientifically proved anatomical and functional differences between the brains of males and females' (Sabbatini 2000, p. 4). Nadeau (1997, p. 330) says 'the human brain, like the human body, is sexed and differences in the sex-specific human brain condition a wide range of behaviours that we typically associate with maleness or femaleness'.

More recently, Baron-Cohen (2004) has theorised that the female brain is hard-wired for empathy and the male brain is hard-wired for understanding and building systems. He also postulates that physical gender does not necessarily equate with brain type – not all men have a male brain or women a female brain; some have a 'balanced' brain that can equally systematise and empathise, but on average, more men have a male brain and more women have a female brain.

What then, are the documented differences between male and female brains from these researchers? We summarise these on page 90.

MALE	FEMALE
Brain Types	
Understanding and building systems	Empathy
How do things work?	How are people feeling?
What are the underlying rules?	How to treat with care and sensitivity
Brain Differences	
Greater spatial awareness	Hear higher frequencies
Visualize 3D objects	More vocal
Greater mathematical reasoning	More skilled in reading/
More skilled in gross motor	vocabulary
movement	Wider range of vision
Thinking	
Action-focused	Detail-focused
Problem-solving	Making connections
Immediate	Internal debate
Compartmental	Global
Intuitive/reactive	Analytical/perceptive
Systemizing	Empathizing
Communicating	
Few words	Many words
About things	About people
Gives information	Seeks information
Competitive	Cooperative
States point straight away	Paints whole picture before reaching point

Fig. 9.2   Summary of male and female brain characteristics

We are not in any way qualified to analyse or debate these differences but there is substantial scientific (and anecdotal) supportive evidence to suggest that these differences may be more than culturally based. We include them here because if it is true that male thinking and communicating is different, then as most playwork theory has been posited by men, it can be reasonably argued that female perspectives could be missing. Surely women's 'seemingly enhanced awareness of emotionally relevant details, visual cues, verbal nuances and hidden meanings' (Nadeau 1997, p. 332) could create potentially absent contributions to our current understanding of play and playwork.

Quadrant C

We come now to the anthropological view. Gender identity development has long been theorised and debated. It is not our brief here to explore that historical or ongoing debate, or to take a particular standpoint. Whatever we believe about gender typing, however, we still have differing cultural perspectives and world-views that will arise from our experiences, perceptions and expectations as men and women.

The divisions between men and women are an ever-moving feast, 'socially created, historically changing, filled with ambiguity and contradiction and continually renegotiated' (Thorne 1993, p. 6). What constitutes and causes these divisions is not the issue here for us: the fact is, they have an experiential and developmental effect on girls' and boys' perception of the world and their place within it. We assert that this in turn must affect our playing, our later understanding of play itself, and our consequent theorising.

Quadrant D

Finally, we come to the sociopolitical quadrant. Despite all the endeavours – of men and women – to tackle sexism and its effects in western society, life is neither equal nor the same for either gender; but perhaps therein lies part of the problem, in that we have tried to make it the same rather than equal.

Goldberg (1993) suggests that patriarchy is inevitable. The neuroendocrinological evidence is that testosterone makes men more aggressive and competitive, whereas oestrogen and progesterone make women more cooperative. This drive for domination will inevitably, in Goldberg's thinking, lead to men taking roles that are of a higher social status. However, the fact that men and women behave differently does not make one gender superior to the other.

Whilst paying due regard to the 'dualistic rut' Thorne (1993, p. 108) refers to when discussing gender differences, we should also not dismiss everything that has not been scientifically researched if it plays out in life.

Our forty-six women came up with many reasons as to why so few women were writing and researching playwork theory. They reflect all four quadrants;

(a) the personal (low self-esteem, fear, isolation, 'what if I get it wrong?' …);

(b) the biological (maternal responsibility and care, global thinking with less focus …)

(c) the cultural (women chat and share, writing and researching is 'not what we do' …)

(d) the sociopolitical ('we don't need that kind of status or recognition', lack of drive or ambition, the glass ceiling …)

However, the consensus was that if the societal power dynamics were different, that might have made or could make all the difference. Women would be more confident and find ways to work together to theorise more creatively, visually and experientially. Men would be more supportive and cognisant of women's ideas and contributions.

Women have much to contribute, but on the whole do not push themselves forward, so playwork theory lacks their perspectives and their contribution to its presentation – some of which we will now consider.

At present these are ideas – based on the recollections, intuition and observations of playwork women. This is not unusual in playwork theory – both Bob and Gordon have presented ideas either based on reflective practice or adapted from other disciplines. Gordon says he 'cannot countenance a definitional perspective for our work that postulates only scientific objectivity' (Sturrock 2003a, p. 43). However, we agree that 'we don't yet have a mechanism for deciding whether these theories hold water or not' (Russell 2004, p. 99) and in fact our sector as a whole has not been good at thinking critically – a situation we feel may be changing slowly. We feel relatively comfortable in presenting these ideas whilst recognising that we are posing more questions than answers and that more qualitative and even quantitative research is needed.

Social Dynamics of Play

'Our focus on the individual child at play has given us many insights, but has, to some extent, not helped with a particular playwork perspective on children's social worlds' (Russell 2004, p. 102). We agree that evidence from a sociocultural perspective, i.e. the bottom two quadrants of the Integral Play Framework, has not been sufficiently examined by the wider playwork sector.

As Russell says, this may be due to the danger that any analysis could use that understanding to socialise and acculturate, but we feel that perhaps more 'male' perspectives might account for the omission.

The 'female' perspective is far more enquiring about how children do (or don't) play together – about negotiation, mutual experience, expression of empathy, issues of power, creation of common culture, cooperation and competition, borderwork, survival techniques, joint fantasy, shared language, emotional risk-taking – to name but a few.

The play cycle (Sturrock and Else 1998) has been of enormous help in giving playworkers a framework to understand play and to reflect more seriously on their impact and intervention in the play space; but it has to date been couched in individual terms. What about group cues and/or group returns? How about describing the metalude in terms of a need to participate, belong or play *with* someone, rather than play some*thing*? Could we not apply our sociological understanding of group dynamics to children playing – the sum of the parts being greater than the whole – and rather than see overlapping frames, see groups themselves as loose parts of individuals forming a collective playing entity?

Many women describe their memories of play in terms of the social experience rather than what they actually played. Who they played with mattered more than what they did. This may well be due to the notion that 'children are so motivated to be accepted in play, that they make sacrifices of egocentricity for membership of the group' (Sutton-Smith 1997, p. 44). We would suggest, however, that it is not simply due to peer pressure.

Holt (1972) gives a marvellous description of a sister and brother aged eight and five playing together in their back yard, with all the frustration and tension of playing out both their own needs and preferences as individuals *and* as social beings. It requires a delicate and sometimes agonising marrying of the two conflicting desires to play 'what I want' and to play with someone else. 'And so, with great subtlety and skill, as they play, they adjust to each other's needs and feelings, respond from one second to the next to what the other says and does' (Holt 1972, p. 17).

Is this adjustment always made reluctantly or resentfully? Is Sutton-Smith (1999, p. 241) indicating this when he says 'much childhood social play is motivated more by a desire to be accepted by the other children than by any special desire for freedom of play choice ... clearly, play is itself a compound of voluntary and involuntary elements, not totally one or the other'. Many women say this is not the case and that often the choice to play with someone is more important and worthwhile than the activity itself.

In a society that is centred on individual will and achievement, we would do well to understand better why the play drive motivates us over and over towards a collective consciousness and experience.

Gender and Play

Gender differences in play have been well documented, although

> for the last quarter of the twentieth century, it has been largely unac-ceptable to study male-female differences and certainly to allow that there could be a biological explanation for differences, at least as important as the explanatory power of socialisation. (Lindon 2005, p. 75)

There clearly are differences and most psychological and anthropologi-cal researchers – including women – have concluded that at least some of the explanation for these must be attributed to biology; but we are still far from knowing 'how large are the *real* sex differences in behaviour and how do they relate to the child's *concept* of gender?' (Konner 1991, p. 160).

The differences mainly noted (F. Hughes 1999, p. 144) are around aggression and simulated aggression (cross-culturally, substantially more boys participate in real and play-fighting), voluntary sex-segrega-tion (especially between the ages of six and eleven), toy selection (e.g. boys like trucks, weapons and construction kits; girls like dolls, fashion and art materials) and choice of games (e.g. boys role-play high-action adventure with complex rules and girls role-play relationships with extensive conversation).

Clearly, the causes of these differences are complex and inter-relate and will include biology, psychology, religion, culture, socialisation, politics, fashion, media, peer pressure, play context ...

What has the playwork sector made of this? Much of current playwork theory, training and education has been strangely silent and only refers to non-gendered children, viz. s/he, 'the child' or 'the children'. Why is this? Surely the professionals closest to children's play would or should have something to say?

We could argue that it is mainly because we have been committed to all children's equal rights to play in the ways they wish without stereo-typical restriction. We could state that it is because we have wanted to stand in the breach and not be subject to sociopolitical will. There will probably be some truth in both of these.

However, might it also be because we have not dared to be otherwise; we have not sufficiently reflected on whether our practice is a knee-jerk response to equality rhetoric or a genuine ludocentric response?

What we can be sure of is that regardless of the array of forces and influences in their lives, children are social actors themselves; 'they are by no means passive or without agency ... children act, resist, rework and create; they influence adults as well as being influenced by them' (Thorne 1993, p. 3). Children shape their own experiences, especially through play. Both boys and girls are, in their ways, wrestling with the concept of gender and its personal application. They know better than we do, that not all boys will be boys and nor will be girls and it is only when they can truly play without hindrance, that they will discover what their gender means to them.

Perhaps it is time for playwork to be more honest and to re-examine gender and play with more open minds. Milne (2000, p. 14) has touched on this from a male perspective. We ask:

1. In our attempts to be anti-discriminatory, have we tried to manipulate play spaces into being non-gendered?
2. Does it matter if boys and girls play differently? Are there better or worse ways of playing if it is freely chosen?
3. Do girls and boys play differently because of their development, or is their development the result of playing differently?
4. What is the impact of the roles that male and female playworkers take in a play space?
5. If a play space is staffed by mostly female, or mostly male workers, does this 'engender' the environment?
6. Can we see (and record) examples of girls and boys playing out the concepts of gender that constrain them?
7. Can we see (and record) examples of within-gender variation that does not fit the male–female culture approach?
8. Do we at the same time, respect the rights of children to play *according to their gender*?

There is much to explore in this!

Emotion and play

We turn now to the subject of emotions.

The sixteen play types listed by Hughes (2002) describe actions, as of course they must, because that is all we can see – we cannot read children's thoughts and feel their emotions and so we can never truly understand what is going on when we observe play. 'Children play with their whole selves: it is a somatic, sensual, emotional, cognitive, social and spiritual engagement with the environment' (Sturrock *et al.* 2004, p. 81).

However, the fact that playworkers describe play in terms of action does mean that the sector has emphasised or been overconcerned with the 'doing' elements of play and therefore less cognisant of the cause and effects of emotion and thought and how these relate to or stimulate each other in play.

The word 'emotion' has Latin roots meaning 'the impulse to act'. Could it be that children play in order to express emotion and that any action on their part is secondary to the emotion that has driven the play? This would mean that play could be alternatively described by the emotion that the play embodies rather than the physical manifestation of the play; for example, playing at being an angry parent could be 'angry' play rather than sociodramatic play. The point of the play might be to feel angry, not to play at being a parent. Deep play could be 'fear' play because the point of the play is to feel and survive the fear.

Perhaps play frames too could be primarily emotional, in that it is sometimes the experience of a particular feeling that holds the play together, rather than a physical or narrative frame. Emotions themselves could be play cues, externally and/or internally.

Sutton-Smith (2001, p. 166) suggests that play may be a 'solution to the paradox of the conflict between the involuntary and the voluntary systems of emotional release'. 'The advantage of playing', says Hendricks (2001, p. 13), 'is that you can test out the action and emotions that would be too dangerous to act out in real life', or, put another way, play out that which otherwise might lead to neurosis (Sturrock 2002, p. 4).

Certainly, the subject of emotion has come to the forefront in recent years, having been long regarded with great disdain and suspicion in western society. Its contribution is being explored in many scientific fields and we are beginning to understand much more how emotions 'work' and how important it is that we become emotionally literate.

Emotions and feelings (for the two are different) pervade play and yet front-line playworkers have not really recognised or explored this in any meaningful way. Else (2003, p. 51) has suggested there may be emotional, impulsive and perceptual play types. Gordon (2002, p. 3) has written much about emotions in play, and sees 'the playing out of affective material as being one of the prime functions of play'. Bob often refers to feelings expressed in play; more notably in his most recent work (Hughes 2006). Drawing on Gordon's idea of affective topography (Sturrock 2003b), we feel that some of Bob and Gordon's work needs overlaying with 'female' interpretation in order to communicate it more effectively to grass-roots workers and to build up what Gordon suggests is the currently 'limited affective/emotional vocabulary to describe our work' (Sturrock 1996, p. 2).

Our playwork women discussed energetically the links between emotions and play and suggested further emotionally related play types such as nurture play, empathic play, sexual play and sadistic play. There will be thinking and feeling aspects to each play type but there may also be thinking and/or feeling types, existent, new and yet unknown, with no observable action at all.

Many of us have suffered from 'a wider cultural tendency to emphasise the cognitive at the expense of the emotional' (Barnes 1995, p. 157) and even a 'culturally transmitted fear of emotions' (Orbach 1994, p. 6). Emotions – particular in the context of play – are not easy to study; they are highly elusive, which is 'inevitable, given the complex inter-relationships of discourse, embodiment, memory, personal biography, sociocultural processes and thought that constitute and give meaning to emotional states' (Lupton 1998, p. 167).

Emotions – 'light' and 'dark' – are a fundamental and essential part of play that deserves more careful consideration, study and communication. This brings us nicely to our fourth contention.

Affective Play Spaces

The fifth principle of playwork talks about the creation of play spaces, but this is often interpreted as just a physical space. An environment that really stimulates play however is much more than its physical attributes; it needs also to address – in a variety of ways – how children feel.

Hughes (1996) acknowledges the importance of both the physical and affective environment in his discussion of content and ambience indicators, saying in later work that environmental modification can 'act as a physical and psychological catalyst that stimulate engagement and triggers sensory and affective engagement' (Hughes 2001, p. 171).

All environments are of course affective in some sense, but we would go further and describe an 'affective play space'; a place where children's inner worlds can be externalised and where the adults present seek actively to support this through attunement, props, ambience and atmosphere. Neurobiology asserts that the more emotions are evoked in children, the better the development of essential chemical structures in the brain (Braun 2004, p. 4). In what ways could a play space do this?

We define an effective affective play space as one in which children can:

(a) express whatever they are feeling – whether this is carried baggage from that day or their lives, or whether it is a response to events and/or people whilst playing;
(b) experiment with different feelings; and
(c) experience new feelings via particular stimuli.

Playworkers in such a space would need to try and ensure that:

- there are neophilic and out-of-the-ordinary experiences from time to time for children to access;
- there are emotionally evocative spaces, loose parts, materials and 'happenings';
- there is an overall ambience of welcome, acceptance, freedom and playfulness;
- they are aware of children's moods and emotional baggage;
- they are not fazed by children's strong feelings and have a supportive repertoire of both positive and playful responses (and props) when required;
- they are comfortable with authentically expressing and talking about their own feelings.

What would an effective affective play space look like and how could one be created? The following factors and the links between them and feelings should be regularly considered by asking the question, 'How does each of these evoke or provoke what kinds of emotions?'

- Lighting: neon, fairy, lamp, candle, torch, darkness, flashing, coloured, filtered ...
- Colours of walls/fabrics/images/equipment: primaries, pastels, mixtures, neutrals ...
- Music: styles, live, created, mood-inducing, background, volume

- Images: abstract, real-life, positive, scenic, of people ...
- Aroma: pleasant or not, cooking, aromatic, chemical, memory-evoking ...
- Layout: different levels, heights, slopes, room for variety, flexible
- Spaces (indoor and outdoor):   open, large, small, natural, private, transient ...
- Familiarity: limited amount of change but still offering rich neophilic stimuli and flexibility
- Noise/sound level: variety right across spectrum including silence ...
- Comfort factors: temperature, cushions, food/drink, etc.
- Sensory stuff: variety of textures, sounds, tastes, sights
- Elements: ways to include earth, air, fire and water (and wildlife)
- Resources and loose parts: especially for fantasy and imaginative use
- Attitudes: all feelings are OK, honesty, acceptance, empathy, support
- Behaviour: rules and unwritten rules that do not block emotional expression – the behaviour of playworkers is crucial to creating the right kind of ambience for affective play.

We have elsewhere (Kilvington *et al.* 2006; Kilvington and Wood 2006) enlarged on these factors and listed possible props, and have explored the reasons why it is so important that children can freely express their feelings in play. These include:

- brain growth
- healing of trauma
- self-mastery
- empathic development/development of empathy?
- experimentation and discovery
- self-expression
- evolution of identity
- creativity and invention

Goleman (1995, p. 195) is emphatic when he says 'the simple neglect of emotional needs can be more damaging than outright abuse'. If this is true, the need for effective affective environments becomes even more acute and playworkers should be seriously addressing how effectively affective their spaces really are.

So, Bob and Gordon, we hope we have not antagonised you with our perspectives. We hope that, in our female agonistic way, we have impressed you with our discourse, as you have us with yours. Our intuition and experience tell us there is much to explore on this subject and we invite you to join with us for inclusive debate.

Chapter Ten

Ludic Discourse: Models and Possibilities

Jayne Shenstone

Introduction

This text was originally based on ideas that were sparked off by a conversation that I had when I first met Gordon Sturrock. This conversation centred around how we have a large vocabulary to discuss art but similar terms do not exist as a common language for playworkers to use about play. A picture or other work of art has a whole range of specialist vocabulary ascribed to it: artists can speak of expressive, tectonic, formal, textural, narrative, generic and symbolic qualities. Within the area of colour alone, one can describe hue, tonality and contrast; colours may be complementary, harmonious or discordant; all these and many more combinations are available from a primary palette of only three essentials – red, yellow and blue. Would it be possible to develop such a rich vocabulary to describe play and playwork?

This chapter sets out the need for expanding communication models that define play and playwork in a professional context. It is concerned with the process of play, and outcomes of play are considered as indicators of ludic processes. At the heart of the paper is Witkin's (1976) conception of the 'holding form', which is described as a transitional mode between sensation and self-knowledge. Thus if the holding form is part of the enactment of play – transforming sensations to intelligible feelings – perhaps the holding form itself can be used as an indicator or signifier of the nature of the sensation that gave rise to that particular enactment of play. If this were true, it might be useful to playworkers to be able to understand playing-out behaviours and thus help us to gauge the nature of the sensations that gave rise to them.

This chapter begins from the premise that children at play, and playworkers to some extent, share a common 'language' that is not always conveyed through words.

The Triune Brain

Paul MacLean's (1976, 1985, as cited in Hughes 2006) work on the triune brain states that the brain has at least three primary parts that link to form the complete human brain. Each of these sections has a distinct character and each functions in different ways. The amygdala is the brain stem, the 'reptile' part of the brain, is primarily instinctual and controls our basic functions: arousal, hormonal secretions and autonomic responses associated with fear, and primary emotional responses. The limbic system is the mammalian emotional part of the brain, controlling secondary emotional responses, mood and motivation, pain and pleasure sensations. The cortex is the intellectual or more rational part of the human brain and is the most highly developed. It is responsible for thinking, perceiving, producing and understanding language. It is also the most recent structure in the history of brain evolution. (Else 2006)

Damasio (2003) expands ideas about sensory awareness: we have sensory organs that collect external signals and internal sensory organs as well. Through these sensory organs, we gain awareness of the world and what is going on within our body and mind. Housed in the 'physical body' the brain is systematically making sense of the stimuli received externally and internally.

Sensate Language

Studies in Neuro-Linguistic Programming (NLP) (Bandler and Grindler, 1982) show that at least three means of communicating (auditory, visual and kinaesthetic) coexist, and that people may have an inclination towards one or more of these modes. This inclination may exist either in the way communications are transmitted or received. Further, linguistic representation (symbolic speech), whether written or spoken, could be said to be tertiary in evolutionary and developmental terms; children communicate more through non-verbal means such as touch and visual cueing – and even noise – than they do words.

Of the five senses, understanding through the sense of touch has lesser 'status' than visual and auditory awareness, though it ranks higher than smell or taste. Perhaps this is because touch, smell and taste belong to a more primeval mode of comprehension or because they remain as sensate experiences, meaning that we do not tend to think consciously about them very much. All humans may share certain symbols and responses to sensory stimulations and other experiences may be culturally or experientially located. Of these symbols, some such as language are acquired through learning and others may be highly personalised, as in the symbolic representations in art or in play. Additional ways of communicating are called for when we attempt to explain playful occurrences with children.

A Psycholudic Focus

The term 'psycholudics,' meaning the study of the mind and psyche at play, was coined by Sturrock and made known in *The Colorado Paper* (Sturrock and Else 1998). This model and the related terms further our understanding of the mechanism of play (see Figure 10.1).

Essentially, Sturrock and Else (1998) describe how playfulness begins and evolves (Metalude: M-L), creating within the child at play a cue that decays over time (T>) and that is returned through playful interaction (@) within the play space, which may be repeated (§) until it is annihilated. The duration of each cycle may vary, and in the therapeutic model of playwork must be within the child's control.

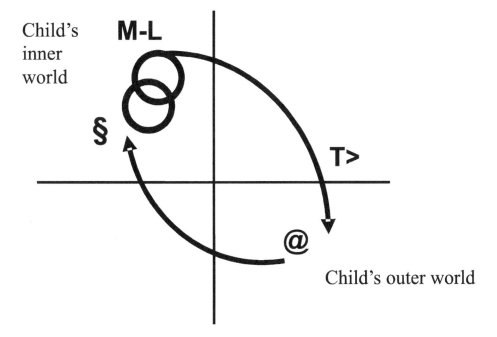

Fig. 10.1   The play cycle (after Sturrock and Else 1998)

Sturrock and Else describe the healing potential of play for children involved in this cyclical process. The play return in particular involves children's perception of changes brought about by playful encounters with play spaces. The nature of the encounters may be environmental, social, material, (objective), or internal, abstract (subjective). Sturrock and Else assert that children are in danger of becoming deprived of play opportunities and appropriate environments, contributing to the increase in perceived behavioural disorders being diagnosed in children. Playworkers also need to be aware of emotional transference between themselves and playing children and the potential for adults to 'adulterate' children's play during this process. (Adulteration as described by Sturrock and Else is when the adult is dominant in the play relationship.)

Playing is a creative process in which infinite variations of a complex and changeable nature are experienced. Children at play experience these potentials in a socioludic context and also a ludic environment. Thus the space shared by the playing child and the playworker in a psycholudic sense might exist not only on the psychological, emotional level but also intellectually and physically too. By developing psycholudics, Sturrock and Else have made two major contributions to the progression of playwork philosophy and the playwork profession: the expansion of the ludic vocabulary and a better recognition of the status of emotional content in children's play. Much of the discussion on children's play refers to abstract forms such as emotion, intuition, sense of belonging, escapism. That is to say, like much of creative thinking, psycholudics is divergent, and suggests that logic belongs to some other form of thinking: cognitive, linear perhaps, but not playful. It is characteristic of play that it combines different types of intelligence, for example, emotional with environmental, in such complex and highly personal ways that they can seem random or even chaotic.

Intelligence of Feeling

The process of the play cycle has certain similarities with the process described by Witkin (1976) regarding *The Intelligence of Feeling*. In his treatise on the means of children's self-expression, he describes the inner and outer worlds of children's experience. The outer world is shared with others, objective and of spaces (environments); and the inner world is one of sensations and feelings. 'There is another world ... a world that exists only because the individual exists. It is the world of [their] own sensations and feelings' (Witkin 1976, p. 1). Witkin suggests that adapta-

Sensate experience →
Intelligible feeling

Transformation through media

Fig. 10.2 The holding form (after Witkin 1976)

tion to the outer world requires impressions that are extrinsic and the inner world requires other means of self-expression; essentially intrinsic. Witkin proposes a transitional 'holding form' between sensation and self-knowledge (see Figure 10.2).

If this is true, then it runs counter to the idea common in the field that play is intrinsically motivated by children; as the model suggests, play can be extrinsically stimulated as well. Brian Sutton-Smith (1997) suggests as much in his discussion of play ambiguities. A playing child might enjoy rolling down a hill, but is stimulated by the hill being there. For Witkin as much emphasis is placed on the environment as the child's opportunity to respond.

Ludic Third

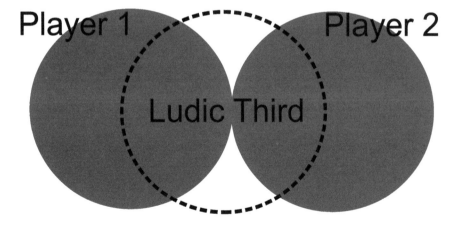

Fig. 10.3 The ludic third (after Sturrock 2003a)

The model of the 'ludic third' echoes this idea (Sturrock 2003a). In therapeutic playwork, the 'third' is the psychological space created by the relationship between the child and playworker (see Figure 10.3). In his treatise, Sturrock demonstrates how a shared psychic space is created between the playing adult and child, or child and child. It is suggested here that it is equally important to consider the Physical, Intellectual and Emotional (PIE) shared spaces of children at play, and that adulteration may be present in all these domains

It may be possible to differentiate between a child's need to play as being PIE, and their conscious experience of play as Feeling, Action and Thought (FAT). In a theoretical model, such discrete modalities are possible, however, in real-life examples, children play within complex and blended modalities, each with their own distinctive characteristics.

The Play Paradigm (Shenstone 2003)

While advancing our understanding and practices in the arena of emotional coherence, Sturrock and Else were not the first to recognise emotion as a component in play and playwork (see Brown 2003 and others). SPICE, an acronym referring to social, physical, intellectual, creative and emotional aspects of play, still has some relevance and resonance for playwork today. In this interpretation, each represents a type of ability that is developed as a by-product of children's play. A problem that presents itself in any analysis of play is that play simultaneously involves children in synthetic processes arising from a range of sources simultaneously. This contrasts with teaching in that learning strategies tend to be developed in isolation and incrementally as in Bloom (1956) (See Figure 10.9).

Itten (2003) uses colour grids to demonstrate various colour harmonies, and oppositions. Translated into play abstractions these might be expressed as in Figure 10.4.

The 'Play Paradigm' (Shenstone 2003) illustrates how SPICE might be more usefully constructed to show how PIE processes apparent in play might be interconnected. Margetts (1990) suggests that 'protective behaviours' are a set of tools to enable children to stay safe by enabling them to recognise when they feel unsafe. The model is in essence a simple means to examine FAT and possible outcomes. What I found interesting was the relationship between FAT and PIE, the PIE aspects of play (Brown 2003). The Play Paradigm (see Figure 10.5) uses a Venn diagram to demonstrate the interconnectedness of Feelings (Emotions), Actions (Physical) and Thought (Intellect). To simplify this idea: when these modes are in equilibrium, the individual is balanced, but if any of the elements is diminished, imbalance occurs. Witkin (1976) suggests that sensations are processed through various media, both subjective and objective, and thus become perceptible and this returns feedback in forms that give rise to new sensations.

SPICE as needs and qualities of processes

Qualities					
Needs	**Social**	**Physical**	**Intellectual**	**Creative**	**Emotional**
Social	Social/Social relationships	Social Physical Interaction	Social Intelligence Identity	Social Creative Esteem	Social Emotional Belonging
Physical	Physical Social Cooperation	Physical Physical Action Movement	Physical Intellectual Motivation	Physical Creative Challenge	Physical Emotonal Sexuality
Intellectual	Intelligent Social Political	Intelligent Physical Coordination	Intellectual/ Intelligence THOUGHT Logic	Intellectual Creativity Divergence	Intellectual Emotional Intuition
Creative	Creative Social Teamwork	Creative Physical Risk- taking	Creative Intellectual Imagination	Creative/ Creative Innovation	Creative Emotional Testing
Emotional	Emotional Social Ritualistic	Emotional Physical Sensuality	Emotional Intelligence Subjectivity	Emotional Creative Expression	Emotional/ Emotional Feeling Sense

Fig. 10.4   Line blend of ideas based on nuances of the SPICE acronym (after Shenstone 2003)

Examples that are cited by 'protective behaviours' practitioners are offered to illustrate how the effects of these internal conditions might be manifest. For example, someone who thinks something needs to be done but feels unable to take the action needed to make life changes, or behaviour that is devoid of emotional content, or a person who takes impulsive action based on emotion without thinking about consequences.

In the PIE Play Paradigm, I am suggesting that Sturrock's (2003a) idea of the ludic third be extended to include the physical as well as the intellectual and emotional spaces, and call it the 'ecolude' (Shenstone 2003).

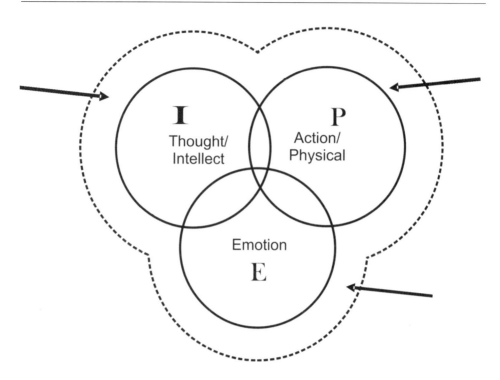

Fig. 10.5   The PIE Play Paradigm (Shenstone 2003)

This playful space could exist in the physical, emotional or intellectual sense where each space is shared between the child and the adult. It should again be noted that the spaces created in the relationships between the playworker and playing child, whether physical, emotional or intellectual, are at risk of 'adulteration'.

Blue, red and yellow are primary pigment colours (see Figure 10.6) and orange, purple and green are secondary pigment colours. Tertiary pigment colours are produced by mixing each of the primaries with a secondary colour. We can further extend this concept by adopting the use of colour from Itten (2003), in which Itten associates colours with intellect, action and emotion, where these are blue, red, yellow, respectively.

Interestingly, Itten's coding links with Eastern belief in the chakra system. The chakras are described as seven levels of power that hold life force and serve to vitalise the body. It is said that when people experience trauma or stress, the energy in one or more of the chakras becomes blocked, and they lose balance and a sense of self. In the chakra system:

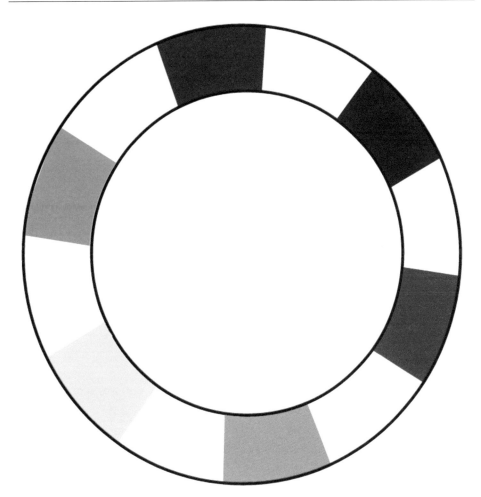

Fig. 10.6   A traditional colour wheel

- Red is associated with the first chakra. It is a hot colour that represents our life energy, our physical strength and vitality. This is where we hold our connection to our family. It is the centre of survival, our roots, our bodies and our foundation. It is about the basics.
- Yellow is associated with the third chakra. It is a warm colour that can stimulate the nervous system and affects the mind and emotions. This is the centre of self-esteem and our personal power and strengths. It is about defining ourselves (becoming an individual).
- Blue is associated with the fifth chakra. It is a cool colour and brings lightness, peace and calm. This is the centre of sound, creativity, self-expression and communication.

(Else 2006)

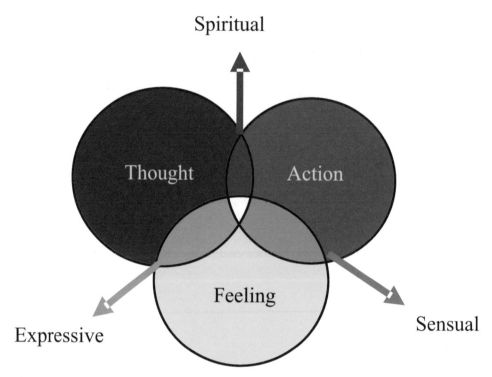

Fig. 10.7: Primary play elements, and proposed secondary play abstract process elements

In this model, Itten's primary colour associations are used to indicate an abstract narrative. As shown in Figure 10.6, the use of primary colours in combination generates secondary colours, and including tertiaries totals twelve nuances. By extension, it is worth blending the concepts with which the colours are associated to provide a more comprehensive, colourful representation of playwork principles (see Figure 10.7).

The diagram is intended to illustrate some of the nuances that may arise from modelling human needs based on this idea.

Assagioli (1965), in his description of psychosynthesis, also discusses the psychological effects of colours, for example cool colours being calming and warmer colours invigorating. Using a model like this could enable exploration of the abstract process involved in play; mapping the expressions, or abstract forms that children give to sensations that arise within them or through their responses to the world around them through the process of playing. Whilst mapping does not pinpoint where or how sensations emerge, it may identify an array of sensations that give rise to playful activity. If the 'holding form' (Witkin 1976) is part of the enactment of play, transforming sensations to intelligible feelings, perhaps the holding form itself can be used as an indicator or signifier of the nature of the sensation that gave rise to the playing. If this were true, it would be useful to playworkers to be able to make sense of this material as an indicator of playing-out behaviours and help us to gauge the nature of the sensations that gave rise to them.

I will now proceed to extend the idea of the 'Play Paradigm' through the use of holistic models and symbolic metaphors.

Hierarchies of Development

Many models of development show a hierarchical, staged development. The current work does not warrant a full analysis of Maslow's (1954, 1971, cited in Santrock 2001) work on human motivation (see Figure 10.8); however experience of young people with anorexia, for example, would suggest that the need for love and belonging (social need) could outweigh a desire for food (physiological). Environmental, extrinsic factors that might influence the play frame might be based on human needs, or something else.

The pyramid shown illustrates Maslow's Hierarchy of Needs (1954, 1971). The model illustrates the five levels of human need; the most basic being physiological and physical safety, shown at the base of the pyramid. As the individual successfully has his/her basic needs met, new needs emerge. These are the need for acceptance in a group, the

Maslow's Hierarchy of Needs

Self-Actualisation	Challenging projects, opportunities for innovation and creativity at a high level
Ego (Esteem)	Important projects, recognition from others, prestige and status
Social (Belonging)	Acceptance, being part of a group, identification with a successful group
Safety/Security	Physical safety, economic security, freedom from threats
Physiological	Physical survival needs: water, food, sleep, warmth, exercise, etc.

Fig. 10.8   Maslow's hierarchy of needs (from Maslow 1954–1971)

need to satisfy the demands of ego and finally in Maslow's hierarchy, self-actualisation, where the individual can make the most of his/her unique abilities and strive to be the best person s/he can be.

Similarly, Clarke (2001, citing Bloom 1956; Krathwohl, Bloom & Bertram 1973; Simpson 1972; Dave, 1975; and Harrow 1972) suggests that cognitive, affective and psychomotor domains, also known as Knowledge, Attitudes and Skills, are developed incrementally through learning. In Bloom's taxonomy these are presented as hierarchies to show how learning can be structured to meet particular learning needs. However, if learning is seen as a by-product of playing out sensations rather than a goal, then a new perspective about the nature of playing and its purpose can be perceived. This supports ideas about play as an innate drive, and the urge to play as involuntary. More useful to play-workers, though, is Bloom's description of *processes* involved in each of the domains.

Within a playwork context, Bloom's taxonomy (see Figure 10.9) could be the foundation for a taxonomy of abstract (process-based) play types. In playwork, we insist that in play the emphasis is on the process, not the product. Note that 'Analysis' and 'Synthesis' emerge at levels 4 and 5 of Bloom's taxonomy, yet these are basic skills to playing children. I suggest these give playwork access to a new genre of play types that indicate what play does for children, to add to Hughes' play types (2002). The basis of Bloom's taxonomies are hierarchical; however, hierarchical systems do not seem natural systems to playwork, as will be explored later. What emerges for children through their play seems not so much knowledge of facts and the ability to evaluate in increasing complexity; it is more about experience of process leading to understanding of themselves and the world.

Bloom's Taxonomy				
Abstract	Affective domain	Cognitive domain	Psychomotor domain	Complex
↑	Internalisation	Evaluation	Naturalisation	↑
	Organisation	Synthesis	Articulation	
	Valuing	Analysis	Precision	
	Responding	Application	Manipulation	
	Receiving	Comprehension	Imitation	
Concrete		Knowledge		Simple

Fig. 10.9   Adapted from Clark (1999)

Symbolism and the Holding Form

The importance and relevance of symbolic representation in human development was recognised by Piaget and Inhelder (1971) and separately by Kellogg (1970), describing respectively children's linguistic development, conceptualisation and drawing and writing skills. Lowenfeld and Brittain (1982, 1987) also describes haptic[1] awareness as demonstrated in children's art. In Lowenfield's explanation of creativity in children, he distinguishes between self expression and the imitative, emphasising that the mode of expression is more important than the content, so 'babbling' and 'scribbling' are seen as different modes of creative exploration. Kellogg (1970) identifies twenty different styles of scribbles from children's drawings.

Saussure (1916) recognised the dualistic nature of signs as having both material and conceptual elements. He called these the 'signifier', (for example, the sound pattern of the word 'sun') and the 'signified', (the mental image of the sun). These cannot be viewed as separate concepts but rather as a mapping from significant differences in sound to a potential differentiated connotation. It is common to take signifiers to be anything one could speak, and signifieds as things in the world, but that would be incorrect in Saussure's structure.

Types of communication differ in their capacity to define qualities and represent objects and abstract ideas either objectively or subjectively. The types or representation include visual, auditory and kinaesthetic (haptic) sensory modes (see Figure 10.10).

For example, children's first experience of the sun is felt, kinaesthetic, experienced by the body as heat and energy and visual as light. The child may later learn a name for the sun and then the word 'sun' becomes a symbol for the sun. The child, in recalling the image, can relate the word 'sun' to the real experience and the visual image.

Visual - seen   Auditory - heard   Kinaesthetic - felt

Fig. 10.10   Depictions of three communication modes

These examples show that some symbols are learned experientially and may be universal, others are culturally determined. In the United Kingdom, a symbol for the sun is generally seen as benevolent, but in a country where the sun's heat is destructive, the symbol for the sun may appear fierce.

> The sun as an aggressive factor was observed in a drawing by a 4-year-old Spanish girl. The sun rather than radiating benignly had sharp aggressive teeth. She also drew around her small hand, and surprised at the image she had produced (paw like) added claws to each digit with a felt tip pen. She then held her hands in front of her face and growled at me followed by giggles. (Jayne Shenstone 1998, 'Observation August Ibiza')

Such playful communication is beyond verbal language, using visual, auditory and kinaesthetic modes. The metalude that Sturrock and Else (1998) describe could be a fusion of all three, perhaps?

Weather is a commonly used metaphor for mood: we talk of sunny smiles, indicating a happy disposition, rain as 'miserable' and of 'gloomy' days. Our moods and environment are inexorably linked, it would seem. As a playworker I noticed that children were more manic during windy weather, a sense of quiet prevailed, however active the children were, on colder days, and warmish weather was the most conducive to playing.

Whereas pictures are two-dimensional representations (symbols) of the real world, toys and other objects are three-dimensional symbols representing real objects, (though often smaller scale) making for a greater variety of possible communication and sharing of ideas. Because play exists in real time and space, a greater variety of meanings can be represented and therefore recognised. A closer approximation of meaning can be symbolically represented using toys rather than language or pictures alone. Play not only enables physical re-enactment of real and apparent events, but seen held up in the reflecting mirror of consciousness, also makes available holding forms that exist in abstraction. That is to say, that they exist in the minds of the player(s) but are held in a form that is other than words or pictures.

Play may be a means by which humans develop the ability and capacity to associate meanings, and interaction between sensate, somatic or haptic awareness and our ability to recall, process and make conscious sense of our inner being and our responses to our physical and psycho-

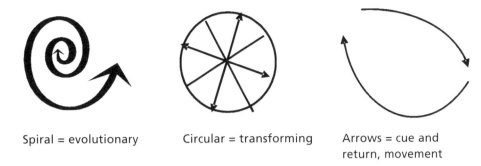

Spiral = evolutionary   Circular = transforming   Arrows = cue and
                                                       return, movement

Fig. 10.11   Linear models of play process forms

logical environments. An ability to read and understand these responses would greatly enhance playwork.

Playwork appears egalitarian in its constructs and more divergent in its forms of expression and inclines, if anything, towards radiating and/ or holistic metaphors. To give these ideas a visual form so that comparisons of meaning might be made, Figure 10.11 may provide useful, diagrammatic ways to express ideas that cannot be conveyed completely in words.

Through the process of symbolising sensations into other forms, they become apparent. As stated above (Witkin 1976), by expressing a sensation through a particular medium, the person comes to a better understanding of it.

Is Psycholudics a Holistic Form?

Circular forms convey holistic ideas; they suggest the planetary motion around the sun, perpetual motion or radiation and thus have cross-cultural significance, and are virtually universal.

The spiral suggests a pathway from which experience can progress and also return, and markers can be set on this journey. Blockages to 'flow' as defined in playwork by Sturrock and Else (1998) and by Csikszentmihalyi (cited in Santrock 2001) can be identified and illustrated using the spiral model – in contrast to a linear model of progression, which places markers only where they fall on the line and may therefore not identify blockages to progress. Furthermore, the spiral is a dynamic form, so more closely represents active rather than passive participation, which is more aligned to the type of progression experienced through play.

In Figure 10.12, the level at which a blockage could occur is indicated

Fig. 10.12   Evolutionary play spiral

by the coloured dots: yellow for emotion, blue for thought and red for action. This suggests an early repression of emotion, a later end to rational thought (for example, unfounded beliefs based on fears) having an effect of limiting positive action.

Circles represent an expanding development, which is balanced, yet boundaried. Circular motifs are common in playwork. In the Manchester Circles, Lester and Russell (2002, building on Bronfenbrenner 1977) use a motif of concentric circles to describe an ecological construct of play settings. Sturrock (2003) uses a similar pattern as a basis for a 'life-worlds' exercise developed for the Therapeutic Playwork course to enable students to reflect on affective inner realities. It should also be noted that it is important in the life-worlds exercise that the experiences are conveyed using pictures, rather than more logical verbal constructs. The reason this is important might be, as Edwards (2001) suggests, that the right side of the brain processes information in an entirely different way from the left at a less cognitive and filtered level.

To develop this further, a potentially useful framework is suggested by the transformational ecological model used by Hope and Timmel (2003) rather than the hierarchical triangular form used by Maslow.

Hope and Timmel (1999, p. 189) propose a Human Needs Model, as a wheel (see fig. 10.11) that can be viewed over a period of time and that has spokes or portions (depending on whether they are perceived as demarcations or sections). If we translate this for playwork as a holistic model of human needs, it shows actualisation not as the apex or summit but as the most deeply congruent, intrinsic experience; in Hope and Timmel's transformational model 'self-actualisation' is within

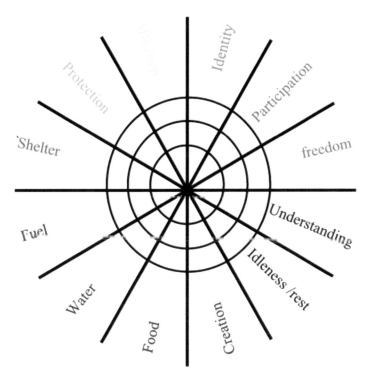

Fig. 10.13   Transformational model of play

the individual and cultural, social and survival factors are equally valued.

Transformational Model of Play

Building on the primary concepts of PIE (Physical, Intellectual and Emotional needs) the Transformational Model of Play can be assembled (see Figure 10.13), using the concept of colour from Itten (2003), terms from Maslow and Bloom and the Wheel of Fundamental Human Needs (Hope and Timmel 2003).

Descriptors have been sorted and colour-coded to correspond (more or less) with emotional, intellectual and physical needs, where yellow is emotion, red is physical, and blue is intellect. The illustration is intended to demonstrate a broad spectrum of human needs; it represents a slice through a three-dimensional model based on the spherical Figure 10.14, at the equator.

Itten's model 53 (2003), from which the above model has evolved, maps a variety of routes possible to enable transition between two contrasting hues. This playwork model, using a similar device, might have any of the main

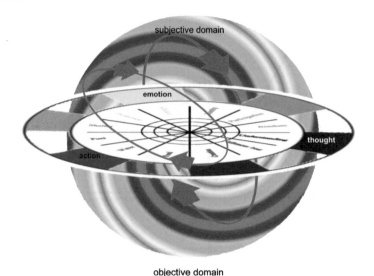

subjective domain

objective domain

Fig. 10.14   Evolutionary, transformational, and cyclical forms with subjective and objective domains

elements of play around subjective or internal and objective or environmental domains exerting influence to a greater or lesser degree on the process of play. The tertiary colours used in the next model (Figure 10.15) are used to show details of elements of play being enacted. Whereas Maslow's hierarchy suggests incremental hierarchical progression, any or all of these needs could be simultaneously or singly fulfilled. The model could be adapted to show a play-oriented spectrum, say by using Hughes' (2002) play types. Work is still needed to be consistent in the terms. For example, creation does not quite work as a gradation between food and rest. I think this is because creativity is really a drive or a process in the same way that play is, a means by which other needs are made to materialise.

As an illustration, a den-building activity is shown in Figure 10.15. The play cues (arrows) though apparently similar in style, might be issued from the same place but for different purposes. They both start in creation but travel through different modes and with different intensities (capacity). Where both examples could be externally satisfied by a den-building activity, shown by the inner cycle line (a), the second repetition of the activity, shown by the outer line (b), might meet an affective or participation need only as part of a *social* den-building activity. Play needs that are adjacent may seem harmonious; however, they explore discordant or oppositional needs such as protection/freedom and combinations that do not immediately make sense together to the casual observer, such as food and identity.

Thus, a = den-building activity, b = social den-building activity,

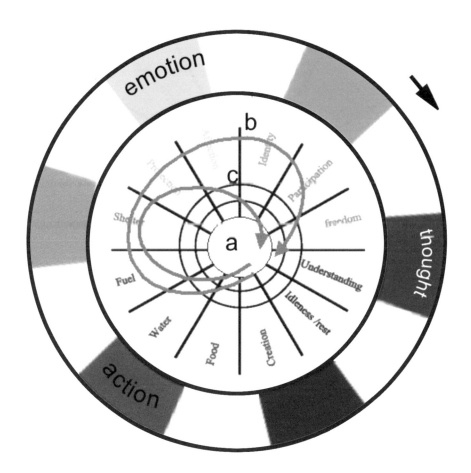

Fig. 10.15   Map to show transformational and cyclical forms

c = possible area for extension between *a* and *b*. It is into that area (and the area not covered by a, b, or c) where playing may extend a child's experiences and where a playworker may support the conditions needed for such experiences to occur. From the concrete or visually perceived representations, the more abstract or kinaesthetic needs can begin to be discerned.

A further development of these thoughts would be to see change and growth as a spiral of development across the model (Figure 10.16).

Conclusion

My aim in this paper was to indicate that a broader spectrum of concepts to describe play could be developed. Play as a process is more than logic, emotion and physical action; it is a holistic combination of some and all

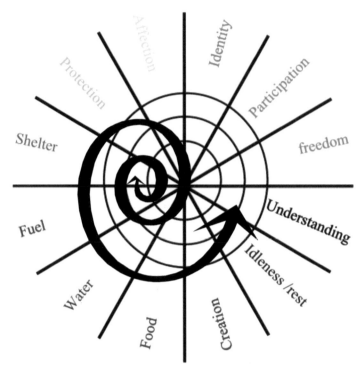

Fig. 10.16   Map to show transformational and evolutionary forms

of these at various times. This change results in the rich pictures of children's activity that we see in play.

These models need to be tested through real-life playwork observations if they are to have any practical meaning. For example, it might be found that patterns emerge in the repetition of play cycles, that perhaps they grow or flow in an outward spiral to begin with, and then spiral back to the centre as they become annihilated, or none of these.

I am grateful to Gordon Sturrock for the original 'provocation', and to Perry Else for his rapid and expert editing skills, any ambiguities or mistakes that remain in the text are entirely mine; also to Wendy Russell for her ongoing support and inspiration without whom none of this would be possible.

Note

1   Pertaining to the sense of touch, from the Greek word *haptein*, to grasp. There are four types of sensory neuron (mechanoreceptor) involved in the haptic modality. The haptic, or tactile, sensory modality is the only active sense that can be used to explore our environment; vision and hearing are passive senses since they cannot act upon the environment (Yates).

Chapter Eleven

The playing that runs through us all:

ILLUSTRATING THE PLAYWORK PRINCIPLES WITH STORIES OF PLAY

Maureen Palmer, Penny Wilson and Arthur Battram

Hello readers, like they used to say in the Beano, this is Arthur talking to you on behalf of the trio, inviting you to let our words play out inside your head. We hope you will indulge them and duck and dive around our interwoven voices.

words were originally magic

This chapter is a playful story about play, and it is made up of playful stories, because **words were originally magic**, and **the highest things are beyond words**. Dreams are play and play is story and we are story. **We live inside the dreams of others.** We might be imprisoned by them. **Writers are dangerous when they tell lies**, and **writers are also dangerous when they tell the truth**. Why are lies plural yet the truth is singular? Bof! There are as many truths as there are stories, and there are more stories than people. **When we have made an experience or a chaos into a story we have transformed it, made sense of it, transmuted experience, domesticated the chaos** (a mash-up made by Arthur playing with his own, and some of **Okri's** and **de Shazer's** words).

> I can imagine spontaneous playful linguistic activity as it springs forth in chil-
> dren ... begin to take on ... story form ... By looking at play as a generator of
> dynamically integrated, affect-laden cortical 'maps' of increasing complexity,
> I believe that play can be considered as a *major* organiser and possible
> sustainer of our human dynamic sense of reality.
>
> (Brown 1998, p. 256)

So, these stories are free-range, organic, whole stories, lovingly plucked from the fertile mulch of playwork experience, processed using only natural words and packaged minimally. There is a point to that metaphor, to be revealed soon. But before we get to them: first a word about principles, followed by a story about some rubbish playwork. Don't worry, nobody will sue, it's my own rubbish playwork.

the noble craft of playwork

Introduction to the Principles
These Principles establish the professional and ethical framework for play-work and as such must be regarded as a whole. They describe what is unique about play and playwork, and provide the playwork perspective for working with children and young people. They are based on the recognition that children and young people's capacity for positive development will be enhanced if given access to the broadest range of environments and play opportunities.

[Arthur] Funny things, principles. It's very easy to get all fired up about them, but, like ethical statements or professional codes of practice, they are useless if all they do is sit in a filing cabinet. (And please note: playwork is not a profession, it is merely an occupation. This is a crucial distinction – let's not give ourselves airs and graces, there is still a whiff of cargo-cult magical thinking about this notion of playwork as a profession. Playwork is our noble craft; be glad that we are not like lawyers. As George Bernard Shaw said: 'All professions are conspiracies against the laity'. Is that what playworkers want? Do we want to be included in the group of professionals described by Simon Barnes below, as 'unpleasant and insensitive people'?)

principles: also originally magic

'Words are originally magic', but the words eventually agreed by a committee have been chewed over and sucked dry. It's unavoidable. Bof! So our key purpose here, and I say this in a non-NVQ way, is to help bring these principles to life. Any set of principles risks becoming like a list of 'the recommended daily requirements of vitamins and minerals needed for healthy living'. Excellent stuff, but we don't eat 893 milligrams of Vitamin A, we eat food. So we're not here to reconstitute the principles like some scary playwork Pot Noodle; we're here to offer you some lovely food that contains all of those essential vitamins and minerals.

Here's an 'amuse-bouche' from our chef, Maureen:

'You could run around like a maniac, or just chill the fuck out and be a miserable barstard if you wanted to.' (One adult's memory of being a child on the adventure playground.)

let me paint you a picture . . .

Let me give you one example – a particularly embarrassing one from the very beginning of my playwork in Spring 1974. There I was in the art room at 'The Priory Youth and Community Centre' in Brighton, in my flared v-knee patch-pocketed loon pants and charity shop jersey, mixing up some poster paint when an eleven-year-old girl came in. I didn't really know the first thing about working with kids, so I said brightly 'Would you like to do a picture?' She was an odd, thin, child, shabbily dressed in a cotton dress and gym shoes and grubby socks, sharp eyes and mistrusting face. These days you would probably jump to conclusions and call Social Services. You might be right. Anyway, 'Sharon' took a piece of paper and made a generic four-year-old's painting of a tree: a big swirly blob of green, done with the brush held tightly, as you would hold a wooden spoon stirring a pan, mashing all the bristles down, followed by a trunk done in sludge brown by moving the brush up and down the paper a few times, pressing hard. Then she put the brush down and looked at me. 'Do you like it?', she asked, or words to that effect. I was being required to express an opinion on her artwork. I said, 'It's very nice.' She looked at me steadily, tore it in two and walked out.

Here are some sentences from the Principles:

2. *Play is a process that is freely chosen, personally directed and intrin-sically motivated . . . children and young people determine and control the content and intent of their play, by following their own instincts, ideas and interests, in their own way for their own reasons.*
3. *. . . essence of playwork is to support and facilitate the play process . . .*
6. *. . . playworker's response to children and young people playing is based on a sound up-to-date knowledge of the play process, and reflec-tive practice.*
7. *Playworkers recognise their own impact on the play space and also the impact of children and young people's play on the playworker.*

playworker teaching

I learnt a lot from that interaction. 'Sharon' was testing me. That was the first time I met her: she was regular at the Junior Club, so I often saw her, but she never paid any further attention to me, at least not willingly. I think I failed her test. Maybe I shouldn't have spoken when she came into the art room, or maybe I should've just said 'Hello' rather than asking her if she wanted to paint. Does that constitute interfering with her 'freely chosen, personally directed play?' One of the things I learnt at the time from playwork was that 'inaction is often better than action', to quote the Tao. I think good playwork often involves **not** doing things, letting things happen, because a lot of the time we don't have a clue what the right thing to do is. As Maureen implies in the kendo story later, it sort of works out, usually.

Now, I am **still** learning from that interaction with Sharon: notice that it is an interaction – not an incident – because an interaction involves at least two entities responding to each other. In Elaine Morgan's book *The Descent of the Child* (1996), she explains that children are often in competition with their parents (and presumably, playworkers), 'manipulating' them to their own advantage. We talk of children learning through play; in this case I think 'Sharon' was **teaching** through play.

ludocentric means interactional

I hope you will agree that interaction with others is central to playwork, but I think we don't pay enough attention to kids playing together and what they might get from it, or even learn from it. In our risk-averse culture, the focus is too much on the individual child: one of the key ways to differentiate playworkers from others such as teachers and social workers is that we do, and should, focus on the group in all its complexity.

Teachers don't usually work with groups, they teach one-to-many or one-to-one; they don't interact with the group as a group, because, of course, if you do, you give up control. Social workers focus almost exclusively on the individual child. So when we say that playwork is ludocentric we are focusing on the play, not the player, and the connections, not the nodes – thus, a ludocentric focus will be a group focus much of the time, and I think we should emphasise this more than we do. It's part of what makes playwork unique – we don't work with individual children, we support the play of children, in what primatologists call 'fission-fusion' groupings of immature primates. And we do that paying ecological attention to the surroundings, the environment, the 'ludic ecology', as Gordon calls it.

speaking the language of ludocentricity

[Penny] Ofsted were inspecting Chelsea Adventure Playground. The inspector had spent her life working with small babies and in nurseries: she wanted written timetables of activities on the walls and spots of paint removed from the floor. She had no concept of inclusive adventure play. I always felt that Kidsactive kept itself separate from the play movement, and it did not arrange any playwork training. Any playwork training we received came through private studies. Consequently, we knew what we were doing and how to do it, but we didn't have the language and were unaware that anyone else had come to the same conclusions as us. Then Bob came and spoke at a meeting of the JNCTP on the site. I found myself laughing at the complexity of language that was used to describe our work. But he pointed out that as practitioners we needed a shared language to describe and discuss our work. At around the same time, Gordon was supervising a student who was working with us. He brought us a copy of *The Colorado Paper*. We welcomed this oasis and saw that we were part of a community of practitioners. We had discovered a voice.

I had a delightful conversation with the people of the Rockwell Design Group in the USA recently, largely concerned with capturing for them the essence of what it is that a playworker does, who they are, where they can find them. They could not 'lasso the cloud' of what we understand in the UK, because they are not used to the sight of a group of what Arthur sometimes calls 'recalcitrants' in steel toe-capped boots and multilayered clothing, capering around like loons at the beck and call of children, who are doing things too messy or too daring or off-beat for them to do in any other space.

this is our place

All children and young people need to play. The impulse to play is innate. Play is a biological, psychological and social necessity, and is fundamental to the healthy development and well being of individual and communities.

[Maureen] We did some brilliant stuff at Cornwallis. We knew that we were getting it right, but we didn't know why.

Many of the children who grew up on Cornwallis Adventure Playground talk about it now it as being 'their place': Vicky says it felt like 'the place we are meant to be', Ryan talks of it being community-based, and Leggy says 'you felt you belonged somewhere – it was part of your identity'.

'How would I have got through some of the devastating events of my childhood?' wonders Vicky, 'without this safe place and this 'extended family' to give the right kind of space and support?' She got what she needed at the time, not what adults thought she needed.

[Arthur] Resilience is rightly a big focus of today's residential work with children. Who survives and goes on to thrive and why? Ann Masten (2001) has summarised the collected evidence, and concludes that the best protections against risk are:

- relationships with competent and caring adults;
- cognitive and self-regulatory skills;
- positive image of self and motivation to be effective in the environment.

There are many ways that these factors can be made available to children, yet I challenge the reader to find a more elegantly effective way than playwork.

[Maureen] Leggy said at a conference, 'It was like a pub is to me now, but without the alcohol, we were able to chill out and be able to relax as children'. Vicky talks about being there 'really late, or it felt really late, and I remember never wanting to leave'.

Lorraine and Sammy talk about being there before the gates opened, and being there all the time, Ryan says 'it was an everyday event, whatever you were doing in the day you knew you were coming here later,' Sam says 'it was every day'.

[Penny] A mum and I watched the complexity of the playing day at Chelsea Adventure Playground as we talked. She told me that she had played at the original Chelsea site with a friend of hers who was disabled. 'Even if my kids had not had disabilities, I would still have brought them here to play', she said. 'I learned that disabled kids are kids like me and it changed the way I thought about the world.'

Following some playwork training in Chicago with a parks team, I learned that the ice hockey coach had told parents off for their competitive behaviour during the four- and five-year-olds' training sessions. 'Just let them play, they are children,' he had told them.

Play is a process that is freely chosen, personally directed and intrinsically motivated. That is, children and young people determine and control the content and intent of their play, by following their own instincts, ideas and interests, in their own way for their own reasons.

[Maureen] Ryan says, 'if something was happening and I didn't like it, then I wouldn't hang about. See you later and do something else, there was always something else to do'.

Debbie talks about being able to do things in your own way, 'not being told you had to be in a crowd and doing things with help if you needed it'.

Sammy says, 'It was entirely your choice'.

Lorraine says, 'you could run wild, go mad, create, and I love creating now'.

two mysterious freedom vignettes

[Penny] A playworker describes a session in which a disabled child – watched closely from a distance by herself – had an idea, sneaked a look around to see if he could get away with his 'mischief', then up-ended a tub of blue paint over his head and rolled around in it until he was covered from head to toe. He found it hilarious. Staff let him do it, then cleaned him up when he was done. Somehow, they forgot to clean his feet. When mum asked why his feet were deep blue, the workers explained. She was delighted.

A young disabled teenager comes on to the site on the first day of the Easter holidays. It is hot and sunny. She communicates through some signs and lots of hummed tunes. She is earnestly trying to tell us something and eventually manages to make us understand that she wants to get the Christmas decorations out. Mock Christmas and silly wrapped-up-anything-presents gave her what she wanted. We never will know why.

[Arthur] To quote Basho, my favourite haiku writer, in a saying I found serendipitously on a website about another Bob Hughes: 'An idea can turn to dust or magic, depending on the talent that rubs against it.'

a virtuous cycle of playwork

The prime focus and essence of playwork is to support and facilitate the play process and this should inform the development of play policy, strategy, training and education.

[Maureen] CACHE Level 3 assignments in Islington have quotes from Leggy and Ryan, from the children who grew up on the adventure playgrounds in the borough; they are informing the learning and practice of the next generation of playworkers. Many of the children who grew up on Cornwallis Adventure Playground now work as adventure playground workers.

Ryan and Leggy describe it as feeling like it was still part of the street, that it still had a street mentality and how what is referred to today as 'street cred' is exactly what children from adventure playgrounds had, 'They had a nice openness, knew what they were about and knew where they were at'.

This summer I worked with a group of the young people at Barnard Park Adventure Playground to do play audits of the area, it was so the right thing to do, they really know where children play and have the eye for quality and for the lack of play value in so much of the fixed play in the area, and they got to comment and feed that back to the play strategy. They are now supporting other children in the borough to do play audits in their patches.

[Arthur] Oh Maureen. So typically, infuriatingly modest. It is clear that your playwork has had, and continues to have, a huge positive impact on the lives of your 'graduates'. Let's get this in its rightful context: who actually raised those children?

Judith Rich Harris (1998) tells us that **children are socialised by their peers, not by their parents**. Shocking notion isn't it? I would amend it slightly, in line with Sarah Hrdy (1999), to say that 'peers' can include not just children, but any **'significant others'**, such as playworkers, or kindly neighbours or even parents – but as part of the **peers** not as a privileged separate class of 'actor'. An IPPR report (Margo *et al.* 2006, pp. ix) tells us that '... British children spend more time in the company of peers, and less time with adults and parents, than young people in culturally similar countries'. It seems clear to me that we, as a society, have to choose:

- we can delinquently allow our children to be raised on the street, in the harshness of an adulterated so-called 'street culture', steeped in violence and bullying and almost totally lacking in stimulation and respect;
- or we can Fed-Ex them around, like a deranged yummymummy, from rugby to ballet to judo to music practice to 'playdate'(yuk – what a vile adulteration) and back home to a lonely bedroom and the companionship of Playstation;

- or we can diligently work to create places in which ludocentric peer-based upbringing may take place. I mean adventure playgrounds, not fixed equipment playgrounds, staffed playgrounds. (I know, I know, it's really 1970s, like Dennis the Space Hopper and being 'curious orange'. Very 1970s colour, orange. We like it.)

from dry play areas to rich playscapes

The role of the playworker is to support all children and young people in the creation of a space in which they can play.

[Penny] Mile End Park was designed by an architect who wanted to create a showcase 'like the Diana Memorial Playground'. Money was thrown at it but ludocentric thinking was absent, so it turned out to be a sterile and dry play place. Play Association Tower Hamlets (PATH) started to work with inclusive groups and to audit the site. Many changes have been made: now we see a broad range of playtypes in the children's play. The park Director had an 'Aha!' moment and 'got' play; now he says that all sessions running from there must be inclusive. Park rangers have been trained in playwork. The Director attends play conferences, advocates play from within the council and in the press and comes up with funding and other resources to enrich the play environment. Recently this playground was chosen for documentation by the NPFA as an exemplar for good inclusive practice. Because of this informed attitude, Integrated Services for Children with Disabilities, including paediatric Occupational Therapists and special and including schools, are using the site on a regular basis. Best yet, families affected by disability are using it as a natural, welcoming and accessible place to play. Local users are cool with this and play with the disabled children in ways that are quirkier and broader than one would normally find in a public park. And hurray! – the Director is getting a firepit built.

PATH has secured funding for a member of staff to offer play access audits to schools. Many schools in the area have very restricted space. One school that took up this offer has a small concrete playground and a rooftop playground. There is a high proportion of children with communication difficulties within the school community. An audit was carried out based on the availability of playtypes and the need to make the most of the available space. This included mirrors reflecting the sky and the height by reflecting the local cityscape of the rooftop site and the creation of a 'stage' in an unused recess in the lower playground. The school requested a follow-up training day for all support and senior staff in play and playwork. In her request for this, the head said, 'I wonder if you could provide this specialised training to our staff. How times have changed', meaning that play sat, formerly, well within the educational remit, but now there are playwork 'specialists' who can inform them.

[Maureen] Beverley describes the Adventure Playground: 'Like a camp you built yourself.'

ludic songlines across the innercity desert

[Penny] Chelsea Adventure Playground is rich in trees, London Plane trees that shed leaves like mad. One day in early autumn, I got a phone call of complaint from the Royal Hospital, our landlord, because our 'Friends Group' had complained that the leaves had not been swept. It was untidy. The weather had been bright and dry and the leaves were crisp and crackling. Irked by the phone call and the prompting of it by our 'Friends', we gathered all the leaves into a massive pile by the splash pool, a small hillock of leaves. One of the staff was Hindu and it was Diwali weekend. Her extended family came to join us on the site and we floated candles in the splash pool, ate food prepared and served with unspoken blessings and had a massive leaf fight, throwing leaves and burying each other in the mountain. It was a remember-for-all-time day, at once raucous, tender and recalcitrant.

[Arthur] Hah! These are not just stories, they are songline stories! Songlines from Cornwallis and across the splash pool to the hillock of leaves! Bruce Chatwin, in the leaves of his book *Songlines*, describes how, by the time they are old enough to walk, the children of the Kalahari Bushmen will have travelled a thousand miles from one side of southern Africa to the other, and how …

> *Even today, when an Aboriginal mother notices the first stirrings of speech in her child, she lets it handle the 'things' of that particular country: leaves, fruit, insects and so forth. We give our children guns and computer games, they give their children the land.*
>
> (Chatwin 1988, p. 78)

What are the songlines of your playground, your childhood, your children, your school, your street? Can you see the 'lines of desire' when they are not marked out by a walker-made track worn into the grass of a leisure area? Marc Armitage (2005) has traced the songlines in the playground of his own primary school in Hull, from the present day all the way back to 1916, and the first recorded instance of the 'Black Pipe', until it was finally blocked by a thoughtlessly-sited Portakabin. *Quel horreur!* Desecration, like logging a rainforest. When a closed-down adventure playground such as White Horse in East London reopens, we must listen to its songlines or the ludic spirits may rise up like mythagos ...

The playworkers' response to children and young people playing is based on a sound, up-to-date knowledge of the play process, and reflective practice.

mistresses of the ludic universe

[Maureen] I heard two playworkers, who have worked together for many years and have that 'professional marriage' which often develops between long-time workers on playgrounds, saying how they were able to have far more effective and enlightening discussions at debriefings since they were on Level 3 training and had done some work with playtypes, intervention modes and other theory. They were surprised and delighted that this could happen after all the time they had worked in playwork together.

[Penny] In solving the problems presented by one disabled child who seemed 'stuck' in his play, the team brainstormed during their meeting. He loves to control, he loves gadgets, mastery and objects. He loves to see cause and effect in his play. The following session it was clear that staff had gone away and thought hard about these problems and his trapped play. They arrived with broken typewriters, computer keyboards, vacuum cleaners and bunches of keys. They were aware that loose parts were the solution for this child. All the devices worked; however, the bunch of keys became a talisman for him. He 'unlocked' everything.

practice magic, ludelic theory

[Arthur] 'There is nothing so practical as a good theory', said Kurt Lewin (1951, p. 169), and if a good theory is one that helps you think about your work, then a superb theory is one that transforms your thinking about your work. We have three examples: intervention modes (Hughes 1996), playtypes (Hughes 2002; 2006) and playcues (Sturrock and Else 1998). Oh sure, we can quibble, until your mum shouts you in, about how many playtypes, and whether they overlap, or not, about whether playcues can be the same as animal cues when humans have consciousness and most animals don't – except perhaps Ofsted inspectors – but the point is, these theories cause almost immediate ludelic improvements in practice. (Ludelic means play-expanding.)

Mr Sutton-Smith, we salute the academic breadth and deep playfulness of your *Ambiguity of Play*, but one way to define a playwork academic is 'someone who reads Brian Sutton-Smith'. Bob and Gordon are not academics; they are playwork thinkers, two giants on whose shoulders we all stand. Budge up a bit.

Leggy speaks of how when he left the playground finally, he had 'much bigger opinions, thoughts, and ideas' and the exposure he had on the playground had really shown him 'how important play is and how important it is that children have this kind of safe but challenging environment to grow up in'. He ends by saying that 'As a parent now, he wouldn't swap that knowledge for anything any one could teach him'.

playscapes and lifespaces

Playworkers recognise their own impact on the play space and also the impact of children and young people's play on the playworker.

[Maureen] Agi talks of his playworkers always knowing about his sexuality, but he also says how hard it was for him to come out to them: he talks of not knowing why he always wanted to be with the girls and how he loved dressing up. The playworkers knew this was what Agi liked and we reflected hard on how we might help him to be himself as a child and not to allow his sexuality to deflect from his right to just be. When he was ready and not before, if he wanted to, he would tell us about himself.

We used to joke about 'Socialism on one Playground' but underlying this was a serious reflection on the nature of our facilitation, a feeling that everything should be up for grabs, nothing should be or should feel taboo: riots; the miners strike; Notting Hill Carnival or industrial action by playworkers; sexuality ... Vicky says 'I felt nothing was taboo, yes, I felt I could talk about anything'. Bev says: 'I felt there were no limits to what I could try'.

[Arthur] This reminds me of the notion, in residential work, of 'lifespace': 'the deliberate and focused attempt to promote individual growth and development within the context of daily events', says Keenan (2002, p. 38), who points out that

> Lifespace work is neither individual casework nor group work, nor even individual casework conducted in a group context, but is a therapeutic discipline of its own ... The life-space is a mini society in its own right ... it has a cultural life of its own.

Sounds very like playwork to me, or rather it sounds like the sustained kind of playwork practised on the few well-resourced adventure playgrounds we have left. (I will not use terms such as 'quality play' or 'quality playwork'. If it is not quality then it is not playwork). We can, of course, trace the idea of lifespace back to Lewin's (1951) 'field theory': without studying the field, he argued, the behaviour of individuals and groups could not be understood. Lewin sometimes called this 'psychological ecology'. Strong echoes of Sturrock's ludic ecology, methinks.

[Penny] *Playworkers' impact upon the site:*
'She was in a bad mood all summer.' (Child talking about senior playworker.)

   'Oi. You two. Dumb and dumber ...' Said by playworker to two disabled children, who then peel off and start to pick fights with younger and more vulnerable children. The playground goes into meltdown.

oh, what a blow that phantom gave me![1]

Child's impact upon the playworker:
A senior worker in a team meeting.

> Look, I know this is difficult but this girl really pushes my buttons. I can feel myself getting angry with her and I feel that she knows it and is winding me up. She does all the things I was told off for as a child. Can the rest of you cover for me when I give you the sign for a day or so,

so that we can break this cycle and I can develop mechanisms for myself?

In an awful play project for children with disabilities: amid the noise and insensitivity and abusive attitudes, a playworker finds a tiny group of friends all who have Down's Syndrome. They are signing and chatting together in an overlooked place. They invite the playworker to join them: a gesture of faith. She sits, in as much like their lotus position as possible and listens. They are making jokes and doing round-robin stories. They frequently translate and explain when she can't keep up. There is a massive and hilarious punchline and a fondness between the group as they split up so as to avoid detection by 'The Man'. The playworker, moved and wonderstruck, goes away and in her free time, researches Down's. 'They are not less, they are more! They have an additional chromosome . . .' She is hooked.

join us in saying to the world . . .

Arthur adds: 'I'm not a saint, just a parent' says *Times* chief sports writer, Simon Barnes, describing life with his five- year-old son Eddie, who has Down's syndrome, in a recent *Times* feature.

> There are various bits of assistance provided by the State: if you have a child with special needs, you will find a cluster of them. Some of these people are great, some less great. There are times when we feel invaded by people with a negative mindset and poor understanding, dominated by an eagerness to fill in forms and keep their arses covered. There are times when we feel that Eddie is state property: a public problem that somehow has to be organised. It seems sometimes that Eddie's principal function is to provide employment for unpleasant and insensitive people. Steps have been taken, words spoken. Problems still occur and are distressing. No doubt there are forms and files that have us down as obstructive and difficult parents.

A parent commented on his article:

> I related 100 per cent to 'I don't have a child with Down's syndrome: I am Eddie's father. There is a huge difference between the two things'. I have also said, many times, that the world is a better place for having Charlotte in it and I join you in saying to the world 'Don't pity us, we are to be envied'.

Playworkers choose an intervention style that enables children and young people to extend their play. All playworker intervention must balance risk with the developmental benefit and well being of children.

default style 1: ludocentrically caring

[Penny] Her life has been dominated by epilepsy. She has had to be watched around the clock. She needs to be watched. This is a very serious aspect of her life. Her playworkers are trying to find a way for her to stop relating totally to 'big brother', the ever-present adult. Bit by bit we move away, make ourselves dull and apparently distant from her, watching closely the whole time, because the fear is real. Gradually, she is able to run away from us within the fenced space of the site and sit alone on the hill experiencing herself and her alone-ness. The playworker watches more closely than if she were within arms reach.

This little lad constantly shadows us. He is silently on our heels. He is little, tiny for his age and he cannot eat. Simply cannot. He tries to be invisible. We know that something is terribly wrong but that he needs to dictate how sensitised he can be at this time. We engineer overheard conversations about 'good secrets, bad secrets'. When he prompts it, we drag cushions under the kitchen counter and sneak in with our lunches. Mine is always filled with extra good things that might tempt him. He says that I am 'Mummy Frog' and he is 'Baby Frog' and we have silly voices and cuddles and stories and everyone gets used to us being 'invisible' beneath the counter. We are not there in the real world. We are living in the world that he needs to be in to feel that he is worthy of tricking himself into taking food from my lunch box. Much later on, we find out what had happened in the family.

default style 2: outrageously ludocentric

[Maureen] We 'knew' that the mother of two of our regular children, who had autism, would 'obviously' not allow them to go to the Play Carnival and be with the playground gang for three days in Notting Hill! So we had to do some real serious thinking after she said: 'But of course I want them to attend!'

Playing at Notting Hill Carnival in 1984/5 called for a risk assessment of mammoth proportions and in the end you had to go for it knowing what a powerful and important event it was for so many children. When you hear those children talking fifteen years later about it as one of their most valuable and important memories, you know you were right to take all those risks.

I watched this summer at Barnard Park as two children played kendo with two broom handles. I waited, knowing that just a shift in mood, attitude or a change in the position they were holding the broom handles could lead to a heavy whack. The children played out in proper kendo style and then moved on to something else – I was relieved I had not had to intervene.

[Arthur] quoting Alan Sutton (2006): "A study of the positive and negative risk factors which may impact on young people shows that adventure playgrounds are invaluable as a local safe, non-judgmental, non-threatening 'home from home' for many children and young people, where they can self-refer for 'normalising' activities which can ameliorate their problem circumstances. An NCB study of accident statistics, funded by the Health Action Zone in 2001, showed that the 25 AP's in Lambeth, Southwark and Lewisham were **actually safer than staying at home**. A 2002 Citizen's panel MORI poll for Lambeth council, carried out as part of the Best Value review of services, showed APs were **top of the list of what parents wanted**, ahead of any other form of provision for children. Where APs are well run and well managed in London, they have largely escaped the cuts, despite pressure from managers to spend on their pet projects and schools to improve league tables, because councillors and local people value them."

[Maureen] Agi says 'Those swings were outrageous'. Yet in all those years he never had a bad accident on them! I recall how workers behaved about Stanley knives; you would regularly hear them, and the children, saying 'Retract the blade', or 'Don't walk with the scissors or blade in your hand, leave it on the table'. Council worker jackets and art tops had nice pockets you could slip tools into if they were on a table, no longer being used, because a child had moved on to something else; often, you would see a worker slip a tool into their pocket as they passed – no big fuss. How do you cut through a big cardboard box?

life just failed its play assessment: what is to be done?

[Arthur] (quoting Keith Johnstone 1987, p. 37) 'When we think of children we tend to think of them as immature adults. Perhaps our understanding would be better if instead we thought of adults as atrophied children, damaged by their upbringing.'

[Maureen] Sammy poses the question now her own children attend an adventure playground: 'I ask my children, do they do this, do they do that and they say no ... Well, what I want to know is if it was safe for us all those years ago, why isn't it now?'

afternote

This piece came into being when Mo was wondering what to write and Arthur suggested using material from her video; then Penny, who also loves stories, joined her, and suggested that Arthur do linking material, so she did. So we did.

acknowledgements

- Thank you to the playpeople at the L.B of Islington, you know who and why, and to these named contributors to Maureen's sections: Beverley Asforis; Samantha Collier; Alex Demarco (Akis Nicolaou); Andrew Legg; Vicky Loki; Ryan Morgan; Samantha Pavey (née Smyth); Debra Smyth; Lorraine Smyth. Thanks also to everyone else at: Cornwallis AP, 1982–91; and Barnard Park AP, from 2005 to the present.
- Thank you also to the inhabitants of the Chelsea AP, 1987–2004. Long may good practice continue!
- Thank you to 'Sharon', wherever you are, I hope you are happy and still wise.
- Thank you to Bob and Gordon, ludic songline explorers.

note

[1] *Oh, What a Blow That Phantom Gave Me!* Edmund Carpenter's (1976) visionary work of visual anthropology and media ecology. A maverick who explored the borderlands between ethnography and media over fifty years, Carpenter looked at the revolutionary impact of film and photography on tribal peoples, much like Maureen. Google him.

Chapter Twelve

The Playwork ABC

(After Alex Glasgow's 'The Socialist ABC')

Bridget Handscomb

When I started my first job in play
My mentor said to me
The time has come before you get too stale
To learn your ABC.
My mentor was a worker in the Adventures of that time
And his alphabet was different from the Enid Blyton kind.

He sang ...

A is for Adulteration, that made us aware of our stuff and
B is for Best Value Indicators, of which the bureaucrats can't get enough.
C is for the Childcare Strategy that led us down a dead end street and
D is for the Danger and Daring that helps us get back on our feet.

E is for Ever-changing landscapes that have kept us so fit for so long and
F is for Fun and for Freedom, without it we'd all go far wrong.
G is for Growth and for Green space that help to keep up our hopes and
H is for Hardworking colleagues who make us more able to cope.

I is for all Interventions, the do-gooders style is the worst and
J is for words like 'jouissance' that Gordon will think of the first.
K is the Killing with Kindness, the controlling nanny state brings and
L is for Loose Parts and Laughter, for all of us essential things.

M is for Memory and Madness, their importance escapes me for now and
N is for Neophilia and Nature that maintain our capacity to 'wow'.
O is for the Over-protection that fear and moral panic create and
P is Play and for Playwork, without which we'd degenerate.

Q is for Quirkiness and Questions, essential tools of the trade and
R is for Recapitulation of which great debate can be made.
S is for Scintillating Stories within each of us ready to tell and
T is for Timber and Telegraph poles which sometimes don't turn out so well.

U is for Unity and Uniqueness, sometimes a challenge to embrace and
V is for Vision and Variety, vital ingredients to the playwork case.
W is for a Worldwide perspective, but that's where the memory fades –
for XY and Z, my play mentor said, would be written on the play balustrades ...

Now that I'm not such a novice playworker
My mentor said to me
Please try to forget the things I said
Especially your ABC.
For he is no longer a frontline worker, he's had to change his plea.
His alphabet is different since he worked for the Big Lottery.

Chapter Thirteen

Dressing Up

The Influence of Play on Fashion

Sarah Atkinson

> It is only shallow people who do not judge by appearances. The true
> mystery of the world is the visible, not the invisible. (Wilde 1891)

Unlike many other areas of play, dressing-up, while commonly acknowledged to be an inherent part of childhood play, has attracted few of the
in-depth studies of other aspects of a child's development. The significance that clothing might play in the formative years of a life has yet to
be seriously considered, although it is recognised by every type of play
provision that a well-stocked dressing-up box is an essential ingredient
of play. It is also recognised by an increasingly child-focused market-
place that costumes and fashion sell. In the past few seasons the increase
in children's dressing-up costumes available to buy has been very
marked; it is no longer the province of specialist toy stores to stock
costumes: they are now available in your local supermarket to be
purchased alongside the essential weekly shopping.

Children love to dress up, to try out different roles, to play at being
adult, or at being magical or scary. Dress is so much a part of the rituals
of childhood, the first pair of shoes, the school uniform, the clothes that
mark out peer-group belonging and membership. Is it any wonder that
as adults we remember the clothes we wore with such nostalgia? Clothes
mark particular points in our lives in a way that is unique. They form
part of our personal identity and our passage into adulthood. What
lasting influence does our experience of dressing-up as children have on
the way we as adults feel about fashion? What does a child learn beyond
the simple pleasure of playing with the way they look or behave through
clothes and costume? What impact does this early playing have on the
adult's sense of dress?

It is interesting that dress is often described in terms of a 'sense'; it suggests that far from being a frivolous pastime, consideration in what we choose to wear is as much an essential part of our nature as deciding what we eat. It is possible to eat just to sustain life, just as it is possible to dress to hide our modesty or keep out the cold. But we do not, we make decisions, we dress-up, we play. This is both part of the child, and adult, play consciousness.

There have been innumerable books on the subject of fashion, costume and dress, but these have been written from a sociological, historical or anthropological perspective. Fashion has many influences, but its ludic qualities have largely been ignored in any serious work. Equally, literature on childhood development pays scant attention in children's play to the theme of dressing up and how this early experience might affect the adult's relationship with their self-image.

These then are the twin themes I will be examining: the relationship between fashion and play, both from the perspective of the child learning the transforming potential of clothing on identity and the adult enjoying the opportunity dress gives us to continue the play of character, role and self-presentation.

> Wantons go in bright brocade;
> Brides in organdie;
> Gingham's for the plighted maid;
> Satin's for the free!
> (Dorothy Parker 1926)

The ideas that I will go on to discuss came about primarily through an association with colleagues actively involved in the field of playwork and with my fellow design lecturers in art and design, who recognised that the key to being a creative person is the ability to continue playing into adulthood. In the application of this idea to the arena of fashion, it became increasingly apparent to me that this was not solely a capacity of designers, that they could tap into the psyche of the public, allowing the continuation of a particular form of play well into adulthood and beyond. You could say that fashion gives a permission to play, to try out different characters, even to adjust the personality to fit. For those of you who love to dress up, you can understand the transforming qualities of a new outfit and, equally, how after a time the novelty 'wears' off. It is as if we were bored with the game. (It is worthy of note that so many of our descriptive words are also associated with dress).

'The most important function of the frame is that it provides the context or stage where the play form is enacted' (Sturrock and Else 1998, p. 11). In understanding the way that children's play evolves, changes and ends, Gordon Sturrock and Perry Else in their joint publication *The Colorado Paper* put forward the concept of the play cycle. This has become widely accepted in playwork and the observation of play cues, frames and annihilation now form the basis of understanding children at play.

The theory can equally be applied to fashion to explain why a mood or look begins and is picked up so rapidly and, why, after a time of playing with a look, the fashion-buying public seek to move on. They have become bored with the frame, bored with the game.

In an industry reliant on people's desire for change, this can only be good, although there are times when the fashion-buying public are so happy with a particular look that it reappears season after season, with only the minimal amount of change; in effect, that the ludic quality, the meaning of the fashion frame is still valid, enjoyed and engaged with. A good example of this is the decorative and feminine look pioneered by Stella McCartney when she was designing for the fashion house, Chloe. It was not long before the stores were bursting with copies of the bias cut, beaded and embroidered dresses and separates that she had presented in the collections. It is now some years since these appeared for the first time on the runways in Paris, but the buyers still want this look.

In order to promote sales the garments have become more and more decorated; at the moment you cannot walk down the high street without being visually accosted by layers of tulle, sequins and beads. If fashion were only dictated by the industry this look would have long since been consigned to the back of the wardrobe, but it is the name of the frame we are playing, a game we like, it is big girls being allowed to play at fairy princesses.

It may be a few seasons yet before it seems inappropriate and we annihilate the play in favour of something new. 'Everybody has a fantasy and clothes give you that – you can be anybody you want to be' (Alexander McQueen 1996, p. 7). There are more designers who demonstrate this playful quality in their work than there is time to mention, but if I might give you some particularly accessible examples:

In the late 1960s and the 1970s Biba was possibly the most influential of labels, but the look Barbara Hulanicki, the founder, promoted had nothing to do with contemporary lifestyles. It was built entirely on her passion for Art Deco and the clothing of the 1920s and 1930s. Such was the influence of Biba that the fashion industry suffered from serious nostalgia in a way that it had never done before. The resulting interest in vintage clothing led to a vast high-street boom in charity shops and second-hand dealers had their best-ever decade.

The American designer Ralph Lauren is a master at recognising that people want to buy into a lifestyle, no matter that it is entirely artificial, it is a game. He markets the idea that you can be British aristocracy, and has been so successful that he has sold it back to us. In the USA his 'preppy look' saw a profusion of college graduate lookalikes, regardless of whether the wearers had ever been beyond second grade.

Vivienne Westwood has made a career out of taking classic costume, from Greek statues to street urchin and subverting it, playing with it. It is no coincidence that her famous orb logo is a pastiche of the Harris Tweed label, the most traditional of tailoring institutions.

The play is in deconstructing the traditional and creating something new, while continuing to reference the inspiration. Her early collections made even fetish clothing wearable on the high-street, certainly for the bolder amongst us. 'We clopped up and down in our mother's high heels wondering how we would ever learn to balance in them, or keep our stockings up with those mysteriously buttoned suspender belts' (Dunmore 1998, p. 61).

It is entirely possible that there is a direct link between the dressing-up play activities of our childhoods and the regular influence of nostalgia for a particular era that informs contemporary fashion. The recent wave of desire for all things seventies that has influenced style, not just for clothing but also interiors, producing endless remakes of old cartoons as feature-length films, owes much to the simple fact that the current generation of designers and stylists have their own childhood memories to replay. For the designers the frame of interest is not spent.

My own experience of working as a designer in the industry allowed me to draw on memories of the clothes my mother had given to my sister and me to play with. We were lucky, as she had been brought up in the war and consequently never threw anything away, so we had a remarkable archive of 1940s and 1950s clothing to dress up in. I still have some of it and often use it to demonstrate a point in my teaching.

A fashion look becomes accessible to the young as the availability of second-hand clothing through charity shops enables them to dress creatively and cheaply. Many the things available through these outlets are about twenty to thirty years old. The mechanics of fashion influence trickles up from the street as well as down from the catwalk, resulting in a rich cross-fertilization of ideas, allowing the public to buy into the nostalgia.

Sometimes a look comes along that has no obvious references to the past, for example in the 1960s the mood was very obviously inspired by the space programme. Designers such as Pierre Cardin and Courreges took their vision of the future and produced ranges of mind-boggling impracticality. The fashion buying public wearing these bizarre costumes were highly unlikely to go beyond the the Earth's atmosphere, but having seen Stanley Kubrick's (1968) *2001: A Space Odyssey,* wanted to play at being on spaceships. Just as children having seen Walt Disney's (1995) *Toy Story* want to be Buzz Lightyear.

'Some of the internalised fantasy material emerging out of the child's play may not fit into practice structured around programme, condition ing, or control, but it must be expressed' (Sturrock and Else 1998, p. 26). In order to investigate whether dressing-up play has any significant, measurable impact on children's creativity, I organised a number of workshops with children aged between 5 and 7 years old. Over and above it being simple enjoyment, play of this type is generally cate- gorised under social play, fantasy play or role play, and there is almost no specific information in this area; books on dressing-up play tend to contain instructions on how to make Halloween costumes out of dustbin bags, and nothing at all about what the children's experience might be, or the value that this particular type of play might have for them. In my observations during the dressing-up workshops that I held, it became very apparent to me that the act of disguise entailed by putting on a costume gives children permission to try out aspects of their character that they do not, under normal circumstances, permit to appear. A child who is naturally very shy, for example, may start to engage much more freely with the other children through the character they become. One such child, N, told me that she liked to dress as a monster because it made her feel brave, and during the time that she was in costume, she took a central role in the play in a way that she had not demonstrated when dressed in her everyday clothes.

Before and after the sessions I had asked the children to provide me with a drawing of themselves. Prior to the play session N's self-portrait was of a demure and smiling self, the figure was diminutive and used up barely half of the A4 paper I had supplied to the children. After the play session her other self-portrait drawn in character was spectacular, bold and dynamic. She used collage and colour in a confident and enthusias- tic way; the contrast was startling. 'When there is a conflict between the outer and inner selves the top layer of clothing may represent the public person and the one beneath his or her private desires or fears' (Lurie 1981, p. 179).

It is not unusual for an actor or performer to describe themselves as being shy and hiding behind or submerging themselves into the characters they portray. As adults we are all capable of adopting different characters in this way and we use dress as a means of illustrating how we feel or to change our personalities to suit certain circumstances. If we lack confidence in a situation we can adopt a dress code to help overcome the way we feel. We 'play the part', outward appearance helps us disguise the insecurities we feel or allows us to 'play down' our dress to fit our mood. This is part of the reason that dress is so closely associated with ritual. Being identifiable as part of a group helps us to support each other. In our society there are accepted forms of dress for most of the major landmarks of life, from the cradle to the grave. These are not always the most practical but are significant of something much more important. For example, in Christianity, the robe that the baby wears to be baptised is up to four times the length of the child it contains, as if an indication of the adult it will some day become or grow into.

It takes a very strong personal conviction or lack of awareness of social conventions to divert from the acceptable in traditional, ritualistic or formal situations. For example, the applicant for a job would almost certainly ensure before the interview the kind of person being sought and would attempt to play that role through dress and manner. Ask yourself if you would feel comfortable wearing jeans and a T-shirt to a wedding, when all other guests are in formal dress? But fashion allows that it is possible to play at different types, so you can be efficient and formal one day and trailer trash the next, if you so desire.

'Gender is not something one passively "is" or "has" . . . . . we "do gender"' (Thorne 1993, p. 5). 'Chanel's personality, like her designs was something of a paradox, a mingling of the masculine and the intensely feminine ...' (Beaton 1954, p. 418). In history and in contemporary culture there have always been examples of play with gender. Many performers, such as David Bowie, Boy George and Eddie Izzard, have made successful careers out of sexual ambiguity and are vociferous in the defence of their right to appear as they choose. Interestingly, this often spawns a period when their fans, people not necessarily in the entertainment or fashion business, will adopt more extreme forms of dress themselves, permission having been granted by the high profile and acceptance of the celebrity.

Under normal circumstances children become very aware of gender role-play, from the age of about four, more or less in line with the start of their compulsory schooling. In one of my dressing-up workshops C, aged six, demonstrated this very convincingly, describing things as being 'for girls'. He was very gender conscious and would only say he liked one type of fabric as the others were not for boys. He drew himself as a skateboarder and said that at home he liked to dress up in leather jacket and jeans. When it came to the dressing-up play session he started out by playing in a skeleton costume and as a pirate, but after a very short while, he had adopted a sparkly wig, high heels and a tutu.

I suspect this is a similar phenomenon to the one that allows men to reach for the drag at fancy dress parties; no one is going to question their sexuality, because it is recognised that they are just playing.

'Clothes are inevitable. They are nothing less than the furniture of the mind made visible, the very mirror of an epoch's soul' (Laver 1937, p. 49). To suggest that fashion is grown-up play is not to detract from its importance as an indicator of social, cultural or historical significance; it is to add to that perspective. Play is recognised as a need or drive in children, it is in their nature to explore their world through play, we should recognise and celebrate that we can continue this exploration in adulthood.

John had

Great Big Waterproof

Boots on;

John had a

Great Big

Waterproof

Hat;

John had a

Great Big

Waterproof

Mackintosh –

and that

(Said John)

Is

That.

(Milne 1924)

Chapter Fourteen

The Meta-maze: Playwork Frames of Reference

Wendy Russell

The chapter

This chapter looks at the concept of *framing* as it can be applied across a number of arenas: play, playwork and playwork theorising. It explores how playworkers can work with the idea of play frames, and how the thinking on this can contribute to a discrete way of articulating how playworkers work – a playwork frame of reference.

As I was writing this chapter I kept finding myself going down dead ends, losing my way, feeling confused and disoriented. To a certain extent, this is usual, yet the ideas presented here seemed particularly resistant to being forced into a logical, rational progression.

To the maze

Halfway through this process, the maze metaphor became clear. I was actually thoroughly enjoying being lost: the dead ends may not lead anywhere (yet) but they were fascinating. The parallels between writing the chapter and the characteristics of playing began to emerge and so I thought it might be helpful, or at least playful, to embrace this maze-like feeling as a frame for the whole chapter. So, apologies if there is no clear pathway through the maze. All I can hope is that the experience is enjoyable and useful in some way, even if we do often come up against dead ends and revisit places that look remarkably familiar.

I would not even have entered this conceptual maze were it not for Bob Hughes and Gordon Sturrock. For me, they have helped to build a contemporary playwork frame of reference. There is no grand unifying theory on play or playwork, nor should there be. Bob has followed his way of thinking in the evolutionary psychology maze, Gordon in the depth psychology and therapeutic maze. Some of their thinking makes sense to me, and with some of it I wish I were better read and so could question a little more. Yet whether I agree with them or not, they have laid the foundations for an approach to theorising on play and playwork that has enabled me to engage with theory, play with ideas and see what happens when I apply these to playwork practice. For this I am eternally grateful. I also need to acknowledge my debt to a very special group of playworkers in Nottingham who have generously allowed me to work with them, observe them, question them and test out my thinking on them. Without them, my theorising would not have been grounded in the reality of playwork practice.

During 2005–2006 I carried out a fascinating piece of research with playworkers in Nottingham (Russell 2006). We were trying to identify what was special about a playwork approach to working with children displaying challenging behaviour. We wanted to move away from the traditional behaviour modification techniques (introducing a system of rewards and sanctions aimed at reducing the unwanted behaviour) or cognitive behavioural therapy (CBT) (finding ways to help people change how they think and feel about things and so break patterns of problematic behaviour).

The research set out to see if an analysis of the children's play behaviour could offer a different perspective. Working from the starting point that the role of the playworker is to support children's play, we began to look at ways of learning more about how these particular children played and exploring this rather than focusing on what the playworkers saw as challenging behaviour. The playworkers drew up 'play profiles' of the identified children. The elements of these play profiles were drawn from the work of Bob Hughes, Gordon Sturrock and Perry Else, namely: play types and play narratives (Hughes 2002a), play cues and play frames (Sturrock and Else 1998).

Applying these tools to look at how the children played gave the playworkers a subtly but significantly different perspective that allowed them to see their work in a new way. They felt that they had much more to work with and that they had something to offer the children. However, I will not take you any further down this pathway – the details can be read in the research report (Russell 2006). Rather, the focus of this piece is on one aspect of the play profiles, namely the notion of frames, and how this opened up the possibility of a particular way of under-standing playwork.

I had initially identified play frames as an element of the play profiles because of their significance in *The Colorado Paper* (Sturrock and Else 1998) and their relationship with Hughes' use of the concept of play narratives (Hughes 2001). As the research progressed, I began to feel that this was key to a particular approach to playwork practice. I decided to return to earlier writings on frames (Bateson 1954; Goffman 1975; and more recently Sutton-Smith 2003).

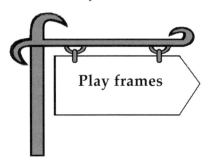

Play takes place within a frame. The frame is metaphorical, it is symbolic. It separates out what takes place within (play) from what exists outside (the real world?). Frames can be seen either as a limiting boundary, or as a containing one. There is a subtle difference here. A limiting boundary is one beyond which we cannot step. For example, playwork-ers often speak of setting boundaries for behaviour. A containing boundary, however, implies the separation of a space that is unperturbed by that which lies outside. (Is the fence around the playground to prevent unwanted visitors or escapes? Come back from that pathway; in this maze, it is a dead end.)

Of course, boundaries can be permeable. There is nothing like a boundary to make someone want to step outside or inside it. Seepage (a term used by Sutton-Smith 2003, p. 10) can take place in either direction, outwards or inwards.

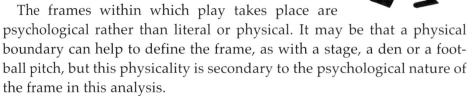

The frames within which play takes place are psychological rather than literal or physical. It may be that a physical boundary can help to define the frame, as with a stage, a den or a foot-ball pitch, but this physicality is secondary to the psychological nature of the frame in this analysis.

At this point in the maze, we come across a junction, two paths from which to chose. They are:

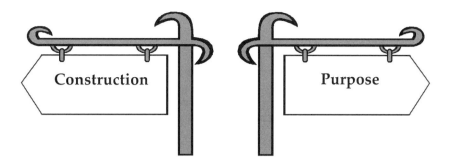

What is the purpose of the frame?
How is it constructed and maintained?

As we have already seen, the primary and immediate purpose of the frame is to separate it from what lies outside. Which leads us to the question – what is outside and why does play need to be separated from it? Here we begin to delve into discussions about play and not-play, the pretend and the real. Although Hughes (2002a) lists 'symbolic play' as one of sixteen types of play, it could be argued that all play is symbolic (Sturrock, personal communication). Certainly, we do tend to think of play as 'not real', although there are qualifications. Garvey (1977, p. 5) states: 'Play has certain systematic relations to what is not play'.

Playing as an activity is real enough: children, and adults, do actually play. Yet 'playing at' something is not the same as doing that something for real. It is, perhaps, the defining characteristic of play, as Burghardt (2005, p. 70) suggests:

The first criterion for recognising play is that the performance of the behaviour is *not fully functional* in the form or context in which it is expressed; that is, it includes elements, or is directed towards stimuli, that do not contribute to current survival [my italics].

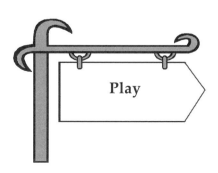

At this stage, perhaps it is necessary to 'frame' a particular understanding of play. The dominant contemporary play discourse focuses on its relationship to development. Even within the playwork sector, where the emphasis is on play being personally directed and intrinsically motivated (SkillsActive 2002; Play Wales 2005), investing public funds in play provision is still justified in terms of the development or progress of individuals (developmental psychology), societies (socio-cultural theories) or species (evolutionary psychology) (for example, see NPFA 2000). Underpinning many of these perspectives is the notion of play as preparation for adult (read 'proper') life, whether this is of specific skills or a more general adaptive variability (Sutton-Smith 1997). We can use the ideas of experimentation (Fagen 1975), combinatorial flexibility (Sylva 1977, cited in NPFA 2000), creativity (Winnicott 1971) and other forms of boundary testing to explain the kinds of playing that we may find pointless or unpalatable (such as nonsense play, fantasy play, deep play, rough-and-tumble play, war play or teasing) within this frame.

It would seem to make sense that playing has something to do with real life simply because much of it simulates real life. Yet the preparation paradigm falls short of an adequate explanation for many kinds of playing, and particularly those in which adults engage. How can it account for ghost stories and horror movies, for deep play so risky that danger of loss or harm is real, for jokes and satire, for toilet humour and obscenities, or for carnivals, contests, theatre and other such play performances?

Sutton-Smith (1997, p. 158) suggests that play simulates the real world not in order to understand it or prepare for a place in it, but '... to fabri-cate another world that lives alongside the first one and carries its own kind of life, a life often more emotionally vivid than mundane reality'.

Certainly, such a view would help explain the kinds of play that mock and subvert the ordinariness and the extraordinariness of real life. In later work, Sutton-Smith (2003) takes this emotional aspect of play further, drawing on Burghardt's (1998) work on the evolution of play. Burghardt suggests that play emerged (or at least greatly increased) at around the same time as mammals did. This was a time when brains grew and changed radically from the early 'reptilian' brain, developing new structures (the limbic brain and the neo-cortex) and new capacities for more complex emotions and conscious thought. Prior to this time, survival had depended on reflexes. These reflexes are closely linked to the six primary emotions: anger, fear, shock, disgust, sadness and happi-ness (Damasio 2000). With the evolution of newer sections of the brain also came secondary or social emotions such as embarrassment, pride, boredom, sympathy and many others. These are less extreme, more reflective and more regulated versions of the primary emotions.

Sutton-Smith suggests that there is a constant tension between these primary and secondary emotions. Play can help mediate this tension, by allowing us to experience primary emotions without the real danger of the situations that might evoke them, thus keeping these emotions alive. He suggests that those who live only on their secondary emotions, without the vitality that experiencing the primary emotions brings, may suffer from depression ('All work and no play makes Jack a dull boy'); whereas those who are psychotic or maladjusted live mostly on their primary emotions unmediated by the secondary ones, and often cannot play. Play allows this mediation to happen by using the secondary emotions to create the rules, rituals and play signals that allow us to recognise the behaviour as playing and therefore not real.

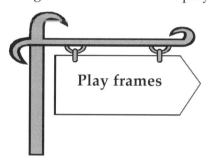

Play frames

Ah, we have gone down a route that has brought us out onto the pathway we were exploring some time back – the concept of play frames.

Playing is a simulation of real life, often of existential or survival crises. Because it is a simulation, it lacks the consequences of the real behaviour that it simulates (Bateson and Martin 1999).

For example, the children who discover lots of wiggly worms in the bark underneath the mat at the bottom of the slide may scream, and they may pick them up and taunt others with them in order to elicit the same expression of fear. The worms do not pose a real threat, so fear is experienced within a safe frame. Sutton-Smith (1999, p. 244) elucidates further:

> although play generates simulations of existential predicaments, it does so generally (but not always) within relatively safe packages. The predictable elements of play that attempt to keep the players safe are those governed by metacommunications, frames, routines, rules, cooperation, stylised performances and the inhibition of hurtful responses. These all provide boundaries against danger and allow excitement to take place without too much anxiety.

We can now return to our two key questions: What is the purpose of the frame? How is it constructed and maintained?

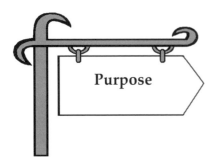

It would appear that the purpose of the frame is to set playing apart from the real world in order to create a safe psychological space where the pretend can allow primary emotions to be experienced without the threat of real consequences. The frame allows the players to understand that what takes place within the frame is play and therefore not 'real'.

This frame is constructed and maintained, as Sutton-Smith says, through the shared use of rules, rituals and 'metacommunications', all behaviours that are possible through the use of secondary emotions. The term 'metacommunications' was coined by Bateson (1954, p. 178) to describe the implicit messages or signals we send to others that communi-

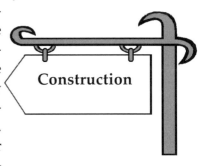

cate our intentions in terms of 'the relationship between the speakers'. So, metacommunications within play send the message, 'This is play'. (Or, just to tempt you down a dead end that we can't explore here, the message, 'Is this play?') Metacommunications include, but are broader than, Sturrock and Else's (1998) 'play cues': cues are the invitation to play, rather than the message itself. Metacommunications can include such signals as smiling 'play' faces, exaggerated movements, speaking in different voices or accents, self-limiting (for example, allowing a weaker co-player sometimes to have the upper hand in play-fighting or competitive games, in order to keep the game going), explicit, implicit or negotiated rules, the use of ritualistic phrases and gestures, and so on.

One playworker in the Nottingham research told me (Russell 2006, p. 16):

> he gets a glint in his eye. It's little telltale signs like that that make you pick up whether they are playing or whether they're actually really feeling something and really having a bad time. And I would say the more you get to know children, the more time you spend with them, that you pick up those things, little mannerisms or the way that they behave in different situations; then that allows you to distinguish easier what they're actually going through, what they're actually

doing, whether they are kind of freaking out or whether … because with him, I've seen him doing a shout, big shouty thing like that, acting all angry but then I've looked at him and noticed the glint and I'm thinking, 'He's playing'.

What this showed me was that there is ample opportunity for misreadings of metacommunications, both between the children themselves and between playworkers and children. Playworkers need to work on recognising when those telltale metacommunications are being employed by children. The other side of the coin is that often children themselves are not very good at making these metamessages clear.

Research by Corsaro (1985, cited in Sutton-Smith 2003, p. 8) shows how very young children have difficulty maintaining the pretence of play, how their play frames fall apart easily:

the children have trouble with the actor's dilemma, which is how to pretend what one is feeling without actually feeling it. The younger they are, the more they want to introduce their own real Freudian or other feelings. But all that does is to frighten off other children. They all have to arrive at a consensus of pretence with which to hold themselves together, and they usually achieve this by exaggerated metarepresentations of what they want to indirectly express.

At this stage, it feels appropriate to take a little peek down the 'playwork' pathway – but just a peek, as there is more to say on play itself yet. I'm sure there are many playworkers who can vouch for older children having similar difficulties, and playworkers can assist here, to an extent, by entering the play frame and indulging in some rather exaggerated metacommunications in order to re-establish the frame itself. A concrete example might be acting as a commentator on the game of football that looks about to fall apart, using names of favoured players; or to squeal in exaggerated terror at the 'monster' whose rage at being taunted looks set to get in the way of the game. I am constantly surprised by how these tactics seem to be effective even with older children – often the more exaggerated and 'childish' the performance, the better. But we're getting ahead of ourselves here.

What this introduces is the notion of some players being better at playing than others. Play may be an innate drive (Hughes 2001; Sturrock and Else 1998), but some develop more effective or sophisticated play skills than others. This is recognised in Sturrock and Else's notion of 'dysplay'. It is also recognised by Smith *et al.* (2002) who cite observational research showing that only 1 per cent of play fights turn into real fights, yet for those who are rejected by social groups the figure rises to 25 per cent, as these children often have difficulty understanding the play signals accompanying play fighting and confuse the playful with the real.

Goffman (1975) speaks of 'keying' as a way of communicating what the frame is, and this can either be implicit (as in metacommunications) or explicit ('We're only pretending!' or 'We're witches, right, and we're going to turn children into mice for our tea.') Playworkers can use both implicit and explicit keying to help re-establish breaking frames.

One of the traps into which we grown-ups often fall is that we take things so literally and we turn small problems into big ones by making them explicit. There is much to be said for working in the realm of the ludic, the subtle and the symbolic rather than the obvious and the literal. If our role as playworkers is to support children's playing, then our first task is to help them to establish and maintain frames that allow that playing to occur. Therefore, if we see behaviour that is threatening a frame that is not yet spent, we can enter the frame playfully and subtly in order to re-establish it, rather than halting the whole thing and explaining why it has fallen apart. Of course, as with all such matters, there are times when the literal approach is appropriate, but there is much value in considering a playful, reframing approach as the default position.

To underline this, our next turning in the maze (which may lead to a dead end or not) is to explore just how far playing is not real. Again, we come to a choice of two pathways: paradox and parody.

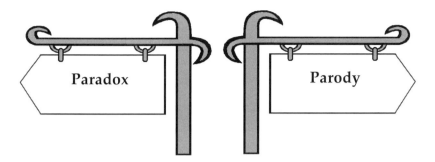

The paradox of playing arises exactly because of its real and unreal nature, and through the construction and elements of the play frame. Winnicott (1971, p. 6) talks of the paradoxical relationship between symbolic transitional object, illusion, playing and reality:

> It is true that the piece of blanket (or whatever it is) is symbolical of some part-object, such as the breast. Nevertheless, the point of it is not its symbolic value so much as its actuality. Its not being the breast (or the mother), although real, is as important as the fact that it stands for the breast (or mother).

Bateson (1954) suggests that a paradox arises because of the very 'false-ness' of what is taking place within the play frame. In play-fighting, for example, the 'nip' represents a bite, but it is not a bite, and nor does the bite that it represents really exist. He suggests that this is similar to Epimenides' paradox. Epimenides was a Cretan philosopher and his logical paradox can be illustrated by the phrase, 'All Cretans are liars.' If Epimenides was a Cretan, and he said this, would he be telling the truth or lying, would the statement be true or false? What might this mean for any statement made thereafter? So, if playful metacommunications make the statement, 'This is play and therefore false', how false or true is the statement? What about bluff and double bluff?

The notion of paradox is a favourite theme running through the work of Sutton-Smith. He sees the constant tension between the need for a sense of disequilibrium (excitement) and equilibrium (safety) as being expressed through play, with the excitement of experiencing primary emotions within the safe boundaries of the play frame (Sutton-Smith 1999). This he calls the 'ludic paradox', an internal paradox between sense and nonsense. He also recognises an 'adaptive paradox' that comes about because of the relationship between playing and the real world – this is much the same as Bateson's paradox.

These structural explanations of the paradoxes of play also go some way towards explaining modal paradoxes too: so, for example, we can now understand why play can be both chaotic (through the vagaries of the primary emotions) and yet ordered (through ritualistic rules, meta-communications and so on), or unpredictable and yet repetitive, or mix elements of the fantastic and the mundane, of mimicry and mockery. In this sense, we can see that play, rather than being a rehearsal for adult life, can be seen as a parody of all the things in life that are scary or boring, and through the experience of playing, give the player some small sense of mastery and control over those events.

An underlying paradox in our understanding of playing is that, despite the playwork sector's insistence that play is intrinsically moti-vated and 'for its own sake', it is still firmly linked to a functional end (for example, helping children practise the skills needed in adult life, or to develop adaptive variability, or as a means of developing one's identity, and so on). Spariosu opened my eyes to the work of the philosopher Hans Vaihinger (1911) and his 'law of the preponderance of the means over the end' (Spariosu 1989, p. 247). A brief and incomplete description is given here. Vaihinger speaks of thought in this way: whereas origi-nally, thought processes were directed towards biological survival, thought has now become overdeveloped, theoretical and contemplative and is indulged in for its own sake. Through asking ourselves unan-swerable questions ('What is the meaning of life?') and through imaginative thought, we create fictions (and there are good and bad fictions) about the world. He uses the term *Spielbegriffe* (play-ideas) to mean the same thing as 'fictions'. It is not the content of the thoughts that matter, as these are mere fictional products of our experiences and create our conceptualisation of the real world; what is important is that the process of thinking helps us find our way in the world. The paradox, of course, is that this then becomes a function.

The purpose of discussing this way of understanding play is that it frees us from the requirement to see play behaviours as indicative of non-play behaviours: for example, play-fighting as actual or potential aggression, or sexual play as a potential indicator of abuse, or fantasy play about death as morbid or neurotic, and so on. Of course, there is no guarantee either way.

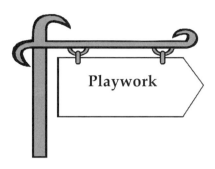

How, then, can playworkers apply this thinking about play frames and meta-communication in their work? The ideas that I explore here may go some way to resolving the paradox of the 'low intervention' paradigm and the fact that playworkers are constantly interacting directly with children at play. Certainly, my recent playwork experience paints a picture of playworkers continuously being cued by children either to join in or support the playing in some way. Even the child who has sat immersed in a creation of some sort will usually seek out a playworker to show off the final production. Although I support the concept of low intervention as a principle whose purpose is to avoid adulteration (Hughes 2001; Sturrock and Else 1998), I have come to appreciate that playworkers' very presence can be supportive to playing and that the children use us as a resource for their play. The hierarchy of intervention proposed by Sturrock and Else (1998) focuses on interventions that support playing rather than those that are aimed at terminating or redirecting it because it has become unpalatable for us adults. Of course, the potential to adulterate is still there.

It was Winnicott who helped me to think further about the idea (that I first encountered in Sturrock and Else 1998) of playworkers being able to 'hold' play frames for children, and for the frames to be a secure and reliable containment for playing rather than being adult-imposed frameworks for acceptable behaviour. Winnicott (1971) suggests that the mother's (or other primary caregiver's) physical holding of the baby enables the creation of the first playground, the space between the mother and infant, and that later this holding can become more metaphorical, where she is not physically holding but is reliably available if the older and more independently playing child should need her. (There is another pathway here that explores the idea of play taking place in the intermediary space between inner psychic reality and external actuality, but I'm afraid space limits prevent us from going down this pathway.) In times of distress, the holding may again become physical.

It seems to me that the playworker can provide a continuation of this holding or containing role (or, for children who have not had this primary experience, they may indeed be able to create it as Dockar-Drysdale (1991) suggests, but that too is another pathway for another time). We can see parallels here with Sturrock and Else's (1998) hierarchy of intervention. Much of the time, if the playworkers have created a physical and affective space where the children can play (Hughes 2001), the playworkers' holding role is one of play maintenance. In my recent playwork experience, I have been asked by children literally to hold frames while they leave them for a while – guarding dens, or making sure no-one spoils craftwork in progress while they go to the shop. We are aware of the playing, and we are reliably available if needed by the children. This is also in line with Hughes' (2002b) intervention modes of 'distance' and 'perceived indifferent' (so that the children do not feel constantly monitored and supervised) and also 'permissional' (where playworkers can convey very subtly that specific play behaviours being manifested are OK in the setting).

Such approaches can also be applied with simple intervention, where, by providing resources to support the play, the playworkers are tacitly saying that the playing is worth supporting. Sometimes the provision of resources may be explicit and in response to direct requests ('Can I have a balloon?'); at others, it may be more subtle, such as the time when I saw a group of children playing in a large puddle, and one of the playworkers, saying nothing, dragged some planks of wood and an old canoe and left them close to the puddle for the children to spot and use if they wished.

Medial intervention is the area where re-establishing the frame or a more significant reframing becomes necessary. Again, this can be done in a number of ways. It may be literal and explicit, for example, helping the children to agree the rules of the game. Or it may be more subtle, such as entering the game and playing it for a while, with exaggerated meta-communications. I have also observed physical reframing taking place, where one child was throwing pieces of clay across the room. The playworker suggested that the child go into a small room and throw the clay as much and as hard as he liked, and where there were no other children to be disturbed by this playing. (As an aside, this playwork intervention was observed by an Ofsted inspector who asked the playworker to explain it and was impressed by the response – a little peek down the pathway that explores how important it is for playworkers to have confidence in this approach and be able to articulate it to others.) This way of thinking helps playworkers to see their interventions as supporting play rather than correcting unwanted behaviour. The child throwing clay was impinging on the play of other children, and this was the reason it was unacceptable. Suggesting that the child physically moves allowed him to continue his playing without it disturbing others. This is an interesting scenario, because the playworkers had previously assumed that the game was 'annoy everyone else', whereas it was, actually, 'throwing clay'.

Recently, during October half-term at a local play centre, I observed a wonderful illustration of playworkers providing a focal springboard for a number of frames to come into being. There is a tradition at the centre of celebrating Halloween. On this occasion, the playworkers decided to make a mummy – basically, stuffing some clothes with shredded paper, sewing it all together and covering it in 15 cm strips of white fabric from the local scrapstore that looked like bandages. A shifting and changing group of children were involved in the core activity for the three hours it took to make the mummy. The playworkers worked with whoever was there, providing the resources, doing the tricky bits, having conversations. This 'holding' and 'permissive' intervention also enabled, amongst other frames:

- a massive shredded paper fight: the whole room was absolutely covered, lots of shrieks, lots of fun, with playworkers dipping in and out of the throwing, as 'permissional' interventions (Hughes 2002b);
- children stuffing the shredded paper down each others clothes and becoming scarecrows (a spontaneous chorus of 'dingle dangle scarecrow' broke out at one point – this is 8– to 12–year-old innercity children playing here) and then becoming Quasi Modo (plastic cricket stumps and hockey sticks were provided as walking sticks as they hobbled their way round the centre);
- a return to the shredded paper fights when one of the playworkers and a couple of children swept up the mess into piles;
- children wrapping each other in the fabric 'bandages' to become mummies themselves; again, later, the playworkers were asked to do the wrapping and so were able to hold the frames through simple intervention.

Somehow, listing the activity of 'mummy-making' in the daybook does not quite capture the number of frames that this core activity gave rise to, held and resourced. In some settings, the paper fight may have been understood as disruptive behaviour and stopped; in this setting, the expectation of being able to play was well established, and so it was clear that the fight was a game for its own sake rather than a game of winding up the playworkers.

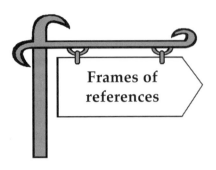

Frames of references

Looking at the role of the playworker as being the holder of play frames is itself a particular frame of reference. Goffman (1975) speaks of 'laminations' of frames, the different layers of frames within frames. So, for example, what you are reading is a chapter (real, a primary framework) about a way of theorising playwork (one lamination) that involves a particular theorising of play (another lamination) that is about play being framed and not real (a further lamination). Each layer has its own paradox of representing something that is real but not actually being that thing (has the maze just become a Russian doll?).

This particular playwork frame of reference allows playworkers to understand their work from a particularly 'ludocentric' (play-centred) perspective, rather than a didactic (teaching) or chaotic (negligent) one (Sturrock, Russell and Else 2004). By understanding that play takes place within a frame that allows relatively safe expression of primary emotions through regulation by the secondary emotions, we can bring a different perspective on behaviour that other professionals may call challenging. We can 'frame' it as seepage of the primary emotions (Sutton-Smith 2003) or we can frame it as a breaking frame (Goffman 1975). Either way, we can frame the role of the playworker as supporting play by helping to establish, re-establish or reframe the play frame. The differences are very subtle, but they are clearly play-centred.

Now, how do I find my way out of here? Bob? Gordon? Help!!

Chapter Fifteen

When Are You Going to Get a Real Job?

Or 'How Bob's work impacted on me' – a personal recollection

Mel Potter

OK, before we go any further let me make something clear: if you are reading this piece looking for a thoughtful and scientific consideration of the impact of Bob's work on playwork practice in the field, then please move on to the next article because I can assure you there is nothing for you here.

   'When are you going to get a real job?' It was something my father said to me on a regular basis back in 1978 when I first discovered playwork (or playleadership, as we used to call it back then). He used to ask me the same question every few weeks for probably the first two or three years I worked on adventure playgrounds. I could sense his disappointment in my choice of career. Well, choice of job would be more accurate – you couldn't really call it a career back then, as the chances of advancement within the work were few to nonexistent. I tried to explain to Dad that I did have a 'real' job; I was working for the council after all! That seemed to make matters worse rather than better. As far as my father was concerned it was doubtful if anyone in the council had a real job unless it was emptying the bins or cleaning the streets (we haven't had the discussion in years but I assume he still feels the same way). I struggled to put into words the feelings I had about my work (I still do, which will probably become apparent as you read on). My first problem was that it really felt as if the work had chosen me. I trained in business studies at college in Dudley and I came to Wolverhampton to carry on those studies at the local Poly (that was before the Government decided all Polytechnics could call themselves Universities so that there wouldn't be a two-tier higher education system!) Anyway, I came from a friendly local college where I was course rep on the Student Union and entertainment rep. My claim to fame was that I booked Slade before they were famous; they cost £50 and a crate of beer.

I arrived at Wolverhampton Poly and for various reasons I failed my exams at the end of the first year. In truth I had every intention of going back the next year and really knuckling down to studying but during the summer something happened. My girlfriend got a job as a temporary playleader on one of the rougher estates in Wolverhampton and I'd dropped her off there a few times but hadn't really taken an interest. However, at the end of 1978 she got a full time job at Phoenix Adventure Playground which was (and still is) the first Adventure Playground in Wolverhampton. When September came I decided I wasn't going back to Poly and instead started volunteering on the Phoenix and in the play team generally. I don't think it was straight away that playwork took over my life but I can say it certainly wasn't long. Years later I would comment to newcomers that playwork had a way of getting under your skin.

Back in those days most of the playgrounds didn't have any indoor facilities except for little tin sheds which we used to keep the tools in, so, because it was dark on weekday evenings, all of the playleaders used to get together and work in teams, either on each other's playgrounds or out in a van 'resourcing'. Resourcing mostly involved driving round local demolition sites trying to beg any scrap wooden beams or floorboards or anything else interesting-looking we thought we could use. I got on really well with the other playleaders and I loved working on the playground, although in the winter of 1978/79 we had lots of snow and I ruined a very fashionable pair of cowboy boots. Since I'm six foot two I probably shouldn't have been wearing three-inch heels anyway.

As I said, I really loved the work; I loved the sense of achievement that came from building a new play structure or getting potatoes to bake in the open fire without burning to a crisp on the outside (I had this theory that we needed to get the heat into the middle quicker, before the outside could burn; we were already wrapping them in foil but I decided that the answer was to stick six inch nails through them to transfer the heat. The kids, it has to be said, were doubtful but they gave me the benefit of the doubt and it actually worked!). Yeah, yeah I know, we couldn't possibly do that with the 'playground users' now. Anyway the point of this rambling, and I could go on for pages but I won't, is that I could see that the kids learnt stuff, that they worked together, that they included me when they wanted and put up with me when they didn't. I knew that this had got to be a good thing, I knew it in my heart and soul, it was a cosmic thing. (Oh no! Old hippy warning but actually I'm not old enough to have been a hippy <grin>.)

So, one thing led to another and I went from volunteer, to getting a job, to being the actual playleader in charge of the site and during that time I moved from Phoenix to Elston Hall (sadly now closed) to Gatis Street Adventure Playgrounds. For some strange reason in 1984 I think my nerve broke and I started to think 'I can't work on an adventure play-ground for the rest of my life.' (To those older play people around, I do now realise the error of my ways.) I didn't want to abandon playwork so I took the unusual step, at the time, of giving up a full-time job to join a government scheme called the Manpower Services Commission (MSC). This enabled me to stay in the play service but I became a manager and eventually a play trainer. And so it was in 1987 I was sent to join a course called 'Exploring Play Policy' at University College Swansea. The course was organised by an organisation called PlayEducation and run by someone called Bob Hughes. I didn't know it at the time but there I met some of the best-known people in the play field including Frank King, Paul Eyre and Mike Nussbaum. There were others there too and if that was you, I apologise that I've forgotten your name, but I have to say it was those few days that started to change my life.

The course was intended to help people write and implement a play policy and I was there because Wolverhampton wanted to adopt a policy and I was to write the draft. I soon became aware that I was hopelessly out of touch with what was often called the cutting edge of playwork theory. During those few days I first heard about 'freely chosen, person-ally directed and intrinsically motivated' and I found out that not only were there other people who knew 'intrinsically' that play was 'a good thing' but that they were organising, networking, helping each other and moving purposefully towards a society where everyone would realise how essential playwork was. To say that I was in shock would be an understatement.

During the course Bob helped me enormously in a way that anyone who knows him will recognise: he was incredibly supportive but also very challenging. I felt proud to be part of something that seemed very special although still rather in awe of my course co-members. If I remem-ber correctly, some of the content was what went on to become Bob's famous *Playworkers' Taxonomy of Play Types*, published in 1996.

I returned to Wolverhampton full of enthusiasm and having also discovered that Bob ran a regular conference which at the time was the only way for playwork's thinkers to share their ideas. I was determined to get Wolverhampton's play staff to those conferences.

Over the years since then, and I've just realised it will be twenty this year, I've managed to get to some PlayEd Conferences where I've always been both amazed and humbled by the work that Bob and people like him have done to underpin and validate the work. In 1999, through some strange quirk of fate, I was appointed as Director of Play to the National Playing Fields Association and although I know I achieved very little in the six months I was there, I am immensely proud that I was able to persuade Bob to commit his thoughts and work to a project which became the publication *Best Play – What Play Provision Should Do for Children* (NPFA *et al.* 2000). I hope that that work at least helped to get the really important facts about play provision out to a wider audience. A while after that, in 2001, Bob gave me the opportunity to read and comment on the manuscript for *Evolutionary Playwork and Reflective Analytical Practice* (Hughes 2001). Although I had been out of direct play-work for some years by then, I was once again overawed by the scale of the achievement. I remember making some comments on the work and thinking to myself, 'who am I kidding, making comments on a work as important and ground-breaking as this?' I think that that work finally brought home to me the massive responsibility I had once held for the future development of the species.

Bob taught me that there could not be a more 'real' job than playwork. He taught me that the work is so important, it is essential that anyone with the power or the ability to do so owes it to the world to do all they can to make sure that that message is heard and understood.

Chapter Sixteen

There's No Place Like the Play Space –

An Appreciation of Disability and Playwork

Stephen Smith and Becky Willans

> It's relatively easy for me to become emotionally close to others. I am
> comfortable depending on others and having others depend on me.
> I don't worry about being alone or having others not accept me.
>
> (James 2002, p. 142)

While working with disabled children and young adults there may be an overwhelming wealth of complexities in all areas of interaction. We find ourselves entwined in our own emotional state and are often faced with children and young people of whom we have limited knowledge, around whom we have apprehension or with whom we have limited means of communicating. If we then add playwork to this equation it becomes apparent that we must at some part in the journey try to understand what we are doing, where we would like to go and how to get there.

> Look at me, look at me!
> Look at me now!
> It's fun to have fun
> But you have to know how.
>
> (Dr Seuss 1958, p. 18)

Sturrock and Else's (1998) play cycle has provided a unique model for looking into play, showing how play begins, the absorption and flow, and the annihilation phase. There is a growing body of work (Sturrock and Else 2005) showing how children play and how as adults we can support this process, through providing and facilitating play environments for children and young adults. From this work we realise the magnitude of the task of self-examination as well as understanding the need for further research in this area.

The adulteration that can occur from our own over-indulgences in the play cycle and how damaging this can be is a critical area of study for those working in a play environment, and who are making decisions about this subject.

> I just can't make friends. I'd like to be on my own and look at my coin collection … I've got a hamster at home. That's enough company for me … I can play by myself. I don't need other people. (Attwood 1998, p. 30)

The field of disability services and studies is vast and we are mostly presented with either an individual/medical or social model of disability (Oliver 1990) that covers a broad spectrum of knowledge, although yields little in the way of learning and understanding of the individual. This can often lead to disabled people being cared for, helped and directed throughout their lives.

From our experience of working in play environments with disabled children and young people, we have often found ourselves in groups of young people who apparently hold no interest in each other as peers or someone with whom to share play experiences. Many are unable to communicate and many have limited mobility. This creates an environment where young people become dependent on adults or peers, and which has the potential to create child redundancy, whereby the adult may find it easier to do something for the child rather than spend time and resources finding ways for him or her to be more independent. It is possibly for this reason that more time is devoted to care work than playwork.

We are discovering new and innovative ways in which to provide care and play opportunities for disabled people and significant work is happening already, in organisations such as Barnardo's through the use of music, drama and play. However, it is apparent that many children and young people with complex conditions still face ridicule and are assumed to be 'idiots' or 'stupid' because they do not conform to the norm expected by society.

The work of Gordon Sturrock and Bob Hughes has greatly informed our work with disabled children and young adults, allowing us to challenge and change these views in order to provide a caring, supportive and informed environment. This has reduced inappropriate behaviour and enhanced communication between these particular children and young people, their peers and workers.

Like many other people in the playwork and youth work professions, we have both worked in and with agencies that supposedly support and provide play opportunities for children and young people with disabilities. We have observed very limited education for staff, which has led to children and young people being presented with minimal choice of play opportunities and in many cases bad practice. Many service providers we have encountered have little understanding of complex conditions or play and therefore are unable to educate their staff or provide a suitable environment.

The work of Sturrock and Hughes has helped to transform the way in which we play and interact, and provides us with more of an understanding about play needs and the importance of environments where play experiences, exploration, adventure and so on to take place. Developing an understanding of play deprivation and its potentially negative impact on human development brings about huge questions that are central to the debate about playwork with disabled people.

When working with disabled children and young adults in a play setting, we understand the difficulties faced in this field. This was highlighted as we learned more about play and youth work through educational experiences and contact. We were providing a play environment for those who challenged the view that people with disabilities are mostly perceived as being unable to interact or play. This was combined with communication barriers and very little or no desire to interact with their peers.

We were in a field of discovery, hostility and nearly complete adult dependency for all play needs and desires to be met. The work of Sturrock and Hughes helps us not to adulterate play and encourages us to support play without taking over. Hughes (2001, p. 18) maintains that 'Interruption by a child or adult destroys the process of the child becoming immersed in fantasy that is so much a part of the dream state which is play'.

Recognising barriers from our own ability to play as adults uncovered a whole range of feelings and emotional responses, self-discovery, fear, trepidation, joy, in fact every emotion and feeling possible. This may be enlightening or destructive, depending on the individual. For many, we have become inhibited by all the social parameters that make us feel self-conscious and vulnerable when playing.

The following case study displays the application of such playwork and guidance.

Layla is a 10-year-old girl who has Athetoid Cerebral Palsy (uncontrolled movements of all limbs) and dysarthia (inability to coordinate the speech muscles). Due to her condition Layla is a wheelchair user. Staff assumed that she was unable to communicate verbally. When her communications were misunderstood or ignored, she often became anxious and aggressive, hitting, biting and pulling hair. Many staff members at the setting became cautious when working with her, owing to the perceived inappropriate behaviour she displayed. A majority of staff had labelled Layla as 'naughty', 'spiteful' and a 'horrible child'. They frowned upon the idea of removing Layla from her wheelchair.

Often, when communicating with the staff and children in the setting, Layla would wave her hands and arms, hitting passers-by. This was partly due to her condition and the frustration she faced when trying to express her wants and needs. As Layla was unable to verbalise her views, she used her limbs to display excitement, anger, sadness and a range of other emotions.

The lack of communication and understanding Layla received led to a display of frustration and inappropriate behaviour. Rarely would staff and children communicate with Layla, as they feared her outburst. We proposed that the work of Sturrock and Else (1998), along with the techniques from Neuro-linguistic Programming (NLP) (O'Connor and Seymour 1990) would be a useful way of assessing communication with Layla, in order to meet her needs.

Sturrock and Else (1998) indicate that children have an internal drive to play, which is evident in the play cue. They elucidate further: 'If we conclude that play is a form of consciousness, the play cue is the signal for the world to engage with the child's developing sense of self and reality' (Sturrock and Else 1998, p. 14). This suggests that Layla was not 'naughty, spiteful and horrible' but quite the opposite, in fact: Layla was a frustrated child who tried frequently but unsuccessfully to communicate with the people in her environment, and their lack of play return was increasing her frustration.

Once Layla's play cues had been acknowledged for what they were, she was able to find a play return.

> The play return will be found by the playing child from the environment or as initiated by another child or adult ... When the return is initiated by another (child or adult), the child's response will be influenced by their own conscious and unconscious emotional state, cultural understanding, physical abilities and sense of power. (Sturrock *et al.* 2004, p. 13)

Therefore, the play return to Layla must be made with awareness and consideration of her needs and abilities, as with all children.

The use of NLP played a crucial part in this area as it provided an insight into how best to return a play cue to Layla. Using the concept of eye-accessing cues, we were able to establish that Layla processed information more often through sound than through sight or touch. She preferred to be spoken to rather than have a visual or kinaesthetic approach, as she was sensitive to touch, especially when people were not in her vision; for example, touching the shoulder from behind without a visual or auditory cue triggered involuntary movement or challenging behaviour, such as kicking, hitting and scratching. Weihs (2000, p. 110) explains:

> It is clear that cerebral palsy is by no means only a motor disability. There is a very considerable sensory element to this condition that manifests essentially in a marked degree of over-sensitivity. It is easy to observe how a child with cerebral palsy reacts with increased muscular contractions to any abrupt noise or even to the approach of someone who does not enter his field of vision gradually.

For Layla to develop to the best of her potential, the play in which she was involved should be varied and not restricted to one area. The aim was to include Layla in as many situations and experiences as possible, improving her socialisation with others. Her general routine prior to this was to be left sitting in the corner with a book, adding to her frustration.

The majority of staff and children ignored Layla, which led to a deprivation of play opportunities. Hughes (2001, p. 217) clarifies: 'The term "play deprivation" at its most extreme, describes a chronic lack of sensory interaction with the world, a form of sensory deprivation.'

In order to facilitate Layla's play, a play plan was then created with her input. Layla was given a drum, allowing her to make an auditory response to a variety of questions asked about activities. She was asked to bang once for yes and twice for no. The activities included in the plan were those with a one-bang response.

The aim was for Layla to be involved in as many play types as possible in order to enhance her play and socialisation. Hughes (2001, p. 47) suggests that: 'Breaking play down into its component play types gives the playworker a tool for focusing expertise, resources and time onto particular areas of need.'

As Layla was generally deprived of many play types in the setting, a plan that included opportunities to engage in more play types was created:

Play type	Activity	Support
Rough and tumble	Wrestling (on soft play mats) – allows Layla to stretch her limbs, as she does not require the use of her wheelchair during this activity.	One-to-one support, one additional playworker
Creative	Use of a variety of malleable materials, clay, paint, cooking – enhances fine and gross motor skills. She does not always require the use of her wheelchair during this activity (good weather – outside activity on grass).	One-to-one support
Locomotor	Hand/ tag games – enhances socialisation with peers, the use of a hosepipe during warm weather helps Layla to tag people. She does not require the use of her wheelchair during this activity; walking frame is appropriate.	One-to-one support, one additional playworker
Exploratory	Indoor sand pit in a tent – allows Layla to explore and dig for treasure. Encourages fine and gross motor skills. She does not require the use of her wheelchair during this activity as she will be sitting inside the tent.	One-to-one support
Imaginative	Use of boat (home corner) – allows Layla to create imaginary role-play games, play with dolls. She does not require the use of her wheelchair during this activity as she can sit on the floor, use cushions for comfort and extra support (if Layla requires them).	One-to-one support

The activities Layla enjoyed and the best way to communicate with her were explained to members of staff and the children accessing the service. Layla's play plan was displayed with an account of the activities she enjoyed. The account provided details of how to interact with Layla in an appropriate way, enhancing her communication and reducing anxiety. Within a week Layla's negative behaviour (outbursts) had dramatically reduced and the other children began to socialise with her with an increased understanding of her play and communication needs.

Layla was able to cue children into her play using a variety of auditory signals; for example, using musical instruments, one tap for yes and two taps for no. As the children were more aware of how to communicate with Layla, they were able to interact with her in play, both verbally and physically. The children would ask Layla questions and wait for a one-tap or two-tap response. The children no longer feared interactions with Layla, and responded to the noises she produced.

Her outbursts rarely occurred as those involved in Layla's play environment were more aware of how to interact effectively. In turn, Layla was much happier as people were able to communicate effectively with her. Layla's popularity grew. Her peers then included Layla on the days she attended the setting. The quality of her play experiences improved, as she was no longer left in a corner on her own.

Prior to the application of our knowledge of play cues and of the different play types Layla enjoyed, it was assumed that Layla had little understanding of the world and how to interact. The use of Sturrock, Else and Hughes' work displayed clearly that in actual fact, Layla had a wealth of knowledge about her own feelings, needs and the world, and that it was ignorance of her condition and ability that caused much of her 'inappropriate behaviour'.

Settings regularly fail disabled children and young people and their families. Due to the lack of knowledge concerning interaction, good practice and the general care and well-being of children and young people, staff are not able to meet their needs. This can cause unhappiness, stress and trauma rather than provide support and understanding. Children and young adults such as Layla have been seen as 'unpleasant' and 'naughty' rather than people who are caring and sociable, with a good sense of humour, who also have complex needs.

Without knowledge of the play cycle, play cues and play types, Layla would have continued to experience play deprivation, as staff in the setting would not have had the ability to facilitate play appropriately. The effects of this are detrimental to a child or young adult's development. Layla would have felt excluded from the setting; this is a regular occurrence for those with such complex conditions.

Both Sturrock and Hughes' work has given us more insight into our own self in the play cycle, and shown us a variety of tools as a means to examine and think about our own material. This has enabled us to work with others and with a platform to deliver both playwork and guidance to those with whom we work.

It is apparent that without the knowledge their work has given us, we would not have been able to provide the disabled children and young people in our care with understanding and support. We are able to comprehend behaviour and use techniques to reduce frustration and enhance communication.

The paradox here is that many of those with whom we have worked are either adult-dependent for their needs or are not given much time alone to play, owing to the required supervision levels. The growing duty for health and safety has a more detrimental effect in this area, as those with high supervision levels are usually at more risk of injury from self-harm. When this occurs the adult will commonly be held responsible.

Our final reflection in this area concerns those who depend on adults entirely. We have both been responsible for supporting children's play experiences and this has the possibility of becoming entirely adulterated, as we are both adults. Adults in this situation can find themselves compromised. Knowledge and education is vital if we are to allow children to develop their own play experience, as well as being able to rediscover or relearn how to play, ourselves.

The play cycle encourages us not to make assumptions about children and young people's ability or play preferences. Although this does not teach the range of complex needs, it helps us to understand that behaviour is not always deliberately inappropriate. It can be the child's way of letting us know they feel anxious, do not like what we are doing, or the way we are communicating.

Knowledge of annihilation is important, as we know not to pursue play if the child or young person wishes not to continue. It has displayed the importance of children and young people being in charge. We are there to support and facilitate play; it could be said that we are honoured to be part of the process.

The work of Sturrock and Hughes informs us so that we can understand the child at another level, support his/her play experience and communicate without actually verbalising in all circumstances.

We learn to look at the whole child and not just take him/her at face value. It would appear an obvious process, but from our experience this is often what happens when merging together more than one complex field: play for disabled children and young adults.

Chapter Seventeen

Playwork Learning –

Sharing the Journey

Bridget Handscomb and Michelle Virdi

> A theme, a thesis, is in most cases little more than a sort of clothes line on which one pegs a string of ideas, quotations, allusions and so on, one's mental undergarments of all shapes and sizes, some possibly fairly new but most rather old and patched; and they dance and sway in the breeze and flap and flutter, or hang limp and lifeless; and some ordinary enough, and some are of a private and intimate shape, and rather give the owner away, and show up his or her peculiarities. And owing to the invisible clothes line they seem to have some connexion and continuity. (Kenneth Grahame, *The Wind in the Willows* cited in Bennett 1994, p. 225)

A long time has passed between the initial idea of writing something as a joint contribution to acknowledge Bob and Gordon's work and getting our shared ideas into a single paper. It has been a difficult, yet entertaining process and the journey has been far more intricate and insightful than the end product is. There is something inevitable about the greater richness of travelling rather than arriving, as is any adventure into the realms of play and playwork.

Early in our discussions we decided to explore the aspects of playwork with which we have had most involvement. These relate to learning, development and reflective practice. We identified some possible titles such as 'The Essence of Playwork' (a parallel to that explored by Guilbaud 2003) or 'Playworkers' Ways' (from a more folklore-like tradition). We asked ourselves some key questions, such as 'Is there a playwork way of being, doing, thinking and learning?', 'How does the playwork way manifest itself in play, work or learning situations?', 'How does the spirit and practice of playwork emerge, evolve and express itself?' This fertile land led us to focus on what, if anything is different and special about playwork and playworkers. And then we spread ourselves so thinly across a vast terrain that there was no substance!

We considered the learning that takes place within individuals as well as between individuals and the significance of the learning journeys on which we embark, whether planned or unplanned. Through our many conversations, we also discussed 'levels' of our learning and understanding and tried to identify 'defining moments' in our own development as individuals and professionals.

Our next stage of discussions focused more on our own experiences of learning and some of the really special experiences we had shared, thanks to both Bob and Gordon either directly (through seminars, speeches, papers and conversations too numerous to recount) or indirectly (particularly through the years of experiencing PlayEd conferences and all they entailed). This took us on a journey of reminiscence and celebration of many weird, wonderful, wacky and even woeful presentations that had influenced our thinking and practice. Many people in the playwork world have probably shared similar moments of nostalgia and revisiting of memorable experiences. That was fun and contributes to reflective practice, but where are we in this journey?

We found ourselves going back to an earlier attempt at expressing some of these thoughts that Bridget had introduced at PlayEd 2004 in a workshop on reflective playwork practice (Hughes 2004) called 'Through the Looking Glass'. The direction from which our discussions seemed to flow here was towards a recognition that perhaps we learn (or certainly approach learning) differently in the playwork world from other practitioners and the rest of the Children's Workforce in general. Standard conference, training and adult learning approaches have their value but do not seem to capture the full essence of playwork learning at its best.

At this point we need to clarify for ourselves, are we concentrating on playworker's learning or playworker development? We were discussing both and going in and out of them with fluidity. Were we talking about the individual and internal process of learning as playwork people or is it about the more collective and external process of facilitating playworkers' development – two sides of the same coin. We realised that throughout our discussions we have been playing with both the idea of how we learn and how we facilitate learning within a playwork context and these notions had become interchangeable and symbiotic as in Wenger's (2005, p. 62) ideas on 'duality of purpose' – it is through their various combinations that we find a variety of experiences of meaning, they are mutually dependent concepts informing both our learning and practice.

We returned to the notion of the 'Playwork Way' and our particular way of learning, educating and training. Does it take a particular type of person to be in this work or maybe we respond to what we learn in a particular and different way because of the nature of the work? Or perhaps, it's both! Of course, all individuals have preferred and habitual modes of learning and to lump all playworkers together as the same is not the intention. The literature on personality types (for example, Boerce 1997), multiple intelligences (for example, Gardner cited in Smith 2002) and learning styles (for example, Honey and Mumford 2002) is vast and essential to inform the repertoire of any educator. In the light of the context for learning touched upon above, we suggest that our relationship to learning is complicated and constructed through our playful perceptions, meanings that we bring from our own play (Lester 2001), and on our playwork conceptions (ideas that we hold about playwork because of our beliefs and experiences).

The narrative of the playworker's life is as significant to the learning process as the curriculum, if not more so. This may be true of many adult learners, but learning about playwork requires a special kind of use of memory, reflection, intuition and creativity (Hughes 2001). Recognising the whole person – not just the learner but a playworker, a child, an adolescent, an adult, a carer – and ensuring that playfulness is integrated into the learning process is vital for effective playwork education to take place. This builds from the general learner issues such as reflection-in-action and reflection-on-action (Schön 1987, cited in Smith 2002) to the more specific playwork learner issues of adulteration and unplayed out material (Sturrock *et al.* 2004).

Palmer (2003) offers the following four suggestions for playwork educators and trainers and practitioners that capture play qualities:

- tell your own story
- talk to each other
- look for clues for how it may be in the future
- read widely.

Without 'knowing' this in a definite way it certainly appeared to be the process that we had accidentally fallen into in our preparation for writing this! Upon reflection, it has also been a feature of our joint and separate professional journeys over the last fifteen years or so, except perhaps for the final suggestion, wider reading having come into our practice relatively recently since we both became 'formal' learners as students ourselves.

Playwork learning and development taps into tacit knowledge described by Polanyi (Smith 2003) as 'all knowledge involving a personal and subjective component' within people's histories and experience, by using models of appreciative inquiry and communities of practice to address the 'how can you, how do you, how have you?' questions as a way of measuring the difference we made and continue to make. This can facilitate a learning culture, where appreciative inquiry becomes a key method of identifying developmental need, moving away from the more popular training needs-deficit model that we have been reliant upon until now.

Having touched on some relevant domains, we need to return to the centre of our position. If we take as a basic starting point an understanding of play as crucial to the evolution and survival of the species (Hughes 2006) and both a form of self-healing as well as necessary for maintaining health and well-being (Sturrock *et al.* 2004) we must connect this knowledge to examining our development as playworkers and playwork facilitators. For the same reasons that we recognise the importance of play for the survival and development of the human species, we need to identify and recognise what the impact of our involvement with people at play is on our own development. This is not purely about biological and cognitive aspects of development – the physical – but also the metaphysical. The social, emotional and spiritual, the more aesthetic experiences that contact with play behaviour brings.

We would like to focus briefly on two core concepts in relation to playwork education from the work of Sturrock and Hughes. These are, firstly, the importance of understanding adulteration, in particular the idea of 'unplayed-out material' (Sturrock 2003) and, secondly, the idea of a 'menagerie' that each individual brings with them (Stevens and Price 2000, cited in Hughes 2006, p. 10).

The purpose of focusing on these examples is to help examine what this means about the content and intent of playwork education. We consider that recognition of our own motivation to be involved with children at play may well be related to our own 'unplayed-out material' and, if we remain ignorant and unaware of this baggage, we will adulterate the play spaces we intend to protect. The same proposition can be made around the concept of 'menageries'. Hughes (2006) is referring not only to the 'crowd' of people we have been in our past life experiences that we carry with us but also the evolutionary ancestry of people that each individual in the species carries within them. A playworker not only requires an awareness of how these concepts relate to the behaviour they witness from playing children but also to their own and their colleagues' behaviour. For playwork education this requires a rethink of how learning opportunities are designed in order to foster this sensitive awareness to less obvious cues.

These two concepts in many ways illustrate the dilemma for playwork education. Where can they fit into the current qualifications and curriculum? How is the confusion about a trainer's occupational competence and who is and who is not competent resolved? How can they be addressed by the generic Children's Workforce priorities? If play is not seen and understood as core curriculum for all professionals working with children, there is little chance for a wider understanding of what it takes to support children's play. In a recent pilot to develop a multi-agency/professional National Induction Programme based on the Common Induction Standards, it was reassuring to see that play and its importance was included, and separately from child development. However, it was programmed in at the end of a day and predictably, ironically and inevitably got left out! In reality, it is probably best left off the agenda than included superficially, risking tokenism.

When we both came into the field (before Ofsted and SPRITO/ SkillsActive) there was not a standardised approach to playwork education and the development of courses was a very creative, novel, precious and ground-breaking experience. The questions that playworkers were asking was whether it was possible to train someone in playwork (was it only from experience and instinct that we developed as good playworkers) and was it desirable to have qualifications at all (or would it be élitist, exclusive and not bring the best people to the forefront of playwork).

There is a level of arrogance around some of these ideas but there is validity in revisiting and exploring the issues they throw up. A historical perspective can really challenge current assumptions and mind-sets, so, to prove that we are not being totally starry-eyed about those 'halcyon days,' we offer this comment from *The Invention of Childhood*, the book that accompanied a recent BBC Radio 4 series on British childhood:

But in the 1960s everything began to be tidied up, to be replaced by adventure playgrounds and play leaders, developments for which the Opies had nothing but contempt. As they put it in 1969, 'nothing extinguishes self-organised play more effectively than does action to promote it'. (Cunningham 2006, p. 129)

This statement is as relevant and as challenging today as it was then. The implication is reinforced through the more recent emerging theoretical base of playwork such as our understanding of 'intrinsic motivation' (Hughes 2001, p. 166) and play frames (Sturrock and Else 1998). The importance of 'not doing' is a central part of playwork practice and the professional development of playworkers.

In the 1980s there was a mixed approach to designing training and educational opportunities derived from the needs and aspirations of playworkers and play organisations. This resulted in huge diversity according to geography, demography, politics and personalities. However, there was a growing consensus about the ethos of playwork training and education. The emerging agreement, largely championed by the Joint National Committee on Training for Playwork (JNCTP), was that the style and content of courses should reflect the nature of playwork. We interpret this as ensuring that the process, mode and experience of learning had resonance with the experience of playwork. The methods and environment used were crucial to integrating a playwork approach in learning and this 'way of being' was often recognised as of equal or of higher value towards developing good playwork practice than the actual curriculum itself. Perhaps the 'low intervention and high response' playwork (Hughes 1996, p. 51–2) should be considered and emulated more in the learning environment.

Since the changes in the culture of playwork and the establishment of the Ofsted regime, qualifications have become more important than the learning experience. The quality assurance processes aimed at ensuring consistent standards stifle the very playful experiences that the ethos of playwork requires us to make possible. Conforming to standardised norms and rigid curricula has been problematic for all adult learning in the creative and people-centred sectors. We would argue that it is especially damaging within the playwork sector as the extremes of philosophy and approach collide.

We also suggest that there was a culture of playwork that influenced the accepted approach to education within the field. Historically, this can narrowly be defined as from the tradition of the adventure playground movement and the context of the free play services of the 1960s to 1980s.

This culture has been influenced by a strong community development, voluntary sector, bottom-up, autonomous organisational history. It has been in decline since the rate-capping Thatcherite era up to the current New Labour, childcare, fee-charging, top-down and outcome-driven agendas. Old playwork managed to keep its name but lose its identity to 'playcare' and in doing so the approach and expectations formulating playwork training has changed in parallel.

Playwork takes place within a constant tension between concepts and approaches such as conformity and individuality; control and freedom; work and play; order and chaos. This creates dilemmas and contradictions for the educative process that require a radical and adaptive response. Therefore, both the playworker and, in a close second place (along with the other playworkers in the shared learning environment), the person facilitating learning opportunities are central to the dialogue and explorative discourse that needs to ensue.

Our approach to playwork education intends to capture the significance and importance of placing the playworker at the centre of the learning process. It should recognise the range of experiences that participants have, including those of the playwork or childcare culture in which they are used to working; the playful experiences of their childhood (and beyond); their internal scripts of parenting and morality; their motivations and aspirations for being with children at play; existing relationships with other learners, providers or commissioners of the training they attend; and the baggage (both positive and negative) of previous educational situations throughout life. Our practice as playwork educators and facilitators needs to be constantly reflective of all of these factors and how they affect our own practice.

Some of the other characteristics of playwork that we might take from Hughes' (2002) intervention modes to inform our facilitation of playwork learning experiences have included:

- distance – observe and listen from a distance when facilitating smaller groups and pairs. Being tuned in without giving learners a sense that they are being watched and looking for cues, direct and indirect, to inform an approach;
- without preconceptions – where the focus is on learners' needs and the learning process. Any interventions are based on the needs of learners and maintaining the developmental capacity of the learning space but not on the basis of external agendas;

- permissional – where environments are facilitated where anything can happen and be discussed, unrestricted by notions of 'political correctness' and saying the right thing. Facilitating an environment in which learners are not censored. This can be difficult, especially in relation to issues around equality, diversity and inclusion;
- de-centred – facilitated learning interventions, which are analytical or diagnostic in a dispassionate way in order to inform the process. An example of this is observing, commenting and giving feedback on group processes, reflecting back to the group, having stood back to enable making sense of it for ourselves. Offering perceptions rather than insisting;
- without stereotypical narratives – where learners do not have to conform to ideas and stereotypes about how training and learning and courses should be based on their previous experiences, often negative, of school or of the organisation. It is about creating an appropriate learning environment in which learners are empowered and in control of both the content and pace of their learning.

Our own professional development journeys have been different chronologically but, through distinctive routes, we have covered much of the same terrain:

- group learning
- peer reflection and teamwork
- self-managed learning
- developmental playwork practice
- academic study
- conferences, workshops, seminars
- organisational development
- managerial and non-managerial supervision
- competence-based assessment.

The continued sharing and comparing of these experiences has provided us with both support and analysis that perpetuates each other's learning and development throughout an 'ever-changing fitness landscape' (Battram 2000). Some of the most enlightening experiences have come from unexpected sources. One such is embarking on Adult Education classes in the Alexander Technique. The total surprise and excitement of making connections between the methodology of observation, the use of kinaesthetic awareness and the philosophy of reflection in relation to making best use of our bodies had total resonance with ideas we were discussing around playwork. F. M. Alexander (2004) emphasises how much we can learn from children using the example of a toddler's posture as they balance their heads in the most effective and least stressful manner when they learn to walk. This recognition that there are things that children do better than adults and that we need to learn through respectful observation is a vital ingredient of our work.

Another rich source of learning was volunteering at ChildLine. The training towards developing a child-centred and non-judgemental empathy has been invaluable to considering communications and relationships between playworker and child. The commitment to preselection training, assessment, reflection, supervision, debriefs (group and one-to-one) and continuous professional development for all staff and volunteers is a model of organisational good practice. These high standards of professional practice enabled rapid and deep knowledge and skill acquisition that has stood the test of time and still impacts on many aspects of our own practice.

In conclusion, through describing this journey we have covered a lot of land but only turned over a few stones on the way. As with the beach, under each stone there is plenty to explore. The main themes seem to have been around:

- person-centred learning;
- the need to integrate the ever-emerging knowledge about play into all aspects of our learning and development;
- the responsibility of playwork facilitators continually to mirror and explore playwork ways through practice.

We are going to have to finish describing our travels thus far. It has been difficult to organise our thoughts into an easily navigated set of clearly marked and labelled information and, for that, we make no apology. The notion of packaging, templating and blueprinting the knowledge that we need to share with each other in the playwork field is a contradiction and leads to the oversimplification of subtle and complex understandings. We do apologise for the times as playwork professionals where we have lacked the knowledge, confidence or conviction to have recognised that our own intuition, memory and experience should have prevailed. We also acknowledge and celebrate the many times that both in our own practice and that of our colleagues we have succeeded in continuing to develop playwork ways.

> Soundlessly collateral and incompatible:
> World is suddener than we fancy it.
>
> World is crazier and more of it than we think,
> Incorrigibly plural. I peel and portion
> A tangerine and spit the pips and feel
> The drunkenness of things being various.
>
> (Louis MacNeice from *Snow* 1935)

Chapter Eighteen

'It's a Playful Life'

A Fantasy in Five Minutes

(with acknowledgments to Frank Capra)[1]

Perry Else, October 2006

The characters and events depicted in this story are fictitious.
Any similarity to actual persons, living or dead, is purely intentional.

'Move over, Lila', I muttered.

It had been a long day on the playground and I was sitting in the shoebox-sized office with Lila, the cat who had adopted the playground when we opened. We were so close in that tiny office that whenever she turned to stretch, her fur tickled my nose. I had just done a nine-hour shift and there was more to come that night at the management committee; we were debating (yet again) how to make our playwork more 'innovative' in order to comply with Big Lottery funding we needed to maintain our staff ratios. I loved my job but here I was with a degree in playwork and I always seemed to be chasing the next funding stream; there must be easier ways to make a living.

On the good days I knew that playwork was the only place for me, but the good days were getting fewer and fewer. On the bad days I thought I'd have been better as a teacher – better pay, longer holidays and no '*Psycholudics*'[2] or '*EPRAP*.'[3] (What did these guys think they were doing, coming up with terms like that??) I set about collecting my thoughts for the meeting; how could I make our work more innovative?

Could I talk about the way children play and the identification of play types?[4] Should I mention the play cycle and *The Colorado Paper*?[5] What about IMEE?[6] What about the metalude[7] and ludogogy?[8] (I remembered why people had complained about the language used in playwork when I had been studying.) What hope had I of convincing people that what we did was innovative; they'd first have to understand what I was saying!

Leafing through my files, I started collecting papers for the meeting. I pulled out many of the papers I had used in writing my playwork essays and made a list of the key ones; first of all Bob Hughes:[9]

- *Notes for Adventure Playworkers*
- *A Playworker's Taxonomy of Play Types*
- *Play Environments, A Question of Quality*
- *Lost Childhoods: The Case for Children's Play*
- *International Play Journals*
- *The First Claim: A Framework for Playwork Quality Assessment*
- *The First Claim: Desirable Processes*
- *Evolutionary Playwork and Reflective Analytic Practice*

Then Gordon Sturrock:[10]

- 'The sacred and the profane'
- 'A diet of worms'
- 'Child X as a case history'
- 'The survival self – An analysis of the effects of survival in a sectarian environment'
- 'The playground as therapeutic space: Playwork as healing'
- 'The impossible science of the unique being'
- 'North of the future – Reverie, imagination and fantasy as a ludic ecology'
- 'The ludic third'
- 'The beauty of play – An attempt at an aesthetic definition of play and playwork'
- 'Towards Ludogogy'

It was daunting looking at those weighty tomes. 'It could be so much easier if these guys hadn't written all these papers', I said aloud.

Only Lila was listening, though I thought I heard a quiet voice say, 'OK'.

Just then the door blew open; 'Who's there?' I said, but no one replied.

I got up and looked around the play building; it was deserted. When I went back into the office, Lila looked at me for a moment with her large round eyes, and then went back to her grooming.

The next ten minutes were spent making notes about our work and then I thought I should put the kettle on to boil, the committee was expected any minute and everyone always wanted a cuppa before we started the meeting.

That night the committee meeting was particularly difficult; no one could agree with a word I said. I'd started by saying that we should support innovation in the way that children accessed play – sadly it was 'innovative' for some children to play outside, build structures, light fires. I listed Hughes' *Elements of a rich play environment*[11] but people looked at me as though I was talking a foreign language.

I'd been shouted down by at least three committee members; too dangerous, too risky, what about the fear of litigation and complaints from parents? The ones who didn't shout stared at me with a puzzled look on their faces and shook their heads. I thought we'd been through these arguments before but tonight the members seemed particularly stubborn.

Another tack; what about promoting free choice through play as a means of supporting the five outcomes in *Every Child Matters*?[12] At last, something I thought we could agree on – until the Chair listed the five outcomes as:

- staying fit
- safety and security
- getting good grades
- being a competent citizen
- earning a wage

'Where's enjoyment?' I asked, perhaps a little too loudly. 'We fought long and hard in the play sector to get that in there. Surely play should be freely chosen, personally directed and intrinsically motivated as it is vital in a child's development …' But then the Chair called order and suggested a brief 'comfort break'. I retreated into my office to collect my thoughts.

The computer was still on, with Lila sat on the monitor to keep warm. I gently pushed her out of the way so I could Google 'five outcomes'. There they were on the DfES website – but just as listed by the Chair – there was no 'being healthy', no 'enjoying and achieving'; things we could contribute to in the playwork sector. I tried again and typed in 'Children's Play Council'. It came up with; 'Children's Council – the agency for promoting good citizens.'

'A different tack', I thought 'Bob Hughes' must be on the web.' He was – but not as I'd seen him before:

- Bob Hughes, Real Estate Agent buying and selling homes in the Central Virginia area

- Bob Hughes, Bottom Diver, Scaffolding, In-water Drinking System
- Bob Hughes Christian School
- Bob Hughes, author of *Dust or Magic* (a study of the history of computer-based media and its working culture)

The 'Toys-R-Bob' Show was the nearest I found, where Bob was lecturing on the importance of change in schools. No references to play, playwork, EPRAP or play types. By now I was getting desperate so Googled 'Gordon Sturrock'. The same thing happened:

- Gordon Sturrock (founder of Squadron 13 and Veterans Against Torture) in Eugene, Oregon
- Gordon Sturrock: Community care: helping others
- Flights of Thought on War and Politics by avatar Gordon Sturrock
- On a Scottish cemetery site: Sturrock, Gordon, d. 23 June 1961

'What's happened?' I asked; this was getting spooky. I tried another approach. Bob Hughes had done a lot of work for Play Wales. I looked for them on the Web – no reference. I typed in 'Spirit of adventure play', their relaunch of the adventure play movement, and all I found was a reference to a poster company. Something strange was happening; it was as if creative and adventurous playwork had been wiped off the Internet.

Looking back at my notes on the playwork papers I'd collected, I saw Wendy Russell in there. I tried her name and found no references to Wendy Russell teaching on the playwork course at Gloucestershire University but came up with hundreds of references to a famous jazz saxophonist who was working with Andy Shepherd and Courtney Pine to explore the 'Third Sax' – a new direction in jazz fusion and world music.

I tried again; I knew that someone called Perry Else had done a lot of work with Gordon Sturrock. But a Google on his name only produced a blog on a guy who was searching for his 'inner child'. He worked in the finance department of a big local authority and was blogging to share his thoughts on new age thinking:

My inner child is sixteen years old!
Life's not fair! It's never been fair, but while adults might just accept that, I know something's got to change. And it's going to change, just as soon as I become an adult and get some power of my own.

Some people need to get a life. I turned to 'Ask Jeeves'. I typed in 'Bob Hughes, Playwork theorist' and pressed 'Enter'.

> Your search for **Bob Hughes, Playwork theorist** did not match with any Web results. Please try your search again.

In desperation I typed in 'What has happened to Bob Hughes, Playwork theorist?' At that moment Lila looking for a warm spot in the tiny office jumped back up on the monitor. 'Scram!' I said and gently pushed her aside. When I looked back at the screen, 'Jeeves' had answered me:

> Your search for **What has happened to Bob Hughes, Playwork theorist** did not match with any Web results. What would you like to know?

I typed in: 'I cannot find reference to Bob Hughes, Playwork theorist. Where is he now?'

> Please define **Playwork** before I can proceed.

The work was all to hand so I entered:

> The key purpose of playwork is to support, rather than direct or control, the play process. This support is effected through the creation, operation and modification of rich physical and social environments that maximise opportunities for children to engage in a wide variety of play types.[13]

Whoever operated 'Jeeves' had a sense of humour:

> Too many words. Please define **Play Process** in fewer words before I can proceed.

Quoting the JNCTP I entered:

> Play is an innate drive and is essential for human development. It is manifested as behaviour that is freely chosen, personally directed and intrinsically motivated. The value of play derives from the play process itself, not from any extrinsic goal, reward or end product.[14]

But I wasn't going to get off that easy:

> Please define **Play Process** (in fewer words) before I can proceed.

I started with ...

> Play is a process that is freely chosen, personally directed and intrinsically motivated. That is, children and young people determine and control the content and intent of their play, by following their own instincts, ideas and interests, in their own way for their own reasons.[15]

... But knew I wasn't going to get away with that so I tried my own words:

> Play is a process where children choose the content and purpose of their actions, following their own instincts, ideas and interests, in their own way for their own reasons.

'Jeeves' answered me:

> Thank you. Earlier you asked: **What has happened to Bob Hughes, Playwork theorist?** Your search did not match with any Web results. Would you like me to search for related terms?

Thinking I was getting somewhere I typed in: 'Search for "play types, Bob Hughes"'.

> Your search for **play types, Bob Hughes** did not match with any Web results. However **play types** has produced the following results:

> West Greenland **Play Types**
> GHEXIS Online, Exploration History. West Greenland: Early Exploration (1970–78), Recent Exploration (1988 to Present Day). East Greenland: The NAD Project ...
> www.geus.dk/ghexis/**play**-typ.htm – 33k – Cached – Similar pages

> Historical Database of Folk **Play** Scripts

> The second main **type** of **play** is the Plough **Play**, found in the English

East Midlands. They are usually associated with Plough Monday (the first Monday after ...
www.folk**play**.info / Texts.htm – 33k – <u>Cached</u> – <u>Similar pages</u>

<u>PartyPoker.com – How to **Play** – **Types** of Wins</u>

There are five **types** of Blackjack wins (Blackjack, normal win, push, insurance   and   surrender)   find   out   about   them   here. www.partypoker.com / how_to_**play** / blackjack / **types**_of_wins.html – 13k – <u>Cached</u> – <u>Similar pages</u>

Play

This page discusses the general **play types** in the North Falkland Basin. ... A variety of **play types** were planned to be targeted by the 1998 drilling ...
www.bgs.ac.uk / falklands-oil / NFB / **play**.HTM – 11k – <u>Cached</u> – <u>Similar pages</u>
Would you like me to search for more answers?

Following them all up only took a few clicks but I was still not getting the answer I was looking for. In my world, Bob Hughes had produced a list of sixteen Play Types:

Symbolic Play, Rough and Tumble Play, Socio-dramatic Play, Social Play, Creative Play, Communication Play, Dramatic Play, Deep Play, Exploratory Play, Fantasy Play, Imaginative Play, Locomotor Play, Mastery Play, Object Play, Role Play, Recapitulative Play

But none of these was listed on the web. I was beginning to realise that something very wrong had happened ... I got up from my chair and went back into the meeting room. People were still chatting and making tea; I needed a bit of space so I went outside. What a shock I got.

In the place where all our play structures used to be was 'catalogue hell'. The private places of the children that we had built over the last year had been replaced by brightly coloured, properly designed, boring 'play huts' and swings. The sand pit had been covered over with 'nice' artificial turf. The handmade benches around the fire pit had been swapped for park benches, with a little sign saying 'For Adults Only'. The fire pit wasn't a pit any more but held a litter bin. The graffiti wall had been replaced by a long set of rules that started with 'No swearing'.

'F@!$ – what's happened?' I said, turning back towards the building.

That's when I got the biggest shock of all. Over the doorway to our building had been a child-painted sign saying, 'Everyone's Adventure Playground – open to all children.' Now it had a bright plastic shop sign proudly saying, 'Everyone's Children's Centre – where play is a child's work.'

Not trusting what I'd get from my committee members, I went back to my inner sanctum to collect my thoughts. 'Jeeves' was still asking,

Would you like me to search for more answers?

In desperation I typed in, 'What's happened? Everything seems to have changed for the worse. Where has real play gone?'

The computer blinked and the download button showed activity, then 'Jeeves' answered me:

Are you not happy? Your wish has been granted.

Confused, I asked 'What wish??'

Earlier you said: 'It could be so much easier if these guys hadn't written all these papers.' Your wish has been granted.

Realisation was dawning but I needed verification: 'You're saying all this has happened because Bob Hughes and Gordon Sturrock have not written all those papers on play?

Strange, isn't it? Each person's life touches so many other lives. When they aren't around they leave an awful hole, don't they?[16]

This can't be true, I thought. That can't be right; lots of other people have had an influence on playwork. I know that Paul Bonel is Director of the Playwork Unit at SkillsActive. I typed in another question; 'show me SkillsActive' and hit Enter.

I felt relieved when the screen showed:

Paul Bonel, Director of the Playwork Unit at SkillsActive, said: 'This is a real achievement for children and young people and delivers a strong message about the Government's commitment to children's play.'

Feeling more confident I typed in Children's Commissioner: I was stunned when the answer came back:

Children's Commissioner for England: Esther Rantzen.

Since her campaigning days on 'That's Life!' Esther has been a tireless champion for children's play safety. Single-handedly she has ensured that every child's play centre has the appropriate safety surfacing. 'I'm proud of the fact that millions of pounds has been spent securing the health of our nation's children,' Esther said recently. 'Now every child can grow up safe in the fact that they will not get a grazed knee on their local playground.'

Looking at the pile of books on my desk I picked a few names at random: 'Show me Mick Conway' and hit Enter.

Mick Conway's National Junk Band

Mick Conway's National Junk Band is alive and kicking as the studio audience for this outrageous concert can confirm. Conway's genius is for a clever combination of the absurd and witty with tremendous musicality. That combination first surfaced in the 1970s when Mick and his brother Jim Conway founded the much loved group, the Captain Matchbox Whoopee Band.

Instruments are many and varied, including sousaphone, the saw, ukulele, phono-fiddle, National guitar, and even a kitchen sink and a garbage can.

Fans have described the band as follows:
'the Sex Pistols meets Bing Crosby'
'bluesy with a touch of Monty Python'
'extreme entertainment'
'layer upon layer of insanity, lunacy, anarchy'

... 'Show me Arthur Battram' and hit Enter.

NAVIGATING COMPLEXITY with DIPLOMACY
with Arthur Battram

Arthur is Director of Californian-based company Plexity. Creator of

PossibilitySpaceDesign, Arthur made his first million through a franchised deal with Microsoft. Since that time Battram and Bill have been close friends ...

... 'Show me Annie Davy' and hit Enter.

Bristol Cathedral School, College Square, Bristol, BS1 5TS
Whom to contact at School:
The Head, Mrs Annie Davy, is available to speak to any pupil or parent on any matter. Please contact her PA on 0117 925 4545 to make an appointment, or email head@bristolcathedral.org.uk.

... 'Show me playwork interventions' and hit Enter; I was terrified by what I saw next:

The Play Intervention of Choice – a joy-inducing neurotransmitter
Now prescribed to over five million children in the UK
Methylphenidate (MPH) is an amphetamine-like prescription stimulant commonly used to treat Attention Deficit Hyperactivity Disorder (ADHD) in children and adults. Brand names of drugs that contain methylphenidate include Ritalin®, Methylin® and Rubifen®.

Like cocaine, methylphenidate is a powerful stimulant that increases alertness and productivity. Methylphenidate and cocaine have similar chemical structures. Their effects, too, are similar; both increase the brain-levels of dopamine – a joy-inducing neurotransmitter – by blocking the ability of neurons to reabsorb dopamine. Methylphenidate is like low-dosage, slow-acting cocaine.

'I luv it' says Dwayne (9), 'I cn play on PS5 fro 12 hrrs non-stop + get loads high scores.'

'Its wikid for him + me,' said Dwayne's mum Kimberline (19). 'I dont need to pay no money 4 skool as hes safe home alone all day.'

'This is all wrong – these guys can't have had all that influence!' I wrote. 'What about all those playworkers at PlayEducation over the years where are they?'

Those playworkers never met to play and share ideas.

'That's a lie! Bob Hughes organised PlayEducation for over 20 years – he influenced playwork for thousands of workers.'

Every playworker found another profession! They weren't there to develop playwork, because Bob wasn't there to run PlayEducation ...

'But the Play Cycle and *The Colorado Paper* have been quoted in 50 play books and on thousands of websites. Gordon Sturrock has taught and presented his work to hundreds of playwork students over the years ...'

Every student found another course in childcare! They weren't there to learn about playwork, because Gordon wasn't there to teach them about the play cycle ...

You've been given a great gift: A chance to see what the world would be like without their contribution. Bob and Gordon really helped the UK have a more playful life. Don't you see what a mistake it would be to just throw it away?

'What have I done!!!' I cried. 'I wish I could take it all back; please take it all back to how it was.' In frustration I pushed the keyboard aside, to rest my head on the table top. Lila came down from her resting place and started nuzzling the back of my neck. She was rubbing her chin on the back of my head and beginning to purr a little.

The door to the office opened and a soft voice asked: 'Is everything OK? You've been in here quite a while ... We need to get on with our application.'

It was Bridget, our Chair; up til now the tireless defender of the adventure playground and all the children who used it. After all that had happened, I wasn't ready for any more nonsense, so I said

'What's the point? It's an anti-play world out there and we've so much to do.'

'Been a long day has it? I see you've been doing lots of preparation on our behalf, Play England, Best Play and all that theory stuff by Bob Hughes and Gordon Sturrock – I don't know how you get your head round it all. But I do know that it's all worth it; if we help give more play opportunities to just five more children, it makes it all worthwhile.'

'What? You can see all this can you?' I agreed with every word Bridget said, but was more amazed that she'd said it after all I'd seen on the Net.

'Course I can', she said, 'But don't ask me to say what it all means – that's your job. Are you coming back in? We have this application to finish!'

'I'll be right there,' I replied – 'Just got one more thing to do.'

I pushed Lila aside and got back on my keyboard. 'Jeeves' was still there waiting for me to type in my search criteria. Feeling confident, I typed in 'eminent playwork theorists Hughes Sturrock' and pressed the key.

Results **1 – 10** of about **30,000** for **eminent playwork theorists Hughes Sturrock** (0.35 seconds)

Amazon.co.uk: Evolutionary **Playwork** and Reflective Analytic ...

Amazon.co.uk: Evolutionary **Playwork** and Reflective Analytic Practice: Books: **Bob Hughes** by **Bob Hughes**. www.amazon.co.uk/Evolutionary-**Playwork**-Reflective-Analytic-Practice/dp/0415251664 – 57k – Cached – Similar pages

Play Wales – **Bob Hughes**

Bob Hughes is the National Co-ordinator for Play Education, an Advisor to the US Committee on Training and Education in **Playwork**, and a member of the NPFA ... www.playwales.org.uk/people/index.php?pg=**bobhughes**&lang=english – 7k – Cached – Similar pages

Play Wales – **Playwork** Principles

The **Playwork** Values and Assumptions were developed during the drafting of the ... **Gordon Sturrock** is more than middle-aged and still enjoys playing. ... www.chwaraecymru.org.uk/values/index.php?pg=faq&lang=english – 19k – Cached – Similar pages

[**PDF**] Scottish **Playwork** Revolution Programme

File Format: PDF/Adobe Acrobat – View as HTML
In conversation with **Gordon Sturrock**. Clyde. Recruitment, Selection. Drew McCanney. TR1. & Child Protection. Exploring the

new SVQ Level 3 in **Playwork** ...
www.vhscotland.org.uk/events/conf/Scottish%20**Playwork**%20Rev
olution%20Programme.pdf – Similar pages

Play Wales – **Playwork** Principles

Bob Hughes, Gordon Sturrock and Mick Conway produced papers
that put the Phase 1 proposals for the **Playwork** Principles into
context. ...
www.playwales.org.uk/values/index.php?pg=supportingmateri-
als&lang=english – 12k – Cached – Similar pages

Things were back to normal. With a smile, I carefully placed Lila back on
the warm spot, picked up my papers and went back into the play room.
We began to fill out that Big Lottery application, and guess what – it was
pretty innovative and playful.

Notes

[1] Title adapted from *It's a Wonderful Life*, directed by Frank Capra (1946). It's a
dark, bittersweet tale in which James Stuart plays a man who never quite
manages to leave his home town, yet has a profound influence on everyone
around him. He only realises the impact he's had when he's shown what the
world would be like without him in it.

[2] Sturrock, G. and Else, P. (1998) 'The playground as therapeutic space:
Playwork as healing' (known as *The Colorado Paper*), Sheffield: Ludemos.

[3] Hughes, B. (2001) *Evolutionary Playwork and Reflective Analytic Practice*.
London: Routledge.

[4] Hughes, B. (2002) *A Playworker's Taxonomy of Play Types* (2nd edition 2002).
Available from PlayEducation, 13 Castelhythe, Ely, Cambs CB7 4BU

[5] Sturrock, G. and Else, P. (1998) as cited.

[6] Hughes, B. (1996) *Play Environments, A Question of Quality*. Ely: PlayEducation.

[7] Sturrock, G. and Else, P. (1998) as cited.

[8] Sturrock, G., Russell W. and Else, P. (2005) 'Towards Ludogogy' in
Therapeutic Playwork Reader Two. Sheffield: Ludemos.

[9] Bob Hughes' papers and books
> *Notes for Adventure Playworkers* (1975) out of print.
> *A Playworker's Taxonomy of Play Types* (1996a, 2002) London: Playlink.
> *Play Environments, A Question of Quality* (1996) London: Playlink.
> *Lost Childhoods: The Case for Children's Play* (1994) London: Demos.
> *International Play Journals* (1993–96) London: E&FN Spon.
> *The First Claim: A Framework for Playwork Quality Assessment* (2001)
> Cardiff: Play Wales.

The First Claim: Desirable Processes (2003) Cardiff: Play Wales.

Evolutionary Playwork and Reflective Analytic Practice (2001) London: Routledge.

[10] Gordon Sturrock's papers and articles (all available from www. ludemos.co.uk):

'The sacred and the profane' (1995)

'A diet of worms' (1996)

'Child X as a case history' (1997)

'The survival self – An analysis of the effects of survival in a sectarian environment' (1997)

'The playground as therapeutic space: Playwork as healing' (1998)

'The impossible science of the unique being' (1999)

'North of the future – Reverie, imagination and fantasy as a ludic ecology'

'The ludic third' (2003)

'The beauty of play – An attempt at an aesthetic definition of play and playwork' (2003)

'Towards Ludogogy' (2005)

[11] Hughes, B. (1996) as cited.

[12] Accessed 14/10/2006: http://www.everychildmatters.gov.uk/.

[13] JNCTP (2002) The New JNCTP Charter for Playwork Education, Training and Qualifications.

[14] JNCTP (2002) as cited.

[15] Accessed 14/10/2006: http://www.playwales.org.uk/values.

[16] Text adapted from *It's a Wonderful Life* directed by Frank Capra (1946)

And miscellaneous websites, too many mention (but most are there, honest!)

With apologies and deep respect to my 'victims':
- Wendy Russell: playwork lecturer, trainer and consultant
- Paul Bonel: author and Director of the Playwork Unit, SkillsActive
- Mick Conway: Play England expert, author and practitioner
- Arthur Battram: author, management consultant and trainer
- Annie Davy: author, manager and practitioner

References

Abernethy, D. (1974) *Adventure Playgrounds – Meeting the Needs of the Community*. London: NPFA.

Abernethy, D. (undated) *Playleadership – Its Significance for the Unattached*. London: NPFA.

Alexander, F. M. (2004) *Constructive Conscious Control of the Individual*. London: Mouritz.

Andrews, I. (1983) 'The creation of play work posts and an analysis of the philosophy underpinning adventure play', unpublished MA Thesis. Anglia Polytechnic.

Armitage, M. (2005) 'The influence of school architecture and design on the outdoor play experience within the primary school'. *Paedogogica Historica,* vol. 41 (nos 4 and 5) pp 535–53.

Assagioli, R. (1965). *Psychosynthesis: A Manual of Principles and Techniques*. New York and Buenos Aires: Hobbs, Dorman and Company.

Attwood, T. (1998) *Asperger's Syndrome. A Guide for Parents and Professionals*. London: Jessica Kingsley Publishers.

Bakhtin, M. (1981) *The Dialogical Imagination*. Austin: University of Texas Press.

Baldock, P. (1974) *Community Work and Social Work*. London: Routledge.

Bandler, R. and Grinder, J. (1982) *Reframing: Neurolinguistic Programming and the Transformation of Meaning*. Utah: Real People Press.

Barnes, P. (1995) *Personal, Social & Emotional Development of Children*. London: Blackwell.

Barnes, S. (2006) 'I'm not a saint'. *The Times*, 13 November.

Baron-Cohen, S. (2004) *The Essential Difference – The Truth about the Male and Female Brain*. London: Penguin.

Bateson, G. (1954) 'A theory of play and fantasy', in Bateson, G. (1972, 2000) *Steps to an Ecology of Mind*. Chicago: University of Chicago Press.

Bateson, P. and Martin, P. (1999) *Design for Life: How Behaviour Develops.* London: Cape.

Battram, A. (2000) *Navigating Complexity.* London: Industrial Society.

Battram, A. (2007, reprint in preparation) *Navigating Complexity: The Essential Guide to Complexity Theory in Business and Management.* Wensley: LudelicPress.

Beaton, C. (1954) *The Glass of Fashion*, London: Weidenfeld and Nicholson.

Beiser, F. (2005) *Schiller as Philosopher.* Oxford: Clarendon Press.

Belenky, M., Clinchy, B., Goldberger, N. and Tarule, J. (1986) *Women's Ways of Knowing.* Basic Books: New York.

Benjamin, J. (1961) *In Search of Adventure: A Study of the junk playground.* London: NCSS.

Benjamin, J. (1972) *Grounds for Play*, London: Bedford Press.

Benjamin, J. (1992) 'Play and Participation,' in *Streetwise* 2 (Autumn), 2–8.

Bennett, A. (1994) *Writing Home.* London: Faber and Faber.

Bloom B. S. (1956). *Taxonomy of Educational Objectives, Handbook I: The Cognitive Domain.* New York: David McKay Co Inc.

Boeree, C. G. (1997) *Personality Theories: An Electronic Textbook* [on-line] Available from http://www.ship.edu/~cgboeree/perscontents.html [Accessed 20/12/06].

Bonel, P. and Lindon, J. (1996) *Good Practice in Playwork.* Cheltenham: Stanley Thornes (Publishers) Ltd.

Bowen, W. P. and Mitchell, E. D. (1927) *The Theory of Organized Play. Its Nature and Significance.* New York: Barnes and Company.

Braun, A. (2004) 'The future of play, learning and creativity', in *Documentation of a LEGO Institute*, Symposium held in Hamburg, Germany.

Bronfenbrenner, U. (1979) *The Ecology of Human Development: Experiments by Nature and Design.* Cambridge, MA: Harvard University Press.

Brown, F. (2003) 'Compound flexibility – SPICE revisited', In: Brown F., (ed.) (2003) *Playwork: Theory and Practice.* Buckingham: Open University Press.

Brown, S. (1998) 'Play as an organising principle: Clinical evidence and personal observations', in Bekoff M. and Byers, J. A. (eds) *Animal Play: Evolutionary, Comparative and Ecological Perspectives.* Cambridge: Cambridge University Press.

Buck, D. (1965) Report on the Relevance of an Adventure Playground to the Study and Control of Juvenile Delinquency (unpublished): NPFA Children's Play Information Centre.

Burghardt, G. M. (1998) 'The evolutionary origins of play revisited: Lessons from turtles', in Bekoff M. and Byers J. A. (eds) *Animal Play: Evolutionary, Comparative and Ecological Perspectives.* Cambridge: Cambridge University Press.

Burghardt, G. M. (2005) *The Genesis of Animal Play: Testing the limits.* MA: Massachusetts Institute of Technology.

Burton, R. (1621) *Anatomy of Melancholy.*

Carpenter, E. (1976) *Oh What a Blow that Phantom Gave Me!* London: Flamingo.

Carse, J. (1986) *Finite and Infinite Games: A Vision of Life and Play and Possibility.* New York: The Ballantine Publishing Group.

Cass, J. E. (1971) *The Significance of Children's Play.* London: Batsford.

Chambers, S. A. (2001) *Language and Politics: Agonistic Discourse in 'The West Wing'* [online] CTHEORY Available from http://www.ctheory.net/articles.aspx?id=317 [Accessed 13/1/07].

Chatwin, B. (1988) *Songlines.* London: Viking.

Children's Play Council (1998) *The New Charter for Children's Play.* London: National Children's Bureau.

Children's Play Council (2002) *More Than Swings and Roundabouts: Planning for Outdoor Play.* London: National Children's Bureau.

Clandinin, D. and Connelly, F. (1995) *Teachers' Professional Knowledge Landscapes.* New York: Teachers College Press.

Clark, D. (1999) *Learning Domains or Bloom's Taxonomy: Three types of Learning.*[online] Big Dog Little Dog. Available from http://www.nwlink.com/~donclark/hrd/bloom.html [Accessed 1/1/07].

Conway, M. and Farley, T. (1999) *Quality in Play.* London: London Play.

Conway, M., Hughes, B. and Sturrock, G. (2004) *A New Perspective for Playwork.* Sheffield: Ludemos.

Corsaro, W. (1985) *Friendship and Peer Culture in the Early Years.* Norwood, NJ: Ablex.

Cowe, E. G. (1982) *Free Play Organisation and Management in the Pre-School Kindergarten.* Illinois: Thomas.

Cranwell, K. (2001) 'Street play and organised space for children and young people in London (1860–1920)' in Jeffs *et al.* (ed.) *Essays in the History of Community and Youth Work.* Leicester: Youth Work Press.

Cranwell, K. (2003) 'Towards playwork: An historical introduction to children's out-of-school play organisations in London (1860–1940)', in Brown, F. (ed.) *Playwork Theory and Practice.* Buckingham: Open University Press.

Cranwell, K (2003) 'Towards a history of adventure playgrounds

(1931–2000),' in N. Norman, *An Architecture of Play: A Survey of London's Adventure Playgrounds*. London: Four Corners.

Cunningham, H. (2006) *The Invention of Childhood*. London: BBC Books.

Cunningham, P. (2002) 'Primary Education', in Aldrich, R. (ed.) *A Century of Education*. London: Falmer.

Daloz, L. (1999) *Mentor: Guiding the Journey of Adult Learners*. San Francisco: Jossey-Bass.

Damasio, A. (1994) *Descartes Error. Emotion, Reason and the Human Brain*. New York: HarperCollins.

Damasio, A. R. (2000) *The Feeling of What Happens: Body, Emotion and the Making of Consciousness*. London: Vintage.

Damasio, A. (2003) *Looking for Spinoza*. London: William Heinemann.

Danby, S. (1972) *Big Hill Adventure Playground*. London: NPFA.

Dave, R. H. (1975) *Developing and Writing Behavioural Objectives*. (R J Armstrong, ed.) Educational Innovators Press.

Davies, B. (1999) *From Voluntaryism to Welfare State*. Leicester: Youth Work Press.

Deleuze, G. (1997) *Essays Critical and Clinical*. London: Verso Books.

de Shazer, S., cited in Jackson, P. and McKergow, M. (2002) *The Solutions Focus*. London: Nicholas Brealey Publishing.

De Sousa, R. (1987) *The Rationality of Emotion*. Cambridge: MIT Press.

Dockar-Drysdale, B. (1991) *The Provision of Primary Experience: Winnicottian Work with Children and Adolescents*. Northvale, NJ: Jason Aronson Inc.

Dunmore, H. (1998) 'The Red Dress', in Dunseath, K. (ed.) *A Second Skin, Women Write about Clothes*. London: The Women's Press.

Edwards, B. (2001) *Drawing on the Right Side of the Brain*. USA: Tarcher/Penguin.

Eibl-Eibesfeldt, I. (1970) *Ethology: The Biology of Behaviour*. New York: Holt, Rinehart and Winston.

Else, P. (2003) 'Play – a beautiful intelligence', in Sturrock G. and Else P. (eds) *Therapeutic Playwork Reader 2*, Sheffield: Ludemos.

Else, P. (2006) Personal communication, 22/12/2006.

Fagen, R. (1975) 'Modelling how and why play works', in Bruner, J., Jolly, A. and Sylva, K. (eds.) (1976) *Play – Its Role in Development and Evolution*. Harmondsworth: Penguin.

Fogel, A., de Koeyer, I., Bellagamba, F. and Bell, H. (2002) 'The dialogical self in the first two years of life: Embarking on a journey of discovery'. *Theory and Psychology*, Vol. 12 no. 2, 191–205.

Freud, A. (1942) *Young Children in Wartime*. London: Allen and Unwin.

Gallese, V. (2003) 'The manifold nature of interpersonal relations: the quest for a common mechanism'. *Transactions of the Royal Society*, 358, 517–28.

Gallese, V., Keysers, C. and Rizzolatti, G. (2004) 'A unifying view of the basis of social cognition'. *Trends in Cognitive Science*, Vol. 8, no. 9, 396–403.

Garvey, C. (1977) *Play*. London: Fontana.

Glasgow, A. (1991) *The Socialist ABC* from *Songs of Alex Glasgow*, MWM Records Ltd.

Goffman, E. (1975) *Frame Analysis*. Harmondsworth: Penguin Books.

Goleman, D. (1995) *Emotional Intelligence*. New York: Bantam Books.

Goldberg, S. (1993) *The Inevitability of Patriarchy*. Peru, Illinois: Open Court.

Gritti, A., Vescovi, A. and Galli, R. (2002) 'Adult neural stem cells: Plasticity and developmental potential'. *Journal of Physiology*, Vol. 96, no. 1–2, 81–90.

Guilbaud, S. (2003) 'The essence of play', In Brown, F. (ed.) *Playwork Theory and Practice* Buckingham: Open University Press.

Harrow, A. (1972) *A taxonomy of psychomotor domain — a guide for developing behavioral objectives*. New York: David McKay.

Harris, J. R. (1998) *The Nurture Assumption*. London: Bloomsbury.

Hendricks, B. (2001) *Designing for Play*. Aldershot: Ashgate.

Hermans, H. (1996) 'Voicing the self: From information processing to dialogical interchange'. *Psychological Bulletin*, Vol. 119, 31–50.

Hermans, H. (2001) 'The dialogical self: Toward a theory of personal and cultural positioning. *Culture and Psychology*, Vol. 7, no. 3, 243–81.

Hermans. H. (2002) 'The dialogical self as a Society of Mind. *Theory and Psychology*, Vol. 12, no. 2, 147–160.

Hermans, H. (2003) The construction and deconstruction of a dialogical self'. *Journal of Constructivist Psychology*, Vol. 16, 89–130.

Hermans, H. (2006) 'The self as a theatre of voices: Disorganisation and reorganisation of a position repertoire'. *Journal of Constructivist Psychology*, Vol. 19, 147–69.

Hermans, H., Kempen, H. & Van Loon, R. (1992) 'The dialogical self: Beyond individualism and rationalism'. *American Psychologist*, Vol. 47, 23–33.

Hermans, H. and Kempen, H. (1995) 'Body, mind and culture: The dialogical nature of mediated action'. *Culture and Psychology*, Vol. 1, 103–114.

Holdstock, R. (2003) *Mythago Wood*. Orb Books.

Holman, B. (2001) *Champions for Children: The lives of modern childcare pioneers*. Bristol: Policy Press.

Holme, A. and Massie, P. (1970) *Children's Play: A Study of Needs and Opportunities*. London: Michael Joseph Ltd.

Holt, J. (1972) *Freedom and Beyond*, Harmondsworth: Pelican.

Honey, P. and Mumford, A. (2002) *Learning Styles Questionnaire*. Maidenhead: Peter Honey Publishers.

Hope, A. and Timmel, S. (1999) *Training for Transformation: A Handbook for Community workers*, Vol 4. London: ITDG Publishing.

Hrdy, S. (1999) *Mother Nature: Natural Selection and the Female of the Species*. London: Chatto and Windus.

Huber, J. and Whelen, K. (1999) 'A marginal story as a place of possibility: Negotiating self on the professional knowledge landscape'. *Teaching and Teacher Education*, Vol. 15, 381–96.

Hughes, B. (1975) *Notes for Adventure Playworkers*. Ely: PlayEducation.

Hughes, B. (ed.) (1993–96) *International Play Journals*. London: E&FN Spon.

Hughes, B. (1994) *Lost Childhoods: The Case for Children's Play*. London: Demos.

Hughes, B. (1996a) *Play Environments: A Question of Quality*. London: PlayLink.

Hughes, B. (1996b) *A Playworker's Taxonomy of Play Types*, 1st edition. London: PlayLink.

Hughes B. (1999) The HPA Design and Build Project, An Evaluation, Ely: PlayEducation.

Hughes, B. (2001) *Evolutionary Playwork and Reflective Analytical Practice*. London: Routledge.

Hughes, B. (2002a) *A Playworker's Taxonomy of Play Types, 2nd edition*. London: PlayLink.

Hughes, B. (2002b) *The First Claim – Desirable Processes*. Cardiff: Play Wales.

Hughes, B. (2004) *PlayEducation Conference Papers*. Ely: PlayEducation.

Hughes, B. (2006) *Play Types: Speculations and Possibilities*. London: London Centre for Playwork Education and Training.

Hughes, B. and Williams, H. (1984) Looking at Play – 1, *Play Times*, Vol. 8. London: NPFA.

Hughes, F. (1999) *Children, Play and Development*, 2nd edition. Needham Heights, Ma.: Allyn & Bacon.

Huizinga, J. (1949) *Homo Ludens. A Study of the Play Element in Culture*. London: Paladin.

Humphries, S. (1997) *Hooligans or Rebels*. Padstow: Blackwell.

Itten, J. (2003) *The Elements of Colour*. Germany: John Wiley and Sons.

James, O. (2002) *They F*** You Up: How to Survive Family Life*. London: Bloomsbury Publishing.

Johnstone, K. (1987) *Impro: Improvisation and the Theatre*. London: Routledge.

JNCTP (2000) *Having Your Say Report* [online] Drawn up in partnership with the SPRITO Playwork Unit, National Centres for Playwork Education, May 2000 Available from http://www.jnctp.org.uk/members/li/docs/having_your_say.doc [Accessed 20/12/06].

Joint National Committee on Training for Playwork (2002) *The New JNCTP Charter for Playwork Education, Training and Qualifications*. JNCTP.

Kane, P. (2004) *The Play Ethic*. London: Macmillan.

Keenan, C. (2002) 'Working within the lifespace', In Lishman, J. (ed.) *Handbook of Theory for Practice Teachers in Social Work*. London: Jessica Kingsley.

Kellogg, R. (1970) *Analysing Children's Art*. Palo Alto: National Press Books.

Kilvington, J., and Wood, A. (2006) *The Enigma of the Missing Female Perspective*. In press.

Kilvington, J., Wood, A. and Knight, H. (2006) 'Affective play spaces'. Unpublished paper presented at *New Directions in Children's Geographies Conference*, Northampton University, 2006.

King, P. F. (2005) 'Give 'em enough rope – can free play exist in children's play environments where adults are present?' M(Res) dissertation; Leeds Metropolitan University.

Klein, M. (1937) *The Psychoanalysis of Children*. London: Hogarth.

Konner, M. (1991) *Childhood*. London: Little, Brown & Co.

Krathwohl, D. R., Bloom, B. S., & Bertram, B. M. (1973). *Taxonomy of Educational Objectives, the Classification of Educational Goals. Handbook II: Affective Domain*. New York: David McKay Co., Inc.

Lambert, J. and Pearson, J. (1974) *Adventure Playgrounds*. London: Penguin.

Lao Tsu (600BCE) *Tao Te Ching* (Book 1, Verse 10)(Many publications in English).

Lather, P and Smithies, C. (1997) *Troubling the Angels: Women Living with HIV/AIDS*. Colorado: Westview Press.

Laver, J. (1937) *Taste and Fashion*, London: George G. Harrap and Co.

Lester, S. (2001) *Playwork Training – A Question of Quality* [online] Cited in the JNCTP Conference report: 21ˢᵗ March 2001 Available from www.jnctp.org.members/li/docs/manchester [Accessed 27/7/06].

Lester, S. and Russell (2002) *Playing for Real*. Manchester City Council (unpublished).

Lester, S. and Russell, W. (2004) 'Towards a curriculum for advanced playwork practice: Background and context for the proposal', JNCTP Study Day, JNCTP.

Lewin, K. (1951) *Field Theory in Social Science; Selected Theoretical Papers*. Cartwright D. (ed.). New York: Harper and Row.

Lewis, M. (2002) 'The dialogical brain. Contributions of emotional neuro biology to understanding the dialogical Self'. *Theory and Psychology*, Vol. 12, no. 2, pp175–190.

Lewis, M. (2005) 'Self-organising individual differences in brain development'. *Developmental Review*, Vol. 25: pp252–277.

Lindon, J. (2005) *Understanding Children's Development*. Bristol: Hodder Arnold.

London County Council (1949) *Conference Report on Juvenile Delinquency*. London: LCC.

Lowenfeld, V. and Brittain, W. (1982, 1987) *Creative and Mental Growth*. New York: Macmillan Company.

Lupton, D. (1998) *The Emotional Self*. London: Sage.

Lurie, A. (1981) *The Language of Clothes*, New York: Random House.

Lysaker, P. and Lysaker, J. (2002). 'Narrative structure in psychosis: Schizophrenia and disruptions in the dialogical self'. *Theory & Psychology*, Vol. 12, 207–20. Cited in Hermans, H. (2006) 'The self as a theatre of voices: Disorganisation and reorganisation of a position repertoire'. *Journal of Constructivist Psychology*, Vol. 19, 147–169.

MacLean, P. D. (1976) 'Sensory and perceptive factors in emotional functions of the triune brain' in Grenell, R. G. and Gabay, S. (eds) *Biological Foundations of Psychiatry*. New York: Raven Press (as cited in Hughes, 2006).

MacLean, P. D. (1985) 'Evolution, psychiatry and the triune Brain'. *Psychological Medicine*. Vol. 15, 219–21 (as cited in Hughes 2006).

MacNeice, L. (1966) *Collected Poems*. London: Faber and Faber.

Marchant R., Jones, M., Julyan, A. and Giles, A. (1999) *Listening on All Channels: Consulting with Disabled Children and Young People*. Triangle: Brighton.

Marcuse, H. (1970) *Eros and Civilisation*. Sphere Books.

Margetts, D. (1990) 'Theories on which Protective Behaviours UK are based. Available from www.protectivebehaviours.co.uk [accessed 29/12/2006].

Margo, J., Dixon, M., with Pearce, N. and Reed, H. (2006) *Freedom's Orphans: Raising Youth in a Changing World.* London: Institute for Public Policy Research.

Markova, I. (2006) 'On the 'Inner *Alter'* in dialogue'. *International Journal for Dialogical Science*, Vol. 1, no. 1, 125–47.

Maslow, A. (1954, 1971) *Motivation and personality,* cited in Santrock, J. (2001) *Educational Psychology.* New York: McGraw-Hill.

Maslow, A. H. (1970) *Motivation and Personality,* 2nd edition. New York: Harper and Row.

Masten, A. A. (2001) 'Ordinary magic: Resilience processes in development'. *American Psychologist*, Vol. 56, 227–38.

Mays, J. B. (1957) *Adventure in Play.* Liverpool: Liverpool Council of Social Service.

McQueen, A. (1996) Quoted in Polhemus, T. (1996) *Style Surfing. What to Wear in the Third Millenium*, London: Thames and Hudson.

Mellor, E. (1957) *Education Through Experience in the Infant School Years.* Oxford: Blackwell.

Miehls, D. and Moffatt, K. (2000) 'Constructing social work identity based on the reflexive self'. *British Journal of Social Work*, Vol. 30, 339–48.

Millar, B. (2002) 'Uncovered; the qualities of an exceptional cook are akin to those of a successful tightrope walker: An abiding passion for the task, courage to go out on a limb and an impeccable sense of balance'. *Art Culinaire*, Spring, 2002.

Milne, A. A. (1924) 'Happiness', in *When We Were Very Young.* London: Methuen.

Milne, J. (2000) 'Men in play', in *Proceedings of Play Education 2000: New Playwork – New Thinking.* Ely: PlayEducation.

Mitchell, E. D. and Mason, B. S. (1934) *The Theory of Play.* New York: Barnes and Company.

Mitton, R. and Morrison, E. (1972) *A Community Project in Notting Dale.* London: Allen Lane.

Morgan, E. (1996) *The Descent of the Child.* London: Penguin Books.

Moss, P. and Petrie, P. (2002) *From Children's Services to Children's Spaces: Public policy, children and childhood.* London: Routledge Falmer.

Nachmanovitch, S. (1990) *Free Play Improvisation in Life and Art.* New York: Tarcher/Penguin.

Nadeau, R. L. (1997) Brain Sex and the Language of Love. *The World and I.* vol. 12, no. 11, 330.

Neville, R. (1971) *Playpower.* London: Paladin.

Nicholson, S. (1971) How NOT to cheat children: The theory of loose parts. *Landscape Architecture*, Vol. 62, No. 1, 30–34.

NPFA, Children's Play Council & Play Link (2000) *Best Play: What Play Provision Should do for Children.* London: NPFA.

O'Connor, J. and Seymour, J. (1990) *Introducing Neuro-Linguistic Programming.* London: HarperCollins.

Okri, B. (1998) *A Way of Being Free.* London: Phoenix Press.

Oliver, M. (1990) 'The individual and social model of disability'. [online] Paper presented at Joint Workshop of the Living Options Group and the Research Unit of the Royal College of Physicians. Available from http://www.leeds.ac.uk/disability-studies/archiveuk/Oliver/in%20soc%20dis.pdf. [Accessed 18/1/07].

O'Malley, J. (1977) *The Politics of Community Action.* Nottingham: Spokesman.

Orbach, S. (1994) *What's Really Going On Here?* London: Virago.

Osho (2002) *Everyday Osho.* Gloucester, Ma., USA: Fair Wind Press.

Palmer, M. (2001) 'Reflections on Adventure Play', unreleased video interviews.

Palmer, S. (2003) 'Does quality training and education ensure quality playwork training? [online] cited in the JNCTP Conference Report: 31 March 2003. Available from www.jnctp.org.uk/members/li/docs/jnctp_conf_report_31.3.03_web_copy.doc [Accessed 18/1/07].

Parker, D. (1926) 'The satin dress', in *The Complete Dorothy Parker*, Middlesex: Penguin Classics.

Petrie. P. (1994) *Play and Care.* London: HMSO.

Piaget, J. and Inhelder, B. (1971) *Mental Imagery in the Child.* New York: Basic Books.

Play Wales (2001) *The First Claim: A Framework for Playwork Quality Assessment.* Cardiff: Play Wales.

Play Wales (2005) *Playwork Principles.* [online] Cardiff: Play Wales. Available from http://www.playwales.org.uk/page.asp?id=50 [Accessed 16/12/06].

Prout, A. (2005) *The Future of Childhood.* Abingdon: RoutledgeFalmer.

Rakic, P. (1998) 'Young neurons for old brains'? *Nature Neuroscience*, Vol. 1, no. 8, 645–47.

Rizzolatti, G., Fogassi, L. and Gallese, V. (2001) 'Neurophysiological mechanisms underlying the understanding and imitation of action'. *Nature Neuroscience Review,* Vol. 2, 661–70.

Rogers, R. (1980) *Crowther to Warnock.* London: Heinemann.

Russell, W. (2004) 'The unnatural art of playwork: BRAWGS continuum', in Sturrock, G. and Else, P. (eds) *Therapeutic Playwork Reader Two,*

Sheffield: Ludemos.

Russell, W. (2006) *Reframing Playwork; Reframing Challenging Behaviour.* Nottingham: Nottingham City Council.

Sabbatini, R. M. E. (2000) 'Are there differences between brains of males and females?' [online] *Brain and Mind* Vol. (11) Available from http://www.cerebromente.org.br/n11/mente/eisntein/cerebro-homens.html [Accessed 13/1/07].

Sarbin, T. (1986) 'The narrative as a root metaphor for psychology', in T. Sarbin, (ed.) *Narrative Psychology: The Storied Nature of Human Conduct.* New York: Praeger.

Saussure, F. (1916) (2006) *Course on General Linguistics*, published in translation. London: Oxford University Press.

Schiller, F (1967) *On the Aesthetic of the Education of Man*, Wilkinson, E. and Willoughby, L. (eds and trans) Oxford: Clarendon Press.

Schön, D. (1987) *Educating the Reflective Practitioner.* San Francisco: Jossey-Bass, cited in Smith, M. K. (2001) 'Donald Schön: learning, reflection and change', [online] *The Encyclopaedia of Informal Education*, available from www.infed.org/thinkers/et-schon.htm [accessed 16/7/06].

Schore, A. (2001) 'Minds in the making: Attachment, the self-organising brain and developmentally orientated psychoanalytic psychotherapy'. *British Journal of Psychotherapy*, Vol. 17, no. 3, 299–328.

Selleck, R. (1968) *The New Education.* London: Routledge.

Selleck, R. (1972) *English Primary Education and the Progressives.* London: Routledge.

Dr Seuss (1985) *The Cat in the Hat.* London: Harper Collins.

Shaw, G. B. (1911) *The Doctor's Dilemma.*

Shenstone, J. (2003) Unpublished essay, University of Gloucestershire.

Simpson E. J. (1972) *The Classification of Educational Objectives in the Psychomotor Domain.* Washington, DC: Gryphon House.

SkillsActive (2002) *Assumptions and Values of Playwork.* London: SkillsActive.

Smith, M. K. (2002) 'Howard Gardner and multiple intelligences',[online] *The Encyclopedia of Informal Education*, Available from http://www.infed.org/thinkers/gardner.htm [accessed 20/12/06].

Smith, M. K. (2003) 'Michael Polanyi and tacit knowledge' [online] *The Encyclopedia of Informal Education*, Available from www.infed.org/thinkers/polanyi.htm. [Accessed 11/02/07]

Smith, P. K. (1994) 'Play and the uses of play', in: Moyles, J. R. (ed.) *The Excellence of Play.* Buckingham: Open University Press.

Smith, P. K., Smees, R., Pellegrini, A. D. and Menesini, E. (2002) 'Comparing pupil and teacher perceptions for playful fighting, serious fighting and positive peer interaction', in Roopnarine J. L. (ed.) 'Conceptual, social-cognitive and contextual issues in the fields of play, Play and Culture studies, 4. Westport, Connecticut: Ablex Publishing.

Spariosu, M. I. (1989) Dionysus Reborn. Ithaca and London: Cornell University Press.

Spencer, J. (1964) Stress and Release in an Urban Estate. London: Tavistock.

Stimson, C. (1948) Education after School. London: Routledge.

Sturrock, G. (1995) 'The sacred and the profane', in Sturrock, G. and Else, P. (2005) Therapeutic Playwork Reader 1, Sheffield: Ludemos.

Sturrock, G. (1996) 'A diet of worms', in Sturrock, G. and Else, P. (2005) Therapeutic Playwork Reader 1, Sheffield: Ludemos.

Sturrock, G. (1997) 'Child X as a case history', in Sturrock, G. and Else, P. (2005) Therapeutic Playwork Reader 1, Sheffield: Ludemos.

Sturrock, G. (1997a), 'The survival self – An analysis of the effects of survival in a sectarian environment', in Sturrock, G. and Else, P. (2005) Therapeutic Playwork Reader 1, Sheffield: Ludemos.

Sturrock, G (1997b) 'Spice a redundant metaphor', in Sturrock, G. and Else, P. (2005) Therapeutic Playwork Reader 1, Sheffield: Ludemos.

Sturrock, G. (1999), 'The impossible science of the unique being', in Sturrock, G. and Else, P. (2005) Therapeutic Playwork Reader 1, Sheffield: Ludemos.

Sturrock, G. (2002a), 'North of the future – reverie, imagination and fantasy as a ludic ecology', in Sturrock, G. and Else, P. (eds) (2005) Therapeutic Playwork Reader ll, Sheffield: Ludemos.

Sturrock, G. (2002b) The Idea of Unplayed-out Material. Sheffield: Ludemos Associates.

Sturrock, G. (2003) Spice a redundant metaphor. Sheffield: Ludemos.

Sturrock, G. (2003a) 'The Ludic third', in Sturrock, G. and Else, P. (eds) (2005) Therapeutic Playwork Reader ll. Sheffield: Ludemos.

Sturrock, G. (2003b) 'The beauty of play – an attempt at an aesthetic definition of play and playwork', In Sturrock, G. and Else, P. (eds) (2005) Therapeutic Playwork Reader ll. Sheffield: Ludemos.

Sturrock G. and Else, P. (1998) 'The playground as therapeutic space: Playwork as healing', (known as The Colorado Paper). Sheffield: Ludemos.

Sturrock, G. and Else, P. (2005) (eds) Therapeutic Playwork Readers l and ll. Sheffield: Ludemos.

Sturrock, G., Russell, W. and Else, P. (2004) Towards Ludogogy Parts l, ll *and lll: The Art of Being and Becoming Through Play*. Sheffield: Ludemos.

Sutton, A. (2006) 'Re: Urban Grimshaw gets his face painted'. *UKPlayworkers*, 18th December.

Sutton-Smith, B (1997) *The Ambiguity of Play*. Cambridge: Harvard University Press.

Sutton-Smith, B. (1999) 'Evolving a consilience of play definitions: Playfully'. *Play and Culture Studies* 2, 239–56.

Sutton-Smith, B. (2001) 'Emotional breaches in play and narrative'. Reprinted from: Goncu, A. and Klein, E. L. (eds.) *Children in Play, Story, and School*. Guilford Publications.

Sutton-Smith, B. (2002) 'Recapitulation redressed', in Roopnarine, J. L. (ed.) *Conceptual, social-cognitive and contextual issues in the fields of play*. *Play and Culture Studies 4*, Westport, Connecticut: Ablex Publishing.

Sutton-Smith, B. (2003) 'Play as a parody of emotional vulnerability', in Roopnarine, J. L. (ed.) *'Play and educational theory and practice'*, *Play and Culture Studies 5*. Westport, Connecticut: Praeger.

Sylva, K. (1977) 'Play and learning', in Tizard, B. and Harvey, D. (eds.) *Biology of Play*. London: Heinemann.

Tappan, M. (2005) 'Domination, subordination and the dialogical self: Identity development and the politics of "Ideological Becoming"'. *Culture and Psychology*, Vol. 11, no. 1, 47–75.

Thomas, D. N. (1976) *On Social Change*. London: George Allen and Unwin.

Thomas, D. N. (1983) *The Making of Community Work*. London: George Allen and Unwin.

Thompson, E. and Varela, F. (2001) 'Radical embodiment: Neural dynamics and consciousness'. *Trends in Cognitive Sciences*, Vol. 5, no. 10, 418–425.

Thorne, B. (1993) *Gender Play: Girls and Boys in School*. New Brunswick: Rutgers University Press.

Turner, H. S. (1961) *Something Extraordinary*. London: Michael Joseph.

UKPlayworkers (2003) Discussion Group. http://groups.yahoo.com/group/UKPlayworkers

United Nations (1989) *Convention on the Rights of the Child*. Geneva: UN.

Vaihinger, H. (1911) *Philosophie des Als Ob* (publisher unknown, cited in Spariosu 1989).

Volkwein, K. (1991) 'Play as a path for liberation: A Marcusian perspective', in *Play and Culture*, Vol. 4, 359–70.

Vygotsky, L. S. (1978). *Mind and Society: The Development of Higher Mental Processes*. Cambridge, MA: Harvard University Press.

Walter, N. and Heiner, B. (1988) Act for yourselves articles, from *Freedom 1886–1907* . Peter Kropotkin. London: Freedom Press.

Ward, C. (1961) 'Adventure playground: A parable in anarchy'. *Anarchy*, Vol. 7, 193–201.

Ward, C. (1978) *The Child in the City*. London: Bedford Square Press.

Ward, C. (1973) (ed.) *Vandalism*. London: Architectural Press.

Weihs, T. J. (2000) *Children in Need of Special Care*: London. Souvenir Press Ltd.

Wenger, E. (2005) *Communities of Practice. Learning, Meaning and Identity*. Cambridge: Cambridge University Press.

Wertsch, J. (1998) *Mind as Action*. New York: Oxford University Press.

Wilde, O. (1891) *The Picture of Dorian Gray*. Middlesex: Penguin Classics.

Winnicott, D.W. (1971) *Playing and Reality*. New York: Basic Books.

Witkin, R. W. (1976) *The Intelligence of Feeling*. London: Heinemann.

Wood, W. (1913) *Children's Play*. London.

Index